IN THE LAP OF THE BUDDHA

SHAMBHALA · 25ᵀᴴ · ANNIVERSARY · 1969-1994 ·

IN THE LAP
OF THE BUDDHA

Gavin Harrison

Foreword by
JOSEPH GOLDSTEIN

SHAMBHALA
Boston & London
1994

Shambhala Publications, Inc.
Horticultural Hall
300 Massachusetts Avenue
Boston, Massachusetts 02115
http://www.shambhala.com

9 8 7 6 5 4

Printed in the United States of America
⊗ This edition is printed on acid-free paper that meets the
American National Standards Institute Z39.48 Standard.
Distributed in the United States by Random House, Inc.,
and in Canada by Random House of Canada Ltd

Library of Congress Cataloging-in-Publication Data

Harrison, Gavin.
In the lap of the Buddha / Gavin Harrison:
foreword by Joseph Goldstein.
p.   cm.   ISBN 0-87773-995-1
1. Meditation—Buddhism. 2. Meditation—
Therapeutic use. I. Title.
BQ5612.H37 1994   94-9907
294.3'443—dc20   CIP

To my teachers, Michele McDonald-Smith and
Joseph Goldstein, with love, gratitude,
and deep respect.

To my mother, Adelaide Harrison, whose love,
care, and support have made the journey
easier in so many ways.

To Carol Drexler, with appreciation
and great respect.

All are nothing but flowers
In a flowering universe.

— NAKAGAWA SOEN-ROSHI

In the midst of winter I finally learned that there
was in me an invincible summer.

— ALBERT CAMUS

The temple bell stops
But the sound keeps coming
   out of the flowers.

— BASHO

Contents

Foreword

I first met Gavin Harrison in Johannesburg, South Africa, in 1981. From that beginning meditation weekend, Gavin has become a longtime student, friend, and colleague whose special gifts now shine so profoundly through this book. Through an extraordinary journey of suffering, shared in these times by so many others, Gavin has forged an understanding infused with wisdom and compassion. It is a wisdom grounded in the meditation practice of the Buddha's teachings, and a compassion born from his own great open heart.

How do we cope with the trauma of abuse, with the onslaught of disease, or with the simple tribulations of our daily life? And in the midst of it all, how can we connect with the purity of awareness that remains our unfailing refuge? *In the Lap of the Buddha* points us to the inner strength and courage we all have, although sometimes overlook.

A deeply personal odyssey gave birth to this book. A timeless wisdom emerges from it. I am grateful to Gavin for this gift of Dharma. Only someone who lives the teachings could have written it.

JOSEPH GOLDSTEIN
Barre, Massachusetts
New Year, 1994

Preface

On July 9, 1989, I was diagnosed HIV positive. Nothing could have prepared me for the impact of this information. It feels as though no part of me has remained untouched by the reverberations of the diagnosis.

Central to the unfolding of these last years has been the practice of insight meditation, which is outlined fully in this book. The inner journey has been deeper, richer, and also more terrifying and challenging than I ever could have imagined. The highs have been glorious and the lows dark and often very difficult. I don't know how I ever could have weathered the storms, had spiritual practice not been a full part of my life.

The impact of the diagnosis opened a door to memories of sexual abuse in my infancy. This information has unquestionably intensified the experience of these last years. Yet it has all been workable, to some degree. Not easy, clearly challenging, but it has been possible to hang in there with the storms as they blow through.

When I look back over the years of meditation practice before July 1989, I see that there was a readying and a ripening happening from the very beginning. The process of inner exploration and inquiry undoubtedly served me at the time of the diagnosis, but the unfolding of the practice clearly began in the moment I committed myself to being more careful and awake.

Of course, a dire illness or a history of abuse is not a prerequisite for serious exploration of the human dilemma. A spiritual journey is the birthright and perhaps even the responsibility of every human being. But suffering certainly serves to bring the importance of inner understanding more sharply into focus. Urgency unquestionably energizes the inquiry, whether or not one is threatened by physical or emotional crisis. I hope that this book will in some way encourage all readers to touch the fragility and preciousness of life, and thereby know that spirit of urgency which is a vital factor for spiritual awakening.

The life and teachings of Siddhartha Gautama, the Buddha, have been an inspiration and guide on my journey. The practice of insight meditation has served this exploration. I am further touched and nourished by the example and message of Christ. I regard Steve Biko, Martin Luther King, Thomas Merton, and Nelson Mandela as important teachers over the years. With time, I see that my heart moves more easily to any place where authentic love and compassion is present, be it a church, prison, monastery, retreat center, or forestland. It is the substance and not the label that truly matters.

My hope and prayer is that this book will provide inspiration and support to all seekers of truth and understanding, whatever their spiritual allegiance or affiliation. Perhaps it may help guide the reader to that path which is most deeply appropriate for her or him. Heeding the call to spiritual warriorship requires enormous courage, patience, and strength. We need and deserve all the inspiration and support we can get along the way! For me, living with HIV and healing from abuse has sometimes been a lonely and isolating journey. One of the blessings of the meditation practice has been a growing understanding of the interconnection and interdependence that are always there. We are never alone; we only think that we are. Perhaps this book will serve as a reminder that we heal together.

In the pages that follow, I draw widely from my personal experience. While the book focuses to a degree on the issues of AIDS and abuse, I fully believe that the themes of suffering, mortality, transformation, and love are universal to every authentic path of awakening. We each have our personal dramas, but we all hurt in very similar ways.

My deepest wish is that the reader will feel both able and inspired to carry along some part of this book on the great journey toward that particular light that draws each one of us to the love, understanding, and freedom that are the birthright of us all.

1
Approaching Suffering

AN ALMOST PERFECT DREAM

Two thousand and five hundred years ago the Shakyan people lived in the foothills of the Himalayan Mountains in what is now Nepal. The tribe was ruled by its royal family, and the kingdom was prosperous and strong. When the queen became pregnant, there was great rejoicing in the kingdom. Sixty-four holy men gathered at the royal palace and foretold that the infant to be born would grow up to be either a powerful universal monarch or a great spiritual leader. The first possibility delighted the king. The second prophecy disturbed him, for it was the king's dearest wish that this child both succeed him on the throne and be a conqueror of foreign lands.

The infant boy was born and named Siddhartha Gautama. A wandering ascetic named Asita visited the palace and asked to hold the newborn child. While Siddhartha was in his arms, Asita began weeping.

The king, concerned, asked, "Why are you crying?"

Asita replied. "This child is going to be a great spiritual savior. He will be a Buddha, a fully enlightened being, and I'm crying because I'll be dead before he delivers his teachings." Asita knew that it was a very rare privilege to live in the time of such a unique person.

The king, perturbed, resolved to prevent the outcome that Asita predicted. He reasoned that if the child knew only the greatest luxury and abundance, and was spared from all difficulty and heartache, the call to a spiritual destiny might remain dormant in him.

Siddhartha grew into a handsome young man. His every whim and desire were addressed with great extravagance and abundance. During each season of the year the boy resided in a different palace best suited to his comfort. He was entertained and served by a vast array of servants and courtiers. He had concubines for his pleasure, royal musicians to entertain him, and beautifully manicured gardens to bring him great delight and joy.

The king was fiercely determined that no harshness, ugliness, discomfort, sadness, or suffering would touch the life of his son. At night, under cover of darkness, gardeners moved through the flower beds and removed all the dead blossoms, plants, and leaves.

And so, within the palace walls, all was beautiful, delightful, and easy. The young prince never ventured outside.

When Siddhartha was twenty-nine years old, he married Yaso-dhara. She was soon pregnant. Now, for the first time in his life, the prince felt stirred to go beyond the palace walls and visit a neighboring grove to see the spring flowers.

———————————

The parallels between the youth of Prince Siddhartha and the society in which we live are poignantly similar. The palace walls that shielded the young prince from the knowledge of suffering have become the many mental, emotional, and behavioral walls within which we try to protect ourselves from the challenging realities of life. Insofar as possible, any discomfort or suffering is kept beyond the threshold of our protected lives. Should something untoward or difficult touch us, this is regarded as wrong and tragic.

The brushstrokes of television, movies, and the print media further embellish our image of the dreamlike life. Youth is sanctified in the beautiful and flawless models that adorn the pages of magazines and television screens. Breathtaking visuals of sleek sailboats in the Caribbean are dangled before us, with picture-perfect couples sipping exotic drinks in balmy, perfect happiness. From our youngest years we are conditioned to aspire to the ideal home, the idyllic vacation, the perfect partner, and the desirable bank account. Like Siddhartha's father long ago, our society invests much energy and time in creating this palace and fortification against that which lies beyond whatever is acceptable to us. Often there is a feeling of intrusion, denial and aversion toward anything that disturbs the shadowless lives we try to create for ourselves. This rejection and avoidance of what is true can be as solid and separating as the thickest of palace walls.

I was born in South Africa in 1950 and grew up in an affluent white suburb in Johannesburg. Our property was surrounded by a wall that grew higher and higher over the years as the political heat intensified. The windows of the house were protected by grid-iron burglarproofing, and a system of sirens and alarms was activated at night or when the house was unoccupied. Our home was no different from any other in the neighborhood. Vicious-looking dogs and electronic gates often provided further fortification. It seemed as though an entire nation was trying to protect itself from the nightmare of apartheid by building huge walls to keep the suffering safely at bay.

Theft was commonplace in the white suburbs where I lived. Whites were almost universally far more wealthy than blacks. Rather than address the inequities, the whites made their fortifications more and more elaborate. The flagrant disparity between the races was kept in place by the walls that divided us.

Because the races were so separated from one another, huge fears and suspicions arose which divided the people. A genuine sense of common humanity and brotherhood between people was lost. Over the years the fear increased, fueled by government propaganda and the media. The walls grew higher and higher as the collective hysteria escalated.

We come to believe that what we choose not to see or acknowledge just does not exist. So, too, we may find that what we are protecting ourselves from is nothing more than a specter born of our fears. In *Waiting for the Barbarians*, a classic anti-apartheid novel, E. M. Coetzee writes:

> . . . last year stories began to reach us from the capital of unrest among the barbarians. Traders travelling safe routes had been

attacked and plundered. Stock thefts had increased in scale and audacity. A party of census officials had disappeared and been found buried in shallow graves. Shots had been fired at a provincial governor during a tour of inspection. There had been clashes with border patrols. The barbarian tribes were arming, the rumour went; the Empire should take precautionary measures, for there would certainly be war.

Of this unrest I myself saw nothing. In private I observed that once in every generation, without fail, there is an episode of hysteria about the barbarians. There is no woman living along the frontier who has not dreamed of a dark barbarian hand coming from under the bed to grip her ankle, no man who has not frightened himself with visions of the barbarians carousing in his home, breaking the plates, setting fire to the curtains, raping his daughters. These dreams are the consequence of too much ease. Show me a barbarian army and I will believe.[1]

Perhaps the most tragic palace wall we build is the one within ourselves. We carry carefully constructed ideas of who we are and how we should behave and then force ourselves into a prison of our own making. We usually expect nothing less than perfection from ourselves. The walls of this self-construction can be so high that there is no possibility for the great light of our hearts to shine or for our growing spirit to soar beyond its imprisonment.

We are often the victims of self-hatred and inner conflict when we hold up the reality of our lives to the impossible standards we expect of ourselves. There is so little self-forgiveness. Again, we separate ourselves from the truth of life.

Often, when we surround ourselves with walls of any kind, we create a space in which secrets thrive. Families project worldly images of perfect accord and happiness, only to retreat back into patterns of dysfunction and even violence, played out within the protection of the walls of secrecy. Without genuine connection and relationship with those around us, family life can become unbalanced and unhealthy. Substance abuse, violence, and other expressions of imbalance thrive in a collusion of silence and disconnection.

Some years ago a close friend of mine revealed to his parents, one of his siblings, and a few close friends that he was HIV positive. Like his homosexuality, his illness now became another family secret. The years of dealing with AIDS were shrouded in secrecy, subterfuge, and withdrawal. After his death, his twin brother asked the doctor how it was possible that his brother had died of pneumonia. It was the doctor who then told him that his brother had AIDS. He had never known. He was angry, heartbroken, and embittered.

In my twenty-ninth year I settled in New York City. I met briefly with a psychologist as part of a job interview process. He asked me about my parents and family life. My response was immediate, certain, and one I've never forgotten: "My family is perfect. My mother and father are perfect." The psychologist's skeptical and disbelieving smirk infuriated me. I was filled with indignation and resentment toward him. How dare he trespass within my walls! When I reflect now on this interaction, I realize how fully I had perpetrated the family's illusion and how desperate I was to keep the dream intact: Ronald, the perfect, loving, providing father. Adelaide, the beautiful, dutiful, flawless mother. Craig and Gavin, the obedient, happy, responsible, successful sons. But there was not much room for humanity in all this perfection!

Yet, despite the familiarity and longevity of all the walls that limit and separate us, there sometimes is a call, far stronger than the isolation. The call beckons us to a place beyond what is familiar. The call challenges all delusion and asks that we accept nothing less than the truth.

BEYOND THE WALLS

SIDDHARTHA INSTRUCTED HIS charioteer to ready the royal horse and carriage for their journey to a nearby flower grove. The king got wind of these plans and immediately ordered all the roads to the grove scrubbed and cleaned. Flowers were to be planted along the route, and all sick and old people were to be removed from the vicinity.

The two men set forth early in the morning. When they had gone only a short distance from the palace, the prince saw a person unlike anyone he had ever seen before. This person was not beautiful at all. Siddhartha immediately halted the chariot and asked his charioteer: "Who is this man I see before me?"

"That is an old man, your highness," replied the man. "Everyone who is born is subject to old age."

Siddhartha was shocked and upset. He had never seen the suffering of old age. They turned around and went home.

A few days later they again set out for the flower grove. Once again Siddhartha called a halt to the journey when they came upon a further strange person beside the road.

"This is a sick person," the charioteer told the prince. "All who are born are subject to sickness and decay."

They returned home immediately. Siddhartha was more shaken and disturbed than ever.

On a third attempt to reach the flower grove, they were again halted by a disturbing sight.

"That is a corpse, sir. A dead person. We are all subject to death, your highness."

They turned around, and on the way back to the palace a mendicant-monk stepped out of a nearby forest. His face was radiant and his head shaven.

"Who is this?" asked Siddhartha.

"This man has renounced the world. He is pursuing spiritual understanding and the true meaning of life."

Instantly Siddhartha knew what he needed to do. He sped home to his wife and newborn son. He bade them farewell and prepared to leave the palace early the next morning. Renouncing his title and worldly possessions, he entered homelessness, wandering the forest in search of truth and understanding.

Like Siddhartha long ago, many of us come to spiritual practice out of deep yearning, questioning, and often pain. We yearn to connect with our essential being. We feel divorced from the truth of who we are. We long to understand ourselves and the world more deeply.

This pain takes many forms. Our lives may feel orchestrated by forces far removed from our center. Often the needs and expectations of parents and friends from childhood still dominate us far into adulthood, perhaps even long after those people have died. We feel unable to live from a place of personal integrity and self-reference. Society as a whole rewards us when we conform and punishes us if we rock the boat in any way. In relationships, we feel caught up in a gridlock of expectations, those we have of ourselves, crosscutting the wishes and needs of partners or friends. We are subject to the enormous manipulative power of media, television and advertising. Battered by such powerful conditioning forces, the sense of being lost becomes very real.

The forces of internal conditioning may also disconnect us from our deeper selves. Storms of fear, anger, envy, and grief may blow us about like helpless leaves. If we are not rooted in clarity and self-understanding, we can only *react* to outer situations and circumstances, instead of *responding* from our center. We are constantly thrown off balance. Powerful forces seem to victimize us within and without. Our hearts feel impoverished and barren.

It is painful to recognize this pervasive suffering within ourselves. It also hurts to realize that most other people also live their lives at the mercy of the many conditioning forces that rage both within and around us.

Yet for some of us there is a stirring. We sense that our spirits must be greater than the conditions that box us in. We feel an urgent need to live by a more profound sense of inner truth. And so we set forth on a spiritual journey. We heed our own particular call to destiny.

I came to spiritual practice out of a great longing to understand why my life, with all its trappings of success and promise, felt so barren and meaningless. There was also a strong feeling of disconnection from and fear of other people, even those with whom I'd been in relationship. What I did not know then was that I had been traumatically sexually abused in my childhood, and that the reverberations of that violence were profoundly affecting my everyday life. For many of us, as the spiritual journey unfolds, we find ourselves opening to the truth of a difficult personal history. And out of the yearning to know why our lives are complicated, why our patterns of behavior are so self-destructive, and why we hurt ourselves and others so often, we set forth on a path that takes us beyond our walls.

For others of us, the walls suddenly come crashing down. Our partner, parent, or friend dies. We witness a dreadful accident or natural catastrophe. We almost die. As we touch directly the fragility of life, we are forced to move far beyond all that had felt safe, sure, and predictable. Like Siddhartha, who came face to face with the difficult truths of human life, we realize that our life can never be the same again. We set forth in our own way to understand who we truly are and why we suffer.

When I was diagnosed HIV positive in July 1989, I felt as though I had been taken by the scruff of the neck and forced to confront aspects of myself that I'd stayed clear of all my life. Even though I had come to spiritual practice many years previously, the impact of the diagnosis brought a sense of urgency and immediacy to my life that were not there before. There simply was no longer any time to waste.

Among one of the tribes in Africa, when a woman decides that she wishes to have a child, she walks out alone from the village. Perhaps she finds a tree and sits down beneath it. Then she listens. She listens for the song of the child that she has decided to bear. The day she hears that song clearly is considered to be the birthday of the child. She teaches the song to her husband, and it then becomes a part of the mating ritual between the woman and the man. They sing the song during her pregnancy and again when the child is born. It is the song of that child, and it will be sung on each birthday and at each important passage of the child's life. On any wedding day, the song of the groom and the song of the bride are sung together. The last time that song is sung is when that child's body is lowered into its grave.

The path of meditation is like remembering or rediscovering our original song. Through the deepening of self-understanding, we reconnect with ourselves and remember all that has been forgotten. Perhaps we have never known ourselves at all, but if we listen inwardly, we may hear again the beautiful strains of our long-lost melody.

When we hear the song clearly, when we discover our true spirit, we stop blaming or praising others for making us feel bad or good. We no longer feel like victims of circumstance. Rooted in truth, we bend within the winds of circumstance, like fir trees. We engage with the forces in our lives instead of running away from who we are and from all that is painful. In that moment when we are willing to open to the ten thousand joys and the ten thousand sorrows of life, the gateway to our real selves opens. This is the gateway through the palace walls that have kept us isolated and limited for so long. Walking through the gates, we access the possibility of a profound happiness and peace that is not dependent on the conditions of our life.

THE SPIRITUAL JOURNEY

FOR SIX YEARS, Siddhartha continued his search for truth and understanding. Sometimes he was alone and at other times he engaged in spiritual practices with fellow seekers. He studied with all the great religious masters of the time and moved on when he felt he had nothing more to learn. He meditated. He studied. He fasted. He engaged in very austere religious practices. After all the years of sincere endeavor, he still was not free.

This rigorous austerity took a huge toll on Siddhartha's body. He described his situation in this way:

> At times I ate only a single grain of rice a day. On other days one sesame seed was all I ate. My joints resembled a wiry creeping plant. My gaunt ribs stood fully revealed and disclosed like the rafters in a tumbledown stable. My eyes were deeply buried in their sockets like the reflection of distant stars in a very deep well. My scalp resembled a withered, shriveled, and shrunken gourd, plucked too early and left to lie in the harsh summer sun.
>
> I would try to grasp the front of my body and found that it was my backbone that I held in my grasp! I tried to stand erect, and each time I collapsed and fell to the ground.

Siddhartha had become a pitiful shadow of the bright and handsome prince who had left his palace six years before. He saw that the extreme austerities had in the end not brought him to the freedom he so longed for.

Starved, exhausted, and depleted, he knew that he was not yet fully liberated from suffering. One day, lying under a tree, too tired to continue, he was offered a bowl of rice and milk by a woman from a nearby village. He accepted the meal and felt so strengthened by the food that he resolved to sit down beneath a nearby tree and not arise until he had gained the understanding he had sought for so long.

He vowed: "Let only my skin, sinews, and bones remain, and let the flesh and blood in my body dry up; but not until I attain Supreme Enlightenment will I give up this meditation seat."

Over the course of the night he wrangled with the forces of greed, aversion, and delusion in his mind, all personified by Mara the Antagonist. Bolts of lightning and the deep rumble of thunder heralded the onslaught of Mara. A searing and blinding flash exploded in front of Siddhartha. A tall tree, split lengthwise and wrapped in flames, crashed down to earth before him.

"Mara!" he exclaimed.

The foliage of the tree above his head began to hiss in the fiery wind. The wind itself seemed to carry the sound of a million screams. The ground quaked and groaned and a huge chasm opened up before him. The very earth trembled and shook.

The army of Mara attacked from all directions. Mara unleashed whirlwinds, cloudbursts, meteor showers, and the darkest blackness in a great effort to seduce the mind of Siddhartha with the forces of greed, aversion, and delusion.

However, the rain did not wet him, the wind did not even flutter his garments, and the flaming cinders that descended from the sky turned to flowers at his feet.

He stretched forth his right hand toward the earth and touched the ground with his fingers. He asked the Earth to bear witness to his right to be sitting where he was.

She did so with a mighty thundering that arose from the depths of the earth. At the same time, an invincible roar overwhelmed the armies of Mara, who immediately took flight.

He had at last attained full enlightenment—he had opened to the deepest wisdom and knew the unlimited compassion of a fully enlightened being. He was a Buddha.

Flowers blossomed everywhere, filling the air with the sweetest fragrances. Ten thousand world systems thundered and quaked in celebration of his Buddhahood. Even the deepest and darkest hells were filled with a great radiance as the entire cosmos acknowledged the immensity of his attainment.

Enlightenment for ourselves can seem a very daunting or even impossible ideal, or it can be viewed as the intrinsic reality of who we fundamentally are: we are all fully enlightened now, just as we are; it is the clouds in our mental sky that temporarily obscure this deepest truth. When we view enlightenment in this way, we may ask, like Siddhartha: "How do I deal with these clouds? Can I be free of all obstacles to freedom? Can my heart be delivered from all forces that keep it closed?"

We all do have moments when we touch a deeper truth and feel fully alive and interconnected with other people and with nature. Perhaps while hearing stirring music or gazing into the eyes of a newborn child, we know some of the contentment and peace that surpasses our everyday experience of life. Often the beauty and perfection of nature can touch us in profoundly moving ways.

For me, one such moment happened on the island of Maui, in the crater called Haleakala, which in Hawaiian means "mansion of the sun." Haleakala rises twelve thousand feet from the surface of the ocean and many more thousands of feet from its roots in the sea bed. Having formed the island eons ago, the volcano continues to dominate the landscape and determine the weather patterns on the island. Very early one morning, I drove to the top of the volcano. I left the tropics at sea level, moved through a cool, temperate zone of tall evergreens, and finally reached the bleak and barren peak. There I found lava rock and no vegetation. Clouds swirled below. If I had been able to go directly through the center of the earth, I would have ended up at home, in South Africa!

Full of feelings of being both near and far away from home, I decided to hike down into the crater. Haleakala is dormant, of course. The trail leads two thousand feet down through an alien domain of magnificent black, red, and gray lava rock, dotted with the huge cinder cones that spewed out lava in prehistoric times. The only plant that can live inside the crater is the silver sword, an endangered species that looks a little like yucca, but without a spike. Silver swords grow for about twelve or fifteen years, bear one flower, and then die. The sharp white leaves of the silver swords reflect the dawn like mirrors, bright against the dull sand and rock.

I was alone. It was deadly quiet. I sat down on a piece of lava rock and looked out on the cinder cones that rose up from the floor of the crater. I was transfixed by the spectacle around me. For a moment my mind grappled and struggled to find some sort of reference for what I was seeing. There immediately arose a deep sense of knowing that this place was simply beyond comparison. There were no references. For the longest time, I sat there, awed, like a child. Nothing stirred, either within or outside of me.

In letting go of the absurdity and even the arrogance of believing that we know what the next moment will bring, we relinquish our grip on reality and surrender into the mystery of not knowing, moment to moment, what will appear next in awareness.

Can we cultivate an attitude that questions the world in a way that is deep and fresh? This is certainly what Siddhartha was doing all those years ago. Can we cultivate a mind that is utterly still, with childlike freshness and wonder? Such a mind is very powerful. It is very different from the adult mind that needs to compare, analyze, judge, and comment. Very often, these separating processes are born of fear. We fear change. We fear the unknown. We codify and solidify our experience so that we have an illusion of control and security. In the grip of fear, we build walls and obscure what is true.

When we are fully present and aware, we experience the world afresh in every moment, free of the governance of confusion, aversion, and greed. Having a childlike mind is so lovely and freeing. No matter how many breaths we breathe, each one is pure and original, and our knowing of those breaths can also be filled with great wonder and interest. This is an experience of the enlightened mind.

The Buddha's experience of full enlightenment mirrors back to us our own potential and possibility for freedom, which is unquestionably the birthright of all of us. As we embrace our birthright and question all that keeps us limited and separate, we move into the presence of what Native Americans call "the great mystery." Can we be present with this mystery, where we are still, silent, utterly clear, and vigilant in its presence, thereby penetrating to the roots of what is happening?

Sadness is the mystery. Pain is the mystery. Joy is the mystery. Thoughts are the mystery. Can we be naked before all of this? We come to understand that our limitation, our separateness, and our fears are actually the material through which we discover the truth of our wholeness. If we can let the inner and outer world rest just as they are, the natural wisdom, joy, and vibrancy of our being begin to emerge. And then, perhaps, we can hear our song again.

As we become more carefully aware of the truth of our experience, we develop the skills that also enable us to be fully and uncritically present with others. On a planet that seems so busy and distracted, a clear awareness of what is true is a priceless gift that we give ourselves, others, and our world.

For me, manifesting this awareness is the deepest gesture of love, inwardly and outwardly. Love is not a matter of doing any particular thing. It is not a matter of fixing our attention on a love object, nor of being sentimental in any way. This love that I am talking about does not gratify the ego. Rather, it is an attitude of receptivity, openness, and profound appreciation without regard for what "I" am going to receive back. Love is utter and complete acceptance.

The yearning for a deep and true love is one reason why we

are called to spiritual journeying. The awakening of love and compassion is the spontaneous response of an open heart in the face of suffering.

The Tibetan teacher Chögyam Trungpa says:

> When you awaken your heart . . . you find, to your surprise, that your heart is empty. You find that you are looking into outer space. What are you, who are you, where is your heart? If you really look, you won't find anything tangible and solid. Of course, you might find something *very* solid if you have a grudge against someone or you have fallen possessively in love. But that is not awakened heart. If you search for awakened heart, if you put your hand through your ribcage and feel for it, there is nothing there except for tenderness. You feel sore and soft, and if you open your eyes to the rest of the world, you feel a tremendous sadness. This kind of sadness doesn't come from being mistreated. You don't feel sad because someone has insulted you or because you feel impoverished. Rather, this experience of sadness is unconditioned. It occurs because your heart is completely exposed. There is no skin or tissue covering it; it is pure raw meat. Even if a tiny mosquito lands on it, you feel so touched. Your experience is raw and tender and so personal.
>
> . . . Real fearlessness is the product of tenderness. It comes from letting the world tickle your heart, your raw and beautiful heart.[2]

2
Opening to Suffering

SUFFERING AND COMPASSION

FOR SEVERAL DAYS after his enlightenment, the Buddha remained seated in meditation. He rested in the vastness of the understanding into which he had opened, and over time he concluded that it would be impossible for him to share the insights and lessons of his experience. He sensed that the ordinary human mind could not grasp the enormous scope of his insight.

However, with a stirring of his great compassion, he saw that indeed there were some people with only a speck of dust clouding their perception of truth. The Buddha decided to find these people and share his understanding with them.

He found the men with whom he had lived and practiced in the forests, and it was to them that he delivered his first discourse. With this teaching it is said that he set the Wheel of Dharma in motion. _Dharma_ means truth, the law, the nature of things.

The Buddha spoke directly from his enlightenment experience, outlining the four fundamental truths of life:

> The Truth of Suffering
> The Cause of Suffering
> The End of Suffering
> The Path Out of Suffering

These are known as the Four Noble Truths.

No one likes pain. No one welcomes adversity. No one wants to feel difficult emotions. If we were to announce someday that we are going to sit down and squarely face our suffering and explore everything that is difficult in our lives, our friends might well be aghast. They might suggest we embark upon some other project, one less morbid, depressing, and difficult. Yet the process of facing our suffering is not necessarily a gloomy one. It can be the first step in learning to relate to our lives with far greater compassion, openness, and kindness than ever before. It is a pragmatic endeavor, too, for if we are honest with ourselves, we will see that we suffer no matter how hard we try not to. Has there ever been a day without its unpleasant moment? Or a lifetime without accident, illness, or loss?

To be happy and free from suffering has been at the center of humanity's age-old quest for understanding. We have invented the wheel, we have split the atom, and we have ventured far into outer space. Yet after tens of thousands of years, and after all the so-called progress we have made, we still have many of the old problems, as well as an array of new ones. There always seems to be a measure of suffering that cannot be eliminated by progress. It has nevertheless fallen to the world's great spiritual traditions to find a way to overcome this irreducible suffering. Though the traditions differ, they all seem to agree that the remedy for suffering comes from within, and involves opening the heart and mind to the truth of reality rather than trying to change it.

An integral aspect of the Buddha's enlightenment was the insight into human suffering. He saw deeply into the nature of reality and forcefully pointed out that suffering is ubiquitous in the world. This is the First Noble Truth. The word that the Buddha used to describe suffering (*dukkha*) can also be translated as "unsatisfactoriness," or the impossibility of finding lasting satisfaction in the outer objects of life.

The next aspect of the Buddha's first sermon was that the cause of suffering lies in the wish for things to be different or permanently satisfying. This is the Second Noble Truth. The Third Noble Truth affirms that there is a solution to this problem—that suffering can be brought to an end. And the Fourth Noble Truth lays out the means to the end of suffering.

The Buddha's words are not a dusty prescription for a distant people who have been dead for more than two thousand years. They are fully valid and meaningful today. Basically, he said that if we engage the suffering, understand it, and open to it, we simultaneously unleash the healing powers of our great heart. What seemed onerous and insoluble before becomes workable in our openness to the truth of things. And far from being a gloomy, depressing, and negative process, this opening of the heart is liberating, joyful, and positive. It is the great human adventure. Hermann Hesse wrote: "You know quite well, deep within you, that there is only a single magic, a single power, a single salvation, and that is called loving. Well, then, love your suffering, do not resist it, do not flee from it. Give yourself to it. It is only your aversion that hurts, nothing else."

As the heart opens to suffering, compassion flowers and inner conflict begins to diminish. Events may not be as we would have wished them to be, but as we accept them, we see the beauty of nature shining through what before were regarded as the difficulties of our lives. An open heart is capable of working with any experience without contraction or aversion. (Specific meditations to strengthen the power of compassion and love in our lives are discussed in part 4, "Meditations of the Heart.")

Awareness meditation is a way of opening our attention to the truth of what is present. We do not selectively pay attention to pleasant things and ignore the unpleasant. We open choicelessly, to what is positive and joyous as much as to the suffering that we find. Meeting each moment without resistance, we discover unsuspected beauty in our hearts, minds, and bodies, and in the world around us. We sense the uniqueness of each fleeting breath. We perceive the movement of nature within us. We feel

sad without needing to justify or eliminate the emotion. We feel
happy without needing to believe that we will never again know
sadness. This is the way of meditation.

In meditation, on every level, we discover that we do not
live in isolation. Other people and other lives deeply affect us.
We do not have to open our eyes too wide to see that we live in
a world of enormous suffering. Billions of people live lives that
are stringently defined by poverty, injustice, and oppression. It
is estimated that famine affects some 45 million people around
the globe. More than 500 million people are chronically hungry.
Despite tremendous scientific and technological advances, over
one billion people—the equivalent of the entire world's popula-
tion two hundred years ago—suffer from some form of food insecurity and malnutrition. Forty thousand children die each day
from preventable malnutrition-related diseases.[1] At the same
time, nations of the world daily spend three times as much pre-
paring for war as they do yearly protecting the peace. The an-
nual ratio of war expenditures to peace expenditures is 1,000
to 1. World military expenditure currently totals 1.035 trillion
U.S. dollars.[2]

It is hard for most of us in the West even to begin to comprehend that in India 360 million people live in such dire need that
they really don't know where their next meal is coming from. In
Africa, entire tribes are being decimated by famine and AIDS.
So many countries seem to be embroiled in a relentless cycle of
violence, upheaval, war, and misunderstanding. In many parts
of the world, people are tortured and imprisoned for their beliefs. The list of endangered species grows by the minute. Rain-
forests are disappearing and the irreplaceable shield of ozone is
disintegrating. Our sacred and beloved sun has become a carcin-
ogenic enemy. Pollution seems ineradicable.

Compared with the suffering of the world, our own lot may

seem quite fortunate. Yet if we examine our lives sincerely, we discover that we, too, have our share of personal misery. There could be a vague sense of unease in our hearts and minds, a feeling that things are not quite as good as they might be. Discontentment may pervade our days. We probably know what it is to feel alienated, fragmented, and lonely. We may feel tried by financial constraint, health problems, or traumatic childhood memories. Indeed, life can be very difficult. And in the end, all of us die. Christ died, the Buddha died, and we shall one day die too. Most of us fear death, and this fear itself is a very painful kind of suffering.

The Buddha saw that the answer to suffering lies in the boundlessness of our great hearts. Another word for this boundlessness might be *compassion*. Compassion is the heartfelt wish that all beings be free of suffering, including ourselves. If we examine our hearts, we will find that compassion resides there naturally. We all hope that the world might be free from pain. We feel happy and relieved when we imagine peace and contentment for ourselves and for others. If we examine any lingering resentment or desire for revenge, we see that it is only the residue of undigested pain. When we picture ourselves perfectly satisfied, the desire to hurt those who have hurt us often vanishes, and we may instead wish them happiness and peace. This compassion is not something that must be learned or forced; it is our nature. It matures through spiritual practice.

If it is true that human nature is basically compassionate, we might ask why there is so little compassion in our world. Each of us yearns for greater gentleness, tenderness, understanding, and forgiveness in our lives, far more than we receive from ourselves or from others. Obviously our planet and all its people could use a great deal more compassion also. This wish for universal compassion is expressed by Ryokan, an old Zen monk, who said:

> O, that my priest's robe were wide enough
> to gather up all the suffering people
> In this floating world.[3]

Why are these qualities of the heart so rare, both within ourselves and in our world? The Buddha saw clearly that we, as human beings, individually and collectively, are largely unwilling to open to the suffering that is there. Our hearts are generally closed to what is uncomfortable and painful. This is why there is often so little compassion, either inwardly or outwardly in our world.

To manifest more compassion, we do not have to be saints. All that is needed is a greater willingness to give attention to the pain that is already there. If we are willing, aware, and open, then compassion must arise, for this is the way of nature.

The imperative for opening to suffering is great. Meditation practice assists us in this process, often by allowing us to understand when and where we are closed. When the heart shuts down, there is a feeling of ignorance and unknowing that arises. In meditation, we can feel this hardness of heart. We catch ourselves in the act of looking away, and we have an opportunity to choose to look more deeply. What is it that we are avoiding? What are the tricks we play on ourselves?

It seems true that we are often shut down and closed. We don't accept situations. We don't accept ourselves. We often do not accept those who are close to us. There is no use in being ashamed of this, for that shame would only add further negativity to a situation that is already painful and contracted. Besides, to realize that we are closed is the beginning of opening, and this is a most important insight. Many people live their entire lives in complete denial that they are suffering. Simply acknowledging that we have reached a limit is the beginning of an opening that can transform our entire life.

Once I spent a weekend at a Catholic seminary north of New York City. It was a gathering for people who, like me, were all HIV positive. There were eighty or ninety people, a cross-section including recovering addicts and alcoholics, middle-class heterosexual couples, prostitutes, former prison inmates, gay men and lesbians, street people and Hell's Angels. Some of us were ill and others healthy. I had never spent so much time among people who had such intense and difficult lives. We all shared the suffering related to AIDS, and there was a willingness to open to one another's difficulties and heartaches.

That Saturday night, we gathered in a tiny chapel high on a mountain. It was a windy night, and the brown-robed Franciscan monks turned off the lights and lit candles below the statues. For several hours in the flickering darkness, people wept, sang, prayed out loud, shared their joy, and told their stories. It was an extraordinary evening, one of the most heartbreaking and moving experiences of my life. There was a strong feeling of love and interconnection among us all. I felt very distant from all that was familiar. My heart gave forth a spontaneous prayer of gratitude that our suffering had brought us together in a way that would not have been possible otherwise. In the willingness to share our personal suffering and at the same time open to the difficulties and heartbreaks of those around us, we created a place of deep healing and truth. The collective faith, hope, and praise of all who gathered there is a treasured memory I'll never forget.

THE WAY OF INSIGHT
MEDITATION

THE BUDDHA CONTINUED to teach and share the Dharma up until he died at the age of eighty. Over the years a vast community of nuns, monks, and laypeople heard the Dharma and began meditating. Many became enlightened. Vast numbers accompanied the Buddha as he traveled and taught.

One day, the Buddha was walking with a number of monks through a forest in northern India. He bent down and picked up a handful of leaves, and, turning to his companions, he asked: "Which is the greater amount? The leaves in my hand or all the leaves in the forest?"

The monks all replied: "The leaves in the forest are much greater in amount that those leaves within your hand."

The Buddha then responded: "Those things which I have realized and which I understand are a great amount, equal to all the leaves of the forest. However, those things that are necessary to know and practice in order to be completely freed from suffering are equal by comparison to the leaves within my hand."

The late Venerable Ajahn Buddadasa, a meditation master who lived in Thailand, commented: "So from this it can be taken that, compared to all the myriad things that are to be found in the world, the root principles to be practiced, to completely extinguish suffering, amount to a single handful. We must appreciate that this 'single handful' is not a huge amount, it's not something beyond our capabilities to reach and understand. This is the first important point that we must grasp if we want to lay the foundations for a correct understanding of the Buddha's teachings."

Meditation practice directly addresses this core issue: the fact of human suffering and the possibility of an end to that suffering.

It is a powerful time in the lifespan of any of us when
we go beneath what is superficial and comfortable and question
the deeper currents of our life. There is perhaps a yearning to
find a meaning that transcends the vicissitudes of living and endures in spite of the ups and downs that come along for all of us.
This is the beginning of a journey of great dignity and courage.

Upon this journey, each of us may be likened to an exquisite
flower bud in the process of opening to the truth of who we are.
If the circumstances of our lives nurture and nourish what is
true, we must open into our fullest loveliness. True spiritual
practice supports a healthy individuation, that process whereby
we unfold into our fullest potential and greatest maturity.

Meditation practice is a tool for bringing us closer to the
deepest truths of who we are. In meditation we come to know
both what is unique in our lives and what is universal to the
human condition. We move beyond the confines of our story and
our circumstances. We go to the center of our flower bud and
feel the pain of where we are closed.

A life of meditation is a welcoming and revealing of all that
is already there, hidden perhaps, asleep, dormant, and quiet.
We bring forward, with time, every facet of our uniqueness for
questioning, knowing, and loving. We are not *told* what is true;
we are invited to see for ourselves what the truth is. Whatever
the circumstances of our lives, this blossoming is always a possibility. In fact, it is often within the storm of crisis and heartbreak
that we move toward deeper contentment, freedom, and surrender. In this movement to wholeness and integration, we are fully
participating in the healing we took birth for.

So many human beings in our world are suffering. Some of us live with physical limitation and disability. Others of us are dealing with chronic or life-threatening illnesses and diseases. Many live with physical pain. There is the widespread suffering of hunger, imprisonment, and warfare. There is emotional and psychological suffering. Some live with depression or uncontrollable anger and rage. There is the suffering of abuse of all kinds. Many of us live with fear, shame, and guilt.

Perhaps there are common questions that we as human beings might ask in response to the suffering.

- Can all of this be workable?
- Is there a possibility of finding a place of balance within all of the suffering?
- Can there be a long-enduring mind that extends beyond and through the ups and downs?
- Can we respond inwardly to these challenges with more love and compassion and less intolerance and self-hatred?

We may find ourselves grappling with these difficult issues and questions long before we ever expected to. We find that through the doorway of the suffering in our own lives, we see more visibly and widely the suffering that pervades all humanity. It is heartbreaking. If we scratch the surface of those whose lives seem together, enviable, and ideal, it is clear that they suffer also, they are not immune.

It is in the dignity and courage of opening to and facing the suffering, both within and outside of ourselves, that the heart begins to open into all its loveliness and power. This alchemy of the heart, the awakening of compassion in the face of suffering, is the essence of meditation practice. Perhaps this is the greatest challenge: to look a little more closely at what is difficult in our bodies, minds, and lives and to engage all of this in a way that is new and potentially freeing. Furthermore, in meditation, we engage our capacity to love, care, nurture, forgive, and trust. This is a true and vital aspect of who we are also. In meditation we are called upon to open to everything.

When we first engage the suffering, we experience an instinctual human response to recoil from pain. We push it away by striking out, denying, and avoiding it. This attitude unquestionably makes matters worse. We contract around what is difficult, out of fear or aversion, and this contraction escalates the situation. Similarly, we see how tightly we cling to what we like. We want more of what is pleasant or gratifying, and then we hurt when whatever we are holding on to ends or changes. Again we suffer. So in truth we make both the difficult and easier aspects of life far worse by patterns of aversion to what we do not like, and attachment to what we want more of. Furthermore, when we examine our responses to life, we see how easily the mind becomes bored, confused, and restless whenever there is nothing alluring or difficult to grapple with. This is suffering too.

In meditation we cultivate a new relationship with what is happening in our lives. Meditation does not take away or add anything to our experience. Rather it offers the possibility of finding balance and equanimity in all the changes. We stop fighting and avoiding the unpleasant, and we accept the easier times with gratitude and thankfulness without holding on for dear life. In meditation we cultivate awareness, attentiveness, and alertness to what is happening. We do this so that we might begin to *live* this attitude in our lives. Buddhist meditation is not a "cushion trip" that begins when we sit down to practice and ends when we get up. Rather it is an embracing of life in a spirited attitude of inquiry, interest, and care, so that we might greet life and each moment with these questions:

- What is going on right now?
- What is the truth of this moment?
- What am I not accepting?
- Where am I attached?
- Who am I? . . . now? . . . now?
- Is who I am permanent? . . . changing?
- Is there anything that is not changing?

With awareness we explore, moment to moment, the truth of what is arising within our experience. True awareness is a strength and maturity of mind that sees life without judgment, comment, resistance, or holding on. The awareness is neither selective nor conceptual. This quality of mind is sometimes referred to as mindfulness, presence, wakefulness, or calm abiding. It is perhaps best expressed in an attitude of flinging one's hands in the air and saying: "Okay, I give up the wrangling and manipulation. I've had it with fighting and holding on. Let's see what's happening now. No moving toward, no pushing away, no confusion, no words, no analysis, no intellectualizing. Simply 'What is this?' " All concepts are extraneous to pure awareness. Can we be simply present with the truth of each moment, without in any way judging, rearranging, or conceptualizing our experience?

There is an array of states of mind that masquerade as true awareness. If in being aware there is an element of wanting what is happening to end or change, this is not true awareness. It is awareness with an agenda. We need to acknowledge, open to, and be aware of the desire or aversion that is there.

Sometimes in meditation we can be in the vicinity of the truth of what is happening, but the mind feels foggy, or there is a train of thought going on concurrently. This is not true awareness either. Perhaps there is a sense that we are not quite fully touching the truth of what has arisen. Here, too, we open to the fog, the thoughts and the confusion.

One of the important qualities of true awareness is clearly knowing what has appeared in one's experience. This knowing is not conceptual. It is beyond words. Furthermore, awareness is nondiscriminating. With balance and equanimity we open to whatever arises, whether pleasant, unpleasant or neutral.

As the practice deepens, so does the quality of awareness. It has been my experience over the years that I am continually humbled and astonished to discover new and subtle levels of resistance and attachment that I had no idea were there. And the challenge is to be aware of these without recrimination, aversion, or denial.

Whenever things start feeling complicated, I'm sure that struggle, nonacceptance, and aversion are somewhere in the neighborhood. At those times, I remind myself that meditation is not about bullying the mind or shaping experience in any way. Meditation is about loving the mind back into the present moment.

As the awareness develops, we come to know even the subtlest shadings of greed, hatred, and delusion. These are the clouds that hide our deepest truth. In this knowing, a deeper freedom becomes possible. We may discover patterns, or perhaps experience our emotions and reactions with a new and startling clarity. And so the meditation moves into our everyday life, and the division between the two begins to dissolve.

INSTRUCTIONS FOR
INSIGHT MEDITATION

Complete instructions for both sitting and walking meditation are detailed on the following pages. You may wish to record the instructions and replay them while actually meditating.

SITTING MEDITATION

When beginning a period of insight meditation, it is customary to be initially aware of the experience of breathing. Once there is a degree of calm and concentration, then open the awareness to include other aspects of experience, such as sounds, sensations in the body, emotions, tastes, thoughts, and smells. Nothing is excluded. We neither cling to nor push away anything that has arisen. Use these instructions in a flexible and soft way.

You may wish initially to sit for twenty minutes and then gradually extend the time to an hour or more. The quality of awareness is far more important than the length of time you sit.

The traditional sitting posture is the lotus position: legs crossed, soles of the feet upturned, back erect. However, few Westerners are able to maintain this position for any length of time, if at all. Again, it is not how you sit that is important; it is the quality of awareness that truly matters.

Certain aspects of the posture serve the quality of awareness. Whether you sit on a cushion on the floor, on a meditation bench, or in a chair, keep the back as erect as possible. If you choose to meditate on a chair, you may wish to sit forward on the chair so that nothing is pressing against your spine. In this way the posture is not slumped or dependent on the chair back. Lift the back of your head up toward the sky, thereby elongating the spine. Tuck your chin in slightly toward the chest to serve this elongation. Hold the posture firmly but without rigidity. If the back slumps, so does the quality of awareness. Try not to move. Sitting still becomes easier with time. By all means move, with awareness, if necessary. Don't hurt yourself. However, do not adjust for every little twinge and tingle. Rather, use the meditation as an opportunity to explore the nature of the body and your relationship with its changes.

- Allow your eyes to close gently once you have settled into the sitting posture.
- In the first few minutes of meditation, give attention to the posture. Whatever it is you are sitting on, it is helpful if the spine is as perpendicular as possible. Feel this. Let go of any rigidity or tension in the posture, but do not slouch.
- Be aware of the feeling of pressure on the buttocks, as well as the feeling of the surface upon which you are sitting.
- Maintain a soft firmness in the sitting posture. This helps the mind be awake and alert.
- When ready, move the awareness to the experience of breathing. Determine that part of the body where you experience the breathing most clearly. It may be the tip of the nose, it may be the arising and falling of the abdomen, or it may be the movement of the chest. Allow awareness to settle at the place you have selected. Do not shift around from one place to another.
- Do not try to control your breathing or its pattern in any way. Allow the breathing to happen on its own.
- Be aware of the sensations of the movement of the breath.

- While you are being aware of the breathing, the mind may wander. If this happens, then without judgment, comment, or aversion to the thought, feeling, or image that has arisen, return attention to the experience of breathing.

- Continue to be aware of the sensations of the movement of the breath without comment or without changing the breathing pattern in any way.

- Be present with the bare experience of breathing. Be aware, if possible, of the beginning of each breath and the end of the breath. Be aware of any space that there might be between the breaths. Feel the differences in temperature between the in-breath and the out-breath.

- Be aware of the sensations of the movement of breathing as the breath enters and leaves the body.

- Without evaluating or imaging, be present to the truth of what is happening. This is the essence of the meditation practice.

- If the attention is called away by a thought, sound, or sensation, be aware of what has happened and return to the experience of breathing. The willingness to begin again and again is vital. In doing so, we cultivate patience and a long-enduring mind. We develop the strength and maturity to simply and willingly return again and again to the truth of what is happening without judgment, aversion, or frustration.

- Without judging the experience of breathing, without manipulating or changing it in any way, allow the breath to happen, and be aware of the changing sensations as the breath enters and leaves the body.

- You may, if you wish, use a soft mental "note" as a tool for supporting the awareness of breathing. For example, note, "in . . . out," or "rising . . . falling." Be sure to keep the note soft and well in the background. It is most important that you be primarily aware of the sensations of the movement of the breath. Do not focus on the note itself.

- After a time, begin widening the focus of awareness to include sensations in the body. Your attention may be called to different parts of the body where there may be tingling, throbbing, stabbing, or heat. Allow the awareness to shift to what now is predominant in your experience.

- Use a soft mental note, if you wish, to help anchor the awareness with the sensation: for example, "heat" or "throbbing." This helps keep the awareness as continuous as possible.

- Return again to the breathing. Use the breath as an anchor to which you return each time the attention is called away.

- If your attention is called to a sound, allow the awareness to move to the experience of hearing. Without commenting or conceptualizing, be aware of the hearing. Do not think, "Oh, it's a bird, it's a yellow bird, it's flying away." Just hearing, without clinging, aversion, or comment. Again, use a soft background note of "hearing . . . hearing" if this is helpful.

- Return to the breathing.

- Emotions may arise, perhaps boredom, frustration, joy, happiness, anger, or fear. If so, allow the awareness to move to the emotion, and bring the same quality of awareness to what is happening. Do not reach out toward the emotion or push it away. Allow the emotion to unfold in its own way.

- You may wish to use a note again: "anger . . . anger" or "joy . . . joy." Return to the experience of breathing once the emotion has passed.

- Thoughts will arise too. Here it is very easy to have the idea that thinking is somehow wrong. This is because thoughts most often remove us from the experience of what is happening. Yet thinking is a natural activity, and the purpose of meditation is *not* to suppress thoughts. If thoughts arise, use a mental note of "thinking . . . thinking," and return to the breathing without judgment, comment, frustration, or aversion.

> Just thinking
> Just a thought
> Just an emotion
> Just a sound
> Just a sensation in the body

- So too with smells. If a smell arises, be aware of the experience of smelling. Note "smelling . . . smelling" and return to the breathing.

- Some people experience internal images of various kinds. These too should be acknowledged and neither clung to nor pushed away. Using a label may be helpful: "image . . . image."

- One aspect of our experience that we usually do not explore in the sitting meditation is seeing, since the eyes are usually closed. Yet, it is possible to see with the same quality of true awareness. We neither retract from nor advance toward whatever is seen. You may wish to experiment with seeing. Open your eyes sometime during sitting meditation, or stand and look at a flower. See what happens in the mind and what responses there are. Is it possible to see without adding words, judgments, or concepts?

- At the end of sitting meditation, slowly open the eyes. Try to carry the same level of true awareness into your next activity.

SUBTLE FACTORS OF MIND

With time, as the awareness strengthens, it becomes possible to know, understand, and be aware of three more subtle factors of mind: feelings, intentions, and consciousness.

Awareness of feelings.   The first subtle factor of mind is feelings. Whatever arises in our experience—whether it be a thought, sensation, sound, smell, emotion, sight, or memory—is accompanied by a simultaneous feeling of pleasantness, unpleasantness, or neutrality. It is important to distinguish these feelings clearly from emotions, as often the two words are used interchangeably. Being aware of the concurrent arising of these feelings with our experience of life is vital. These feelings condition clinging if the feeling is pleasant, aversion if unpleasant, or confusion if neutral. When we are aware of the feelings, we can interrupt the cycle of suffering that the conditioned responses bring about. We no longer habitually reach out with desire toward pleasant feelings. Neither do we push away with aversion all the unpleasant feelings. When the mind is relaxed, present, and aware, we observe the feelings of pleasantness, unpleasantness, or neutrality that arise from moment to moment with our experience of life. We become aware also of the tendency or movement of mind in response to these feelings.

With awareness we open to the possibility of relating to these feelings with balance, detachment, and acceptance, and thereby sidestep the potential suffering that results if we cling to, or push away from, what is happening.

Awareness of intentions.   The second subtle factor of mind is volition. Prior to every action of body, speech, or mind, there is a moment of volition or intention. It is vital that we be aware of intentions. If we are able to open to the moment of volition that precedes action, we have a choice whether or not to continue with what is intended. There is a moment of intention before reaching for a cookie, before speaking, before taking a step, and so forth. We include moments of volition in our awareness.

A good place to begin is the moment of intention before moving the body. Be aware of the mental urge to shift posture, prior to the movement. If we are aware of the urge, we are not on automatic: we have a choice whether or not to actually move. When we open to the intention to speak, we have a moment of decision and reflection to decide whether or not we really do wish to say what is intended. We do not run off at the mouth and say something that we later regret. We are not a victim of our careless words. (See part 6, the section titled "The Third Precept"). We see clearly the cause-and-effect relationship between our mind (volition) and our body (speech, movement, etc.) (See part 5, the section titled "Karma.")

Awareness of consciousness.   The third subtle factor of mind is consciousness, the knowing faculty of mind. In every moment there is an arising of different aspects of experience (thoughts, sounds, sensations, smells, emotions, etc.) and the simultaneous knowing of them. This knowing quality is consciousness, and it is possible to be aware of both the moments of consciousness and the flow of objects which are known.

It is easiest to observe consciousness in relationship to the body. The leg moves, for example. There are the physical sensations of that movement. Separate and simultaneous is the knowing of these sensations. This knowing is consciousness.

Do not try to pinpoint consciousness. Do not strain to find it somewhere. It is intangible, not to be found in a specific location. In Tibetan Buddhist texts, consciousness is sometimes referred to as the cognizing factor of emptiness. When the mind is alert and relaxed, be aware of the knowing factor of mind. Once there is awareness of consciousness, we see that there is no one being aware. There is no one moving the leg, no one walking, and no one speaking. There is just the arising of aspects of experience and the knowing of them. This is a deeply freeing insight into the nature of things.

WALKING MEDITATION

Walking meditation is an alternative to sitting practice. As in sitting meditation, here too we cultivate the quality of true awareness.

- Find a stretch of ground about twenty steps long. Stand at one end of this length of space. Feel the ground beneath your feet. Feel the pressure where your body contacts the earth. Be aware of sounds and perhaps the feeling of a breeze on your cheeks.

- In the walking meditation we rest the attention on the physical sensations of walking. We cultivate the same quality of awareness by bringing our focus either to the soles of our feet or to the sensation on the calves or in the entire leg. If you do very slow walking meditation, it is natural to focus on the sensations at the soles. If the walking is more rapid, it is easier to give attention to the sensations of clothing touching the skin of each leg or on the movement of the leg itself.

- Be sure that your walking space is clearly delineated. Move from one end to the other, stop, turn, and return to where you started. If the parameters of walking are not clearly defined, this can very easily lead to discursive thinking and wandering of the mind.

- You may wish to keep your eyes downcast a few feet in front of you. This helps contain the mind and focus it more directly on the experience of walking.

- You may use a soft mental note of "left . . . right" or, if the walking is very slow, it is possible to note the "lifting . . . moving . . . placing" of each foot.

- Each time the mind wanders, bring it back to the experience of walking.

- If some other aspect of experience predominates, you may wish to stop walking and give full attention to what has arisen. This might be an emotion, sound, smell, or sensation in the body. What is important here, too, is the quality and continuity of awareness.

- If you are doing alternating periods of sitting and walking meditation, be particularly aware of the times between meditations when the mind can easily wander and get lost. Developing a continuity of awareness that extends through every facet of our lives is the heart of meditation practice.

A FEW SUGGESTIONS FOR PRACTICE

Daily practice.   Meditating as regularly as possible is vital for developing the quality of true awareness. Many people find it useful to set aside a specific period of the day in which to meditate. You may wish to sit twice, at the beginning and at the end of the day. It is a good idea to choose a specific length of time (such as twenty or thirty minutes), and then allow the rest of the day to unfold around those times.

Once you've chosen your time and decided to meditate at that time every day, you avoid the problem of having to decide anew each day when to practice—and possibly be tempted not to if you don't happen to feel like it. You know that, for example, 7:00 A.M. each day is meditation time. Often it's easy to make the excuse that we "don't have time" to meditate. If we consciously make the meditation a priority, so that other activities fall into place around it, we may discover that all the day's activities unfold with greater awareness. Another advantage of choosing a regular time and place for sitting is that the time and place chosen seem to take on a supportive atmosphere, so that each time you go to your place at the designated time, it feels very conducive to practice.

You may wish to create a sacred space specifically for meditation. A separate room or even a separate corner of a room, arranged in a way that is comfortable, would make a difference. Some people create a shrine with sacred images, photographs, candles, and incense for inspiration and focus. A book of beloved poetry, a Bible, and a bowl of flowers are other possibilities. Be creative.

Retreat.   If it is possible for you to do a retreat, this is a very precious and valuable way to support the process of meditation and get a fuller understanding of the practice. Retreats vary in length from one day to three months and even years. On retreat, full meditation instructions are offered, and there is opportunity to discuss difficulties and questions with a teacher. On longer retreats it is often possible to meet with the teacher alone. Otherwise, group discussions and question-response sessions are scheduled. Usually meals are provided and every care is taken to ensure that the meditators are fully supported in their practice. The day is divided into periods of sitting and walking meditation. Much emphasis is given to continuity of awareness, and in this special, protected environment, with the support of fellow meditators, the practice deepens and becomes clear. Please see the back of this book for a list of centers where retreats are held.

Silence.   Silence has traditionally been the context in which meditation retreats are held. If it is possible for you to do a retreat, this is a very precious and valuable way to support the process of meditation and get a fuller understanding of the practice. You may wish to experiment with silence in your daily life:

- Have a time of the day when the television is off, the telephone is unanswered, and conversation is avoided. Do this in order to see more clearly what is going on within yourself.
- You may wish to have a short period of silence before meditation, during which you read a book of inspiring poetry or a spiritual text.
- You might prepare and eat one meal each day in silence, being aware of the whole process necessary for the nourishing of yourself: Be aware of the spirit in which the food

is prepared, of the cutting of the vegetables, and of the whole way in which the meal eventually comes together on the plate. Before eating, you may wish to reflect with gratitude on all that made the meal possible—farmers, harvesters, shopkeepers, you as the cook, and of course the living substances that are the food itself. The sunlight, rain, soil, and insect life are also part of the interconnections that enabled the food to arrive before you. During the eating of the meal, be truly aware of tasting, chewing, and swallowing. Notice the colors and appearance of the food also. In these ways, the eating of a meal becomes a meditation in itself.

Patience.   Because it is not always easy to take an honest and frank look at the truth of yourself, being patient with what you see in meditation is important. In our willingness to begin again and again in meditation, we cultivate patience. We ride the ups and downs with increasing balance and equanimity. In the end we come to see that there are no good meditations or bad meditations. There is just the truth of what is happening.

Our first look at ourselves can often be fairly discouraging. We start meditating and endeavor to be inwardly aware, and our life appears to be far more scattered and confusing than ever before. That was how I felt on my first retreat. I felt swamped, disappointed, and exasperated. One of the retreat teachers gave a talk in which he quoted the Buddha as saying that the Dharma is beautiful in the beginning, beautiful in the middle, and beautiful at the end. I later met with him and said, "There's nothing at all beautiful about what I'm dealing with. It's horrible!"

He answered, "There is a point where you break even. Just wait and see."

The break-even point comes. All we need is great patience and a sincere willingness to be present. Breaking even means finding balance and spaciousness in the midst of change and having access to breathing room when powerful events and mental states arise. Can we be with everything without reaction? Can we be patient?

According to Buddhist texts, there are four ways in which meditation practice deepens. Some people deepen slowly with a lot of suffering. Some deepen slowly with no suffering. Some deepen rapidly with a lot of suffering, and some deepen rapidly with no suffering. I've always considered myself to be one of the first kind of meditator—the slow ones who suffer a lot. But I have come to realize that time is not important, for in the end there is only one moment: the present. When we are truly aware in the present, this is enough, this is everything.

True awareness is the essence of the meditation practice. Anytime this factor of mind is strong, the practice is sufficiently deep, and each moment is experienced as absolutely new and fresh. This powerful, childlike quality of mind is central to freedom. The Zen master Shunryu Suzuki said:

"People say that practicing Zen is difficult, but there is a misunderstanding as to why. It is not difficult because it is hard to sit in the cross-legged position, or to attain enlightenment. It is difficult because it is hard to keep our mind pure and our patience pure in its fundamental sense. . . . I am interested in helping you keep your practice from becoming impure.

In Japan we have a phrase, *shoshin*, which means "beginner's mind." The goal of practice is always to keep our beginner's mind. Suppose you recite the *Prajna Paramita Sutra* only once. It might be a very good recitation. But what would happen if you recited it twice, three times, four times, or more? You might easily lose your original attitude towards it. The same thing will happen in your other Zen practices. For a while you will keep your beginner's mind, but if you continue to practice one, two, three years or more, although you may improve some, you are liable to lose the limitless meaning of original mind. . . .

Our "original mind" includes everything within itself. It is always rich and sufficient within itself. You should not lose your self-sufficient state of mind. This does not mean a closed mind, but actually an empty mind and a ready mind. If your mind is empty, it is always ready for anything; it is open to everything. In the beginner's mind there are many possibilities; in the expert's mind there are few."[4]

Slowly, with patience, over time, meditation shifts our perception from the conceptual to a deeper perception of reality. This reality is a direct apprehension of experience, impossible ultimately to convey in words.

The *Kena Upanishad* uses the tactic of emphasizing what reality is not: "Eye, tongue, cannot approach it nor mind know; not knowing, we cannot satisfy inquiry. It lies beyond the known, beyond the unknown."

The *Tao-te Ching* tries, too: "The Tao that can be expressed is not the eternal Tao."

The Taoist sage Chuang Tzu remarks with exasperated good humor, "If it could be talked about, everybody would have told his brother!"

Nothing that is said in this book is meant as a final, definitive statement of truth. Everything is presented as a suggestion for your investigation. This attitude is expressed by the Buddha in a discussion with the Kalamas, the people of a town called Kesaputta:

> The Kalamas of Kesaputta asked the Buddha:
> "There are, sir, many different teachers that come to Kesaputta. They illustrate and illuminate their own doctrines, but the doctrines of others they put down, revile, disparage, and cripple.
> "For us, sir, uncertainty arises, and doubts arise concerning them: who indeed of these venerable teachers speaks truly, who speaks falsely?"
> The Buddha replied:
> "It is indeed fitting, Kalamas, to be uncertain, it is fitting to doubt. For in situations of uncertainty, doubts surely arise.
> "You should decide, Kalamas, not by what you have

heard, not by following convention, not by assuming it is so, not by relying on the texts, not because of reasoning, not because of logic, not by thinking about explanations, not by acquiescing to the views that you prefer, not because it appears likely, and certainly not out of respect for a teacher.

"When you would know, Kalamas, for *yourselves*, that 'these things are unhealthy . . . these things, when entered upon and undertaken, incline toward harm and suffering'—then, Kalamas, you should reject them."

OUR PERSONAL DRAMA
AND BEYOND

Human suffering is both unique and universal. We all suffer, but how we suffer is personal and specific to our lives. While the experiences of fear, anger, and pain may be common to all of us, the circumstances that give rise to these difficult aspects of life are different.

Unlike the many psychological therapies that focus primarily on the story of our lives, our personal drama, meditation focuses on the level of experience that is common to all human beings. Beneath the circumstances of our lives and the effects of our personal history are patterns of aversion, denial, confusion, fear, and anger that are similar for each of us. Understanding these deeper patterns contributes to our understanding of the drama of our everyday lives. Similarly, our engagement of the difficult aspects of living, in psychotherapy, bodywork, or any of the other ways that are possible, also serves understanding on the meditative level.

Each serves the other, like two hands washing each other. In meditation we go beyond the words, thoughts, stories, and drama to an experiencing of the truth of life, which is both non-conceptual and impersonal. On this level we come to know the interconnection and unconditioned love that are aspects of the truth of things. In meditation we do not deny the circumstances of our lives; we merely move to a deeper level of experiencing what is happening.

In my own personal drama, AIDS and abuse are principal players. Yet I see more and more clearly that the insight and wisdom born of meditation and strengthened by the impact of AIDS and abuse, are universal and not individual to me alone.

I was diagnosed HIV positive in 1989 and probably contracted the virus five to seven years before that. The virus has become a touchstone, changing almost every aspect of my life in ways I could never have foreseen. Most of my preconceptions about the virus have shown themselves to be stumbling blocks as I try to cope with the challenge of bringing balance, care, and clarity to my situation.

Since 1983 I have also been dealing with issues related to childhood sexual abuse. For me, the line between recovery from abuse and living with AIDS is often blurred. The pain, rage, and frustration are similar in both areas. Healing the emotions stemming from abuse heals my relationship with the virus; and relating to the virus with balance, acceptance, and skill heals the panic, projections, and rage that are the legacy of sexual abuse. Opening to these difficult areas becomes easier with time and patience.

Meditation helps establish balance and acceptance in all I deal with. I constantly remind myself to open to whatever is present. Allowing the feelings surrounding abuse and HIV to surface in a space of tenderness, I see that they do not define who and what I am. They are simply feelings. They will change. They are conditioned by my situation. They do not emanate from some fixed core of who I am. As I allow feelings of unworthiness, helplessness, fear, and rage to come and go, this creates an atmosphere in which I find more and more of life to be acceptable, with all its suffering, happiness, and fleeting beauty.

In meditation I deal with physical pain. I also grapple with the fear of death and the insecurity of life. This is all part of both my personal drama and the terrain of meditation. In a world that contains so much that is frightening and painful, a meditative mind that is a little more peaceful, open, and loving is a great blessing.

3
Aspects of Meditation

BEYOND THE GRIP
OF FEAR

WHENEVER THE BUDDHA was asked about the origin of the universe and about the beginnings of life, he responded in this way:

> Inconceivable is the beginning of this cycle of birth and death. Not to be discovered is the first beginning of beings who, obstructed by ignorance and ensnared by craving, are hurrying and hastening through this round of rebirths.
>
> Which do you think is more: the flood of tears which, weeping and wailing, you have shed upon this long way, hurrying and hastening through this round of rebirths, united with the undesired, separated from the desired—this, or the waters of the four great oceans?
>
> Long have you suffered the deaths of fathers and mothers of sons and daughters, brothers and sisters, and while you were thus suffering, you have shed more tears upon this long way than there is water in four great oceans.
>
> And thus have you long undergone suffering undergone torment, and undergone misfortune, and filled the graveyards full.

The endless round of birth and death is referred to as *samsara*. In his teachings the Buddha clearly laid out the reasons why samsara keeps turning from one lifetime to the next: the mental factors of greed, hatred, and delusion are the forces that keep us locked into this cycle of rebirth.

He emphasized that although the beginning of samsara cannot be discovered, its cessation is clear. This freedom from suffering is the substance of the spiritual path. The Buddha's enlightenment brought him to the deepest realization of this, and out of compassion he devoted his life to helping others discover the same liberation in their own lives.

The Buddha said "I teach one thing, and one thing only. The truth of suffering, and the way out of suffering."

The forces of greed, hatred, and delusion are the cause of this suffering. One of the most powerful expressions of hatred is the energy of fear. The Buddha spoke often of the need to confront, grapple with, and understand the true nature of fear.

———————

The path of meditation is a process of recognizing, understanding, and eventually letting go of all painful patterns of mind. In this letting go, the truth of who or what we are begins to emerge. This truth was always there, hidden, latent, and perhaps quietly asleep. Slowly the beauty and perfection of our being emerges. This is our true essence, our birthright—what some call "Buddha-nature." This perfection is the deepest truth of who we are. As we explore the clouds that obscure our Buddha-nature, we undoubtedly discover the emotion of fear. Fear prevents us from opening to the truth of ourselves, for who we are is largely unknown, and fear arises at the threshold of what is unexplored.

Fear is an inward manifestation of aversion, the second of the three forces that perpetuate birth and death. The outward manifestation of aversion strikes out in the form of anger and frustration. The inner manifestation is the paralyzing and contracting energy of fear, terror, panic, anxiety, angst.

If we can learn to acknowledge fear, to engage it and wrestle with it, we give ourselves a wonderful gift: the possibility of great freedom. Of course, it is fear itself that keeps us from acknowledging the fear within. It may help to realize that fear is as much a part of our human birthright as the perfection. As such, it can become an instrument for releasing that innate perfection, when we accept its presence, work with it, and transform it.

Saint Thomas, in the Gnostic Gospels, says: "If you bring forth what is within you, what you bring forth will save you. If you do not bring forth what is within you, what you do not bring forth will destroy you." If our meditation practice is true, it must acknowledge the entire range of our experience. Nothing lies outside the scope of meditation. Everything that arises is potentially and ultimately workable, no matter how difficult things might seem in the moment.

As meditation practice deepens, we come again and again to our limits. These are places where we have probably not been before. They are also the edges of possibility. We come to the edge of what is acceptable and what is known, to places where the familiar ends and the unknown begins. Here, too, we might find that fear is the signal that we have touched a boundary. If we respond to that signal by obeying a fear-filled command to retreat, we remain bound within our habitual patterns. If the emotion of fear is workable, we have the choice to expand the limits of what is acceptable.

The question then is, Can we go beyond the fear that lurks at the edges of what is unexplored in our life?

I do not mean to imply that whenever we find fear, we must push past it. Sometimes it requires great courage to say, "I'm not ready for this one right now," and to back off with wisdom and compassion. Neither is it a feasible goal to pursue an end to fear. Some fears, like the one that arises when we step in front of a moving train, are highly justified and very important. They protect us from physical and psychological harm.

When fear does arise, some reasonable questions to ask of oneself might be:

- Can I open to the fear completely?
- Can I acknowledge, examine, and explore the fear whole-heartedly?
- Is it possible to become totally naked in the presence of fear?

- Can I be completely vulnerable in the face of this fear?
- Can I feel the fear completely? Can I feel it in every cell of my body as long as the fear has life, again and again and again?

This is a movement from fear into fearlessness. We do not eliminate fear, but we do move beyond the grip of fear.

Kabir, the fifteenth-century Indian mystic poet, speaks of fear and bondage:

> Friend, hope for the Guest while you are alive.
> Jump into experience while you are alive!
> Think . . . and think . . . while you are alive.
> What you call "salvation" belongs to the time
>   before death.
>
> If you don't break your ropes while you're alive,
> do you think
> ghosts will do it after?
>
> The idea that the soul will join with the ecstatic
> just because the body is rotten—
> that is all fantasy.
> What is found now is found then.
> If you find nothing now,
> you will simply end up with an apartment in the
>   City of Death.
> If you make love with the divine now, in the next
>   life you will have the face of satisfied desire.
>
> So plunge into the truth, find out who the Teacher
>   is. Believe in the Great Sound![1]

Making love with the divine requires opening to all of our fears. It is not easy. In times of trial, you may find it useful to consider this gentle suggestion offered by the Dalai Lama: "Lay your head in the lap of the Buddha." For me the thought is soothing and comforting.

Chögyam Trungpa, Rinpoche, speaks vividly of fear:

Going beyond fear begins when we examine our fear: our anxiety, nervousness, concern, and restlessness. If we look into our fear, if we look beneath its veneer, the first thing we find is sadness, beneath the nervousness. Nervousness is cranking up, vibrating, all the time. When we slow down, when we relax with our fear, we find sadness, which is calm and gentle. Sadness hits you in your heart, and your body produces a tear. Before you cry, there is a feeling in your chest and then, after that, you produce tears in your eyes. You are about to produce rain or a waterfall in your eyes and you feel sad and lonely, and perhaps romantic at the same time. This is the first tip of fearlessness, and the first sign of real warriorship. You might think that, when you experience fearlessness, you will hear the opening to Beethoven's Fifth Symphony or see a great explosion in the sky, but it doesn't happen that way. . . . Discovering fearlessness comes from working with the softness of the human heart.[2]

The softness of our great hearts allows us to go beyond fear. This process is neither simple nor easy. We must first recognize the fear and then acknowledge it.

Often, when first we suspect its presence, fear seems to lack a clear form or shape. It apparently has no beginning or end. It perhaps lurks just outside the edges of our awareness and comprehension. When awareness of fear feels imprecise, then imprecise awareness of fear is the truth we need to open to. Patience is vital when grappling with fear. This strength of mind is simply the acceptance of whatever is present. Patience is the willingness to be with suffering. Rilke writes: ". . . have patience with everything unresolved in your heart. . . . Don't search for the answers, which could not be given to you now . . . but take whatever comes, with great trust."[3]

The patient willingness to begin again and again is the essence of meditation practice. We allow each moment to be new and fresh, free of comparison, judgment, or comment. We meet these moments with innocence, as if they were the first of their kind. Even if we wander off, we willingly return again, whether it be to the breath or to the edge of fear. Gradually, the many faces of fear begin to emerge. The process is slow, requiring care, attention, and courage.

We get to know fear as we become more willing to acknowledge its presence whenever and wherever it arises, at any time of the day or night. We neither trivialize nor underestimate the situation or our feelings. When we feel some movement of energy in our hearts or in our bodies, we ask:

- What is this?
- What do I feel right now?
- Is this fear, perhaps?
- Where do I experience it in the body?
- Where do I experience it in the mind?
- What are the images and the thoughts of this moment?
- Is there resistance or contraction of any kind?

This patient investigation must eventually yield fruit. One day we will confidently announce, "I see you, fear. I see you clearly now!"

As we lose our fear of fear, we may come to know that a surprising amount of fear has governed our lives for a long time. There is great joy and celebration in making this discovery and a sense that we can never again be dominated to the same fearful degree. When I came to recognize all the possibilities I'd sacrificed to fear, I felt a deep sadness. So much suffering! The sadness slowly turned into a profound tenderness, toward myself and toward all who are fearful.

Trungpa Rinpoche speaks of this tenderness as being like the first growth of a reindeer's horns, which he compares to the birth of the warrior spirit within us:

At first, the horns are very soft and almost rubbery, and they have little hairs growing on them. They are not yet horns, as such: they are just sloppy growths with blood inside. Then, as the reindeer ages, the horns grow stronger, developing four points or ten points or even forty points. Fearlessness, at the beginning, is like those rubbery horns. They look like horns, but you can't quite fight with them. When a reindeer first grows its horns it doesn't know what to use them for. It must feel very awkward to have those soft, lumpy growths on your head. But then the reindeer begins to realize that it *should* have horns: that horns are a natural part of being a reindeer. In the same way, when a human being first gives birth to the tender heart of warriorship, he or she may feel extremely awkward or uncertain about how to relate to this kind of fearlessness. But then, as you experience the sadness more and more, you realize that human beings *should* be tender and open. So you no longer need to feel shy or embarrassed about being gentle.[4]

Accepting fear is difficult because of its unpleasantness. Fear is uncomfortable. We often try not to feel it. Furthermore, society wishes us to be brave, optimistic, and in control at all times. Thus, the typical conditioned responses to fear are denial, resistance, and aversion. However, if we are to accept fear, we must engage all the levels of resistance and denial. Each of us has a personal style of both fighting with and hiding from what is difficult. Thus, exploring the workings of resistance is a personal inquiry too.

- Where do I hold the resistance? In the body? . . . in the mind? . . . in the heart?
- Do I feel it in the neck? . . . the chest? . . . the throat? . . . the back . . . the gut?

As we investigate the resistance and feel the contraction, our task is simply to open to what we find. We open to the aversion and tightness, not in order to make them go away, but so that we might fully understand the workings of fear and aversion in our lives. We also open to our fear of fear, with the same patience and tenderness. With loving acceptance, we become a friend of fear. Joseph Goldstein imagines a child filled with fear and asks, "Do we beat the child because it is fearful? No! Do we feed the kid's fear in any way? No! Are we able to treat our fearful selves like that child, with a tenderness toward the fear, giving it space, care, time, and patience?"

With discriminating wisdom we realistically evaluate all situations of fear. We acknowledge our limits. We may need to back off from a situation. We don't have to be like kamikaze pilots, crashing into the center of everything that arises! We may choose to back off and let a situation quiet down for a while. Or we may decide to stay with the situation.

Wisdom enables us to make choices that are discerning and appropriate. Over time we become familiar with the many voices of fear. As they lose their charge, the voices become obsolete relics of an earlier period of our lives. We may choose to move onward and to act in spite of an old fear that still lingers.

In my experience in meditation, if the power of awareness is weak, I find that when I try to get close to the fear, I am easily deflected and get lost in a proliferation of thoughts. So when mindfulness and concentration are not strong, I've found it useful to allow the mind to expand even wider than the fear itself. I give the fear great space. When the concentration and mindfulness are strong again, I come closer to the fear and become intimate with its energy. There is a time for each strategy. The objective is to make the fear workable in whatever way we can in the moment.

Fear requires a willingness to work our edges again and again. If we observe the fear in order that it might go away, we are still standing within our limitations. This attitude is filled with aversion, one of the hindrances to clear perception of what is truly going on. Chances are that the fear will remain and endure. Fear has taught me much about the subtleties of unconditional awareness and acceptance of what is happening.

The challenge is to open to fear without any agenda or preference. This attitude brings great possibility to the meditation practice. A place of fear may well be a place of great potential and understanding. Can we receive the fear with a mind that is open and interested, without cringing every time fear arises?

Continuing the image of the reindeer horns, Trungpa Rinpoche writes:

> When you begin to feel comfortable being a gentle and decent person, your reindeer horns no longer have little hairs growing on them—they are becoming real horns. Situations become very real, quite real, and on the other hand, quite ordinary. Fear evolves into fearlessness naturally, very simply, and quite straightforwardly.
>
> The ideal of warriorship is that the warrior should be sad and tender, and because of that, the warrior can be very brave as well. Without that heartfelt sadness, bravery is brittle, like a china cup. If you drop it, it will break or chip. But the bravery of the warrior is like a lacquer cup, which has a wooden base covered with layers of lacquer. If the cup drops, it will bounce rather than break. It is soft and hard at the same time.[5]

Since the landscape of AIDS is riddled with fear of many different kinds, knowing and dealing with fear instinctively feels like the direction of healing. For me, whenever there is struggle in the mind, fear is usually not far away, either. In meditation, I have at times felt great depths of anxiety and terror, down to what has felt like a cellular level of experience. It seems logical, then, that healing needs to emerge from these levels also. Allowing love, forgiveness, and acceptance to enter into the very cells of our being is the stuff of meditation. Fear often seems to be a subtle and thin veil through which I experience life. It is immediately clear that the awareness needs to be that subtle and sensitive to perceive it.

There are many ways of working with fear, as I have shown. Sometimes we need to be innovative in our efforts to understand the different levels of fear that constellate around the issues of life that are most scary for us. I have tried to do this in my relationship with the AIDS virus.

The virus is now indisputably part of my life. I know that when I relate to the virus with anger, fear, or guilt, I exacerbate the pain of the experience. Furthermore, if I believe myself to be a victim of the virus, I am in certain trouble.

One way in which I have re-visioned my relationship with the virus is by giving it a name. I chose the name Sipho (pronounced *see*-poe), which is a Zulu name that I love. Each morning, I check in with Sipho:

> "How are you feeling today, Sipho?"
> "I feel a little under the weather."
> "What do you need today, Sipho?"
> "Rest and quiet."

Then we discuss our needs:

> "I'm busy today, Sipho; please don't act up. Please be co-operative. Tomorrow is a clear day. Hang on till then."
> "Gavin, I need to rest today. I need a break. We've been so busy."
> "Well, Sipho, I'll do as little as possible today, and we'll certainly rest whenever we can. OK?"
> "It's a deal, Gavin."

And then we affirm our relationship:

> "I die, you die. I live, you live."

> "Keep moving, Sipho." (I imagine Sipho on roller blades, moving through my body.)

"Don't stop anywhere, Sipho. Go fast through the nerves and muscles, down the back and through the colon."

When Sipho travels in the areas of the kidneys, I imagine that he churns up all the potentially harmful HIV factors and pushes them over the blood vessels, into the kidneys. I wave goodbye as they pass through the bladder, out of the penis, and into the toilet bowl with my urine.

A friend who is HIV positive refers to the virus as the Time Bomb in his bloodstream. Over time, I have found that I prefer to envision my relationship with the virus differently. As I cease to view myself as a helpless victim and the virus as an impersonal enemy, I experience far less fear. Instead of a time bomb, Sipho feels more like an equal or a dance partner these days.

After three years of friendship and conversation with Sipho, I recently learned that his name means "gift" or "blessing." Certainly our ongoing dance is both a gift and a blessing, for instinctively and intuitively, I sense that our relationship has played a major part in the considerable lessening of fear in my life.

With time, meditative awareness moves into the full and ordinary bustle of our lives. As we come to know the workings of fear and fearlessness within us, we are able to respond to the people we encounter with more love and less fear. To the extent that we understand and have grappled with the many faces of fear in our own lives, we more easily recognize and work with the fears of others—not with contraction and further fear, but with compassion and wisdom. This is a great blessing that we bring to a world enmeshed within the grip of fear. Our society's frenetic pace of life usually keeps us from opening to difficulty or unpleasant feelings. Terrified of what we do not want to feel, we keep ourselves busy at any cost. Frantic momentum is our refuge. Should we inadvertently slow down, we feel desperate and confused. We have a cup of coffee. We rev up the engine again and keep running. We fidget and twitch. We chew our nails. We doodle and fiddle and play with our hands in our pockets. Our faces are stretched, our bodies tight, tense, and rigid. We are adept at creating strategies to keep our minds off the fear, off all that is difficult.

From a fearful point of view, slowing down seems dangerous. Winding down, we might realize what we have done to ourselves. Then fear might have the space to emerge, and our anxieties might rise to the surface. Difficulties would become obvious. This must be avoided at all costs!

It is not hard to understand how fear influences the very structure of society. Having grown up in South Africa, I am intimate with apartheid, one of the most tragic manifestations of fear run wild in a nation. Even though apartheid is now outlawed, its consequences will live in the hearts and minds of South Africans for generations. In the United States, fear has plenty of power, too. There is a great need to create enemies. Who are America's enemies today? The Russians? the Iraqis? the Serbs? the Somalis? Once fear creates our enemies, we risk losing touch with our humanity.

Our efforts in meditation have a radical quality. As we engage our fears, and as we come to know greater fearlessness in our lives, we simultaneously change the world in which we live. We challenge the cycle of violence and the forces of delusion. We stop the craziness for a blessed moment. What a gift this is, in a world so paralyzed with fear.

When I visited Hawaii not long ago, each Tuesday I would go to a support group of women and men whose lives had been affected by AIDS. At one session a new person came in whom I'll call Peter. Peter had great big cancerous lesions on his skin, which he tried to hide under his clothing. One night, he told us, he went out in his long sleeves. A total stranger came up to him and lifted the sleeve. He took Peter's arm and kissed the lesions there. The stranger said, "My hope and prayer is that these are soon healed and gone forever." He hugged Peter, turned around, and disappeared.

Such expressions of love strike to the heart of fear. Trungpa Rinpoche says:

> The genuine heart of sadness comes from feeling that your . . . heart is full. You would like to spill your . . . blood [and] give your heart to others. For the warrior this experience of sad and tender heart is what gives birth to fearlessness. . . . Real fearlessness is the product of tenderness. It comes from letting the world tickle your raw and your beautiful heart. You are willing to open up, without resistance or shyness, and face the world. You are willing to share your heart with others.[6]

Peter was clearly both self-conscious and ashamed of his lesions. I believe the stranger sensed this pain and conflict, and his loving and compassionate gesture obviously unraveled much of the fear and contraction that Peter was feeling. Of course, an act of compassion that is simple and inconspicuous would be just as vital in this suffering world. The great Indian master Meher Baba says:

> The scope of service is not limited to great gestures, like giving big donations to public institutions. They also serve who express their love in little things. A word that gives courage to a drooping heart or a smile that brings hope and cheer in the midst of gloom has as much claim to be regarded as service as onerous sacrifices and heroic self-denials. A glance that wipes out bitterness from the heart is also service, although there may be no thought of service in it. When taken by themselves, all these things seem to be small; but life is made up of many such small things. If these small things were ignored, life would be not only unbeautiful but unspiritual.[7]

As awareness deepens, we become increasingly aware of the reality of death, birth, and change. The evidence is everywhere. For me, the abuse, the physical pain, and the whole catastrophe of AIDS fit more and more naturally into the vast tapestry of arising and passing away, the perpetual changing of things, and the inevitability of death. When I go for a walk in the countryside in western Massachusetts, as I try to do each day, I always notice the frogs, salamanders, and bugs squashed to death on the road. I receive these impressions with a combination of grief for the suffering which each creature may have gone through, an acknowledgment that the life it had to relinquish was a sacred thing, an awareness of the many lives and deaths constantly arising within the greater scheme of things, and the sense that it is not simply a useless, depressing cycle, because through those many lives and deaths there can be a meaningful movement toward realization of the truth and liberation.

Visiting my homeland recently, I was shocked to realize the extent to which death is a part of the birthing of a new South Africa. Many people die each day in violence. There are bomb blasts. People are thrown off trains, murdered in bed, or "necklaced" to death in burning tires. Tragically, all this dying is part of the birth of a country that I pray will one day know peace, justice, and freedom from fear.

Last fall in New England, as the leaves all died in a spectacular display of colors, I came upon millions of the tiniest caterpillars, hanging down from the branches above my head, all suspended on fine golden threads. It was so beautiful and hopeful. Seeing and feeling change, understanding that birth and death occur everywhere in life, makes living with physical and emotional suffering more understandable, more workable, and much less fearful.

Jae Jah Noh says in his book *Do You See What I See?*:

When the fears of the mind have been worked out upon the field of the heart, the mind sinks into the heart, into reality, and becomes one with it. Conscious relationship is established, in fact. Now the heart can be lived, faith can be lived, not in ignorance, but in true understanding. Understanding now no longer serves as proof of faith. One can live in his knowingness and unknowingness without fear or inhibition. Ignorance is not a limit to those who live in faith, but only for those who, living in ignorance, without faith, seek knowledge as security against fear.[8]

WORKING WITH PAIN

Pain in the body is an obvious kind of suffering, far more defined and tangible than emotions, which can often seem vague and indistinct. As we deal with physical pain in a meditative context, we develop a foundation that makes it easier to work with difficult emotions and interpersonal reactions when we are called to deal with these also. The flexibility we learn while practicing the lessons of the body goes out with us into the world.

I am speaking here not only about pain associated with illness or disability. Most meditators, whether they have practiced for a long time or are just beginning, experience a degree of pain in the practice, including discomfort in the knees or back and other nonserious but distracting painful sensations.

To work with pain in the body, true awareness is essential, unmediated by concepts or images. As we attend to a strong physical sensation, we see that it does not speak to us in words, nor does it contain in itself the image of the body part where it occurs. Experiencing the body nonverbally, independently of images, we come to understand that all that happens in our bodies arises and eventually passes away. No pain or discomfort is fixed, permanent, or unchanging.

Buddhist texts speak of the "four great elements": these are the four general types of sensations. First is the element of fire, which includes all sensations of temperature, including both heat and cold. Second is the earth element, which encompasses sensations of pressure and heaviness. Air, the third element, includes the sensations of movement, touch, and feelings of hardness, softness, and piercing. The water element has a quality of cohesiveness that holds the other elements and binds them together. This element cannot be directly experienced.

As we open to our physical life with true awareness, free from words, images, clinging, judgment, or aversion, we experience the physical body as a manifestation of these four elements or energies. This perspective is very freeing. Concepts and ideas, such as attractive or unattractive, pleasant or unpleasant, healthy or diseased, lose much of their power. Although these concepts may have their usefulness in everyday life, it is helpful to separate them from the true nature of the body as it is in each moment. When we are sick, for example, each ache and pain can take on a horrible meaning. We may lie awake at night, consumed by images of doom and destruction. But if we are able to be precisely aware of the difference between a twinge and the worry that is caused by that twinge, the situation is immediately more workable. We find more rest. This distinction reveals the very nature of spiritual freedom. We do not become free *from* events, but we become free *within* events. Circumstances lose their power to lacerate our minds.

Having seen the difference between sensation and the thoughts and emotions that might arise because of the sensation, we begin to explore the edges of what we call pain. Rather than becoming lost in projection and distress, we ask, with balance, "What is the truth of this sensation? What is its real nature?" We see that ultimately all physical sensations are energies like heat, cold, tightness, piercing, twisting, or tingling that have arisen. If the mind is steady and clear, it is possible to move into the center of physical pain and ask again, "What is this?" Curiosity and interest arise. We see perhaps that the individual sensations arise and pass away. They are ever moving and never solid. The label "pain" is no longer meaningful. The conditioned chain of reactions, usually involving fear, anger, and self-judgment, have been short-circuited by true awareness of what is happening. In this seeing, joy and elation often arise. It is as if we have emerged from a jail cell onto a mountaintop.

Meditation offers a very different way of dealing with our bodies. Bit by bit, we open our hearts and minds to what is difficult within us. We develop compassion right at home, within our bodies. We come to know an openness that is gentle and accepting of what is happening.

There will naturally be times when the heart and mind are neither open nor clear. The mind may feel foggy and the attention scattered. Of course, it is not possible to be always crisp and clear, for it is the nature of all things to open and to close, just as the sky itself is not clear all the time. So, in meditation, we make peace with the clouds. We accept a heart that at times will shut down for various reasons. This is a critical aspect of meditation. We direct compassion toward our limitations. We are only human! With kindness and acceptance we come to know our ways of coping with suffering. And sometimes we cope by shutting down.

What strategies do we use to deny pain? Suppose we are meditating and feel a sudden pain in the back. (Let's assume that this twinge simply arises as a result of the stillness of our posture and is not an urgent signal of imminent injury that would require an adjustment in posture.) The first strategy is usually to deny that anything is going on. We try to stay with the awareness of breathing or whatever else we are giving our attention to at the time—anything but the back pain! The thought may arise, "It'll go away." We avoid paying attention to the pain, clinging to another object and hoping all the while that the backache will evaporate.

But the pain endures. So now, out of the corner of our eye, we give the pain a sideways glance, as if some minuscule dose of attention will cure the problem. We give the pain a few of those cursory glances; still it does not respond. So we decide to bargain with the pain: "OK, I'll give you some real attention, and then you must go away." We bring awareness to the back pain, but in truth our heart and mind are saturated with the idea that we are doing this in order to get rid of it. This idea is a thinly disguised manifestation of aversion and dislike. But we do not experience the aversion clearly and are actually further than ever from a true awareness of the sensations arising in the back. In all likelihood these mental efforts to push the pain away will only exacerbate the situation. Not only does the aversion increase the total quotient of unpleasantness that we experience, but often the physical pain seems even more intense.

Finally, after the denial, after the bargaining, there eventually comes a letting go. We surrender to the pain. There arises a willingness to simply be present with what is there. This is the birthing of equanimity. We are fully present with the truth of what is happening. We do not interfere. We are truly aware of things as they are. This is a sacred moment of great possibility, for the power of this surrender can be taken out into the world. It is a rare and precious strength.

For most of us, when we begin meditation practice, one of the first things we are afraid of are physical aches and pains that we imagine will arise. It is difficult to be accepting of all that happens in the body, particularly in the beginning. If we sit still for some time and the twinges get strong, we may feel afraid of physical damage to the knees or back. Whenever any kind of difficulty arises, it is inevitable that thoughts of fear will come up. Some meditation teachers instruct students to sit without moving for an entire hour! This is a way of encouraging students to confront the pain and at the same time deal with fear. What seems most important is that we be as carefully aware as possible of the changes happening in our body! If we do this, it soon becomes clear that having bodies means trouble for us, whether we move or are still.

Pain is an intrinsic part of being born in a physical body, as the Buddha has taught. In reality, aging and sickness begin the moment we enter the world. Yet we are conditioned to ward off all pain. We are unwilling to allow the pain to simply happen. There are some important and challenging questions relating to physical pain and our bodies:

- Are we comfortable with the truth of our bodies?
- Do we feel a need to control the changes in our bodies?
- Do we need to change things in any way?
- Can our mind be sufficiently spacious and receptive to allow all that appears to arise without our resistance or aversion?
- Can we be OK with heat, pressure, tingling, cold, and throbbing in the body?
- Is it all OK?
- Can it be workable?

Paradoxically, once we are willing to work with pain, we feel that it is not all bad. Pain is a riveting object of attention; to paraphrase Samuel Johnson, it concentrates the mind wonderfully. If we leave the breath and direct attention to whatever physical sensation is in the body, allowing ourselves to be present with whatever has arisen, the mind doesn't tend to wander very much. If we are truly aware of the sensations, we find that pain can focus and calm the mind. There can be a joy that arises with this concentration. We are not scattered. The mind is happily focused.

What else do we discover in our examination of painful sensations? With careful observation we find that the sensations are dissolving all the time. What previously seemed like a solid mass of misery is in fact changing from moment to moment. We may also discover that it was our aversion that made the pain seem really intolerable. When the aversion dissolves, what is left is much simpler and much less intimidating.

Each time we reach a threshold of pain, fear of course will be present, generating thoughts such as:

> I can't do this.
> I'm going to be crippled.
> I'll never be able to get up after this meditation.
> I'm permanently damaging myself.

Perhaps you have heard these voices in your head? They make the experience of pain far worse. They escalate the suffering far beyond what it originally was. Instead of being calmly aware, you find yourself caught in a great struggle.

I have known such voices of fear that whisper and scream of disfigurement, doom, and misery. I know the wild panic, the nameless terror that threatens to overwhelm me at the slightest provocation. My own HIV-positive diagnosis was really a dual diagnosis: It was a physical diagnosis and a diagnosis of fear. With this virus come the collective terrors, irrational phobias, and ignorant fears of a humanity that lives in deep dread of something it can neither understand nor control.

This whirlwind of collective terror can strike at the slightest ache, pain, cough, bump, or blemish. Examining some bump, my fear may easily escalate to a level of unbridled panic. Legitimate concern blooms into fear of things I've had before, fear of things that have happened to friends, fear of what I've heard or read about or even invented in my mind. Simone Weil has accurately described this state of mind:

> When thought is obliged by an attack of physical pain, however slight, to recognize the presence of affliction, a state of mind is brought about, as acute as that of a condemned man

who is forced to look for hours at the guillotine that is going to cut off his head. Human beings can live for twenty or fifty years in this acute state. We pass quite close to them without realizing it. What man is capable of discerning such souls unless Christ himself looks through his eyes?

The challenge is to let a cough be just a cough, an ache be just an ache, and a blemish just a blemish. Then I can respond appropriately to what is actually happening. I can respond with wisdom and tenderness rather than in terror and panic.

On a recent retreat I experienced excruciating physical pain in my belly. The cramping and fire profoundly affected my back and peripheral nerves too. Hell 101! Obviously the physical sensations were the primary object of attention. However, day and night, day after day, it all became grueling, gray, and very difficult. Several things came clear in the light of the continuous awareness. The resistance to the pain was itself in the belly, and this exacerbated the pain. The fear was centered in the gut too, and the tightness of aversion to the fear was in the belly also.

One day, in the midst of all this pain, it felt as though my heart broke with a feeling of immense compassion for all of this suffering. For the remainder of the retreat I directed lovingkindness and compassion into my belly, which has endured so much conflict.

The Buddha said that thoughts of the future and past are one of the principal hindrances to the development of a concentrated mind. My own experience certainly shows that fearful thoughts about the future can be very painful, particularly if they proliferate and I believe them. The origins of these patterns in my thinking are clear. Early in my life, the trauma of abuse deeply shattered my ability to trust. Ideally, a growing infant is surrounded by basic goodness, kindness, and love, which enable the child to bond with others in a relationship of trust. The violence of sexual abuse can sever this bond. The child's terror of the present develops into the idea of a fearful future. With this predisposition, it is so easy for the mind to paint terrifying pictures of what a future with AIDS might bring. If I don't see clearly what has happened within my mind and heart I find myself petrified by what I have imagined and am well within the grip of fear again. Certainly the unfolding of the AIDS disease process can be excruciatingly painful and challenging, but to anticipate all of this with terror and panic in the imagination can only be hurtful to oneself. To do so is also to deny that there might be an altogether different outcome that we cannot even imagine. In some instances, people may imagine the worst as a way of "trying on" a situation, to prepare for how to deal with it if it happens. I don't believe there's anything wrong with such imaginative trying on, as long as it is a conscious activity.

If I get enmeshed in this gridlock of fear and worry, there is little space for healing to occur. It is all just too solid and unchanging.

Compounding the load of extra baggage is the fear, ignorance, and anxiety of others. I choose to be as free as possible of these fears also. I need to be particularly careful when people act as if I am already halfway in my grave. Ironically, at this time in my life there are many ways in which I feel more alive than I've ever felt before. The experience of being present with whatever is happening in life feels like the greatest and most precious gift I can give myself. In this presence I am impervious to the projections and fear-filled imaginings of others.

And so the fearful thoughts relating to the future must fall within the light of our awareness too. We open to the fear and the thoughts that both condition the fear and those that are born of the fear.

Here, I have found a playful attitude to be a great help.

For me, one of the most tenacious patterns relating to the future consists of somber thoughts such as:

> "This pain can only get worse."
> "This pain can only progress into complete disability."
> "I'll never manage."
> "It is going to be hell."

On a recent retreat I decided that instead of noting in the usual manner ("Thinking, thinking"), I would label these thoughts in a special way. I was experiencing physical pain, and the fearful future-oriented thoughts were coming thick and fast. Soon I had labeled each one:

> "What a preposterous thought!"
> "Another preposterous thought!"
> "Yet another . . ."
> "So preposterous . . ."

I kept the tone soft, light, and chirpy. This was a great contrast to the gloomy content of the thinking. Soon the process became playful, and the absurdity of thinking that I indeed had any idea of what the future held became very clear. As the charge and sting of the thoughts fell away, they became more and more empty. They were just another phenomenon passing through, another cloud. (In labeling thoughts in this way, I was somewhat departing from the basic instructions of noting: "Thinking . . . thinking." Terming the thoughts "preposterous" is certainly judgmental. However, this innovation was very helpful at the time, even if not completely in line with basic Buddhist instruction.)

Working with physical pain is probably my central practice now. Even before I was diagnosed HIV positive, I had some problems with my back because of a separated lumbar vertebra. Digestion has been difficult for a long time, and neurological pain is now a part of life also. In fact, I deal with some degree of pain almost all the time. I have found that meditation practice is a powerful tool for making this pain as workable as possible. It is so easy to banish areas of pain from the warmth and love of my heart. Aversion to discomfort is a rejection of the pain. It also marginalizes a central part of the truth of what is happening. Opening to pain is a persistent practice, and at this edge I learn much.

I have found that it is vital to touch discomfort with an awareness that is forgiving, accepting, and loving. Sometimes I extend loving-kindness to the fiery nerve ends or the cramping belly. At each level of pain, I explore the possibility of finding a space that can hold the pain and surround it. This means I'm no longer overwhelmed, no longer a victim, but rather an active participant in what is going on. Often it is difficult to be calmly present with the sensations of burning, tightness, stinging, and heat. This is usually because of the fear and aversion that accompany the situation. At these times, a soft mental note, silently spoken in the background of my mind, helps to stabilize the awareness and bring out clearly the components of the episode. As I feel the pain directly, I voice soft, background labels like this: "Breathing. Heat. Heat. Fear. Tightness. Tingling. Heat. Breathing in . . . out. Aversion. Heat. Heat." I simply label whatever is predominant, whether it is a sensation or a thought or an emotion. It feels important to keep the label very quiet, so that it helps rather than hinders me from giving full attention to what is happening.

Another strategy that I find helpful when dealing with pain is to allow the mind to rest in a state of vast, open awareness. Into this awareness appear different objects of experience like thoughts, emotions, smells, sounds, and bodily sensations. Perceiving that intense pain arises and disappears into this open awareness seems to create less identification with and attachment to the sensations. Furthermore, sounds, thoughts, and other impressions often arise concurrently with the bodily sensations, thereby diluting and diminishing the intensity of the experience. You may wish to experiment with this: allow the mind to be vast and spacious and open, like the clear, wide sky above. Rest in this openness. Allow every aspect of your experience to appear in the open awareness, like clouds in the sky.

Whatever strategy we use to deal with pain, it is always true that pain becomes rigid if it is surrounded with concepts. I have found that to say, "I have peripheral neuropathy, I have muscular dysfunction, I have gastrointestinal dysbiosis," is dangerous, for these bleak self-descriptions etch the pain in stone. In truth, the pain is changing always. Sometimes it feels better. Sometimes it's worse. If I do not hold gently to the truth of change, I ignore the possibility of transformation and healing. Perhaps the pain might disappear altogether. It has certainly happened for some people. Perhaps there will even be a cure.

A while ago I had shingles, which produced the most intense physical pain I have ever known. The suffering was enhanced by sleeplessness, depression, and despair. Altogether, shingles was like a mental and physical avalanche, making it incredibly difficult to be simply present. Too exhausted to do anything, I let go of all meditation forms. Sleep was impossible. Painkillers and sleeping tablets only seemed to render the experience more dull and exhausting. I fought and finally I surrendered. I let go into the truth of the shingles. The unwinding and the disappearance of conflict were a blessed relief. I still feel the shingles sometimes, and now I use them as a reminder to stop fighting. They remind me to be a friend to the pain and not a soldier at war with myself.

I certainly don't want to give the impression that I'm always able to deal with pain in a noble and valiant manner, for that would be far from the truth. Working with pain is a moment-to-moment practice. It is humbling. Sometimes I am able to find an inner space of serenity. At other times, peace is completely elusive. When times are hard, there is a margin of peace in just feeling OK about being overwhelmed. Feeling that pain is unworkable, feeling hopeless, and opening to despair are all part of the process of being present to our experience as it unfolds. Our task is not to alter the process in any way, but to bring a careful awareness to the truth of what arises in our body from one moment to the next.

Guided Meditation
Bringing Loving-kindness and Compassion into Areas of Pain

- Allow your eyes to close gently.
- Center attention on the breathing.
- Move awareness now to a part of the body where there is pain and discomfort.
- Rest there.
- Be aware of any sensations that there might be.
- Allow whatever you find to be OK.
- No fight.
- No struggle.
- Be with the truth, with acceptance.
- Continue attending to the breath for a while. If possible, breathe into and through the pain, as if this were actually the place where the breath enters and leaves the body.
- Direct the following phrases quietly to the area of pain (or use your own meaningful phrases). Allow the words to echo within you.
  - "I welcome you into my heart."
  - "I accept you."

- "I care about this pain."
- "I hold you deep in my heart."
- "I accept what is happening right now."
- "May I be free from fear."
- "May I be happy, just where I am."
- "May I be peaceful with what is happening."

- You may wish to lay your hands gently on the area of discomfort.
- Allow feelings of loving-kindness and compassion to flow through the body. If there are no feelings of compassion, that is OK also.
- Continue repeating the phrases.
- End by returning to the breathing for a short while.

FACE TO FACE WITH
MORTALITY

All great spiritual traditions give importance to exploring the issues of birth and death. The Buddha encouraged his disciples to come to terms with old age and sickness, and out of compassion and kindness, he helped them to recognize and accept their mortality. He knew that true freedom is possible only when we appreciate the inevitability of our death.

We protect ourselves very carefully from the truth of our aging, from disease and death. Youth is worshiped and old age is painfully shunned. The palace walls that separated Siddhartha from life's difficulties have become the walls of nursing homes to which we relegate our old people and the walls of hospitals where people are sent to be processed through their final illness. When people die, their bodies are whisked away and often subjected to a complex and expensive embalming procedure. They later reappear on display, in a waxen imitation of serenity and peace to mollify the bereaved.

With all this subterfuge and denial, how can we connect with the fundamental truths of death and aging?

One of the ways we come to a deep understanding of mortality is through meditation practice. As we observe the arising and passing away of physical sensations, thoughts, and sounds, we witness the continual birth and death of our experience in each moment. We begin to see the constant change. Yesterday is gone. Last year is just an idea now. Our childhood is a distant memory.

In May of 1989, I returned to my parents' home in Zululand, South Africa. I was sitting with my mother in the living room when my father cried out from the bedroom. We rushed in and found him in the throes of a massive heart attack. After calling the doctor, my mother and I knelt down beside him, held him in our arms, and whispered words of encouragement, love, and letting go in his ears. He was clearly in enormous pain. We felt a great sadness. There was also great presence in those moments as we held him.

I watched each of my father's breaths more closely than any breaths of my own that I had ever watched. Recalling that moment, I am reminded of the words of Nagarjuna, a great second-century Buddhist philosopher: "Life is so fragile, more so than a bubble blown to and fro by the wind. How truly astonishing are those who think that after breathing out, they will surely breathe in again, or that they will awaken after a night's sleep."

My father died in our arms. When the doctor arrived, I arranged for us to be with the body for a long while before it was removed from the house. My mother and I went outside into the garden and gathered branches of bougainvillaea, and put them beside the bed. We washed him and combed his hair, put fresh pajamas on him, and changed the sheets. We lit candles. For many hours we sat and held him, meditated, and prayed. We kidded him, too, and said all the things we wished we had said while he was still alive. As his hands turned slowly cold in ours, I realized that this was one of the most sacred and special times of my life.

I had to stay in South Africa for a month longer than I had planned. I had gone there to be with two friends who were living with AIDS. Roy, who had been a lover many years before, died before I arrived. My friend Michael died soon after I left. It was a heartbreaking trip for me.

It was two weeks after I returned to the United States that I found out that I too was HIV positive. In the moment of my diagnosis, I took my place in the community of fifty or so of my friends who have been affected by the AIDS virus, some of whom are still alive, many of whom have died. What I had feared so much was now a part of my life. I suddenly found myself in that place of fragility and unknowing that the Buddha had spoken of so often.

Of course, I would not choose to have the AIDS virus, but it is now a given in my life. I've certainly learned lessons that I believe I would never have learned otherwise. The first days after the diagnosis were a surprise: I felt a sense of excitement, anticipation, and joy. The feeling was strong and quite bewildering. I now realize that it had to do with the relief of knowing the truth, after having been fearful for so long. It also had to do with my heart protecting itself from the enormity of the information that I had received. But most of the feeling had to do with a deep knowing that there were going to be some big changes in my life. I knew that I could no longer postpone the things that for so long I had most wanted to do.

The first thing I did was end my career as a financial consultant. It was an activity that was not nurturing me at all, and there seemed no place for it anymore. Also, many relationships which were serving neither me nor the other person began to fall away. There seemed to be much greater honesty in my dealings with people. Ways of being in the world that were petty, unnecessary, or hurtful began to fall away. This seemed to happen naturally and spontaneously.

The most wonderful decision I made during this time was to begin teaching meditation and sharing the Dharma. My teachers had been encouraging me to do this for some time. I had felt unprepared and consequently had not followed their advice. Now, doing this work brings great joy and the deepest sense of fulfillment I have ever known. I am able to reach out to others and to life when I might be tempted to withdraw instead.

Unfortunately, the honeymoon didn't last long. The next months were a nightmare of blood tests and medical examinations. I sometimes felt as if there couldn't be any more blood left for them to take, but they still managed to find more! The stream of specialists and alternative-health-care people with whom I began working seemed endless and exhausting.

In the fall of 1989 I decided to sit a three-month silent meditation retreat at the Insight Meditation Society in Barre, Massachusetts. This time felt like a rite of passage into a future that of course I knew nothing about. When I began the retreat, it seemed as though a volcano erupted within me. Huge fear, terror, and rage moved within me, greater than any I'd felt before.

Early one morning I was standing under a tree. The leaves were very beautiful in their fall colors. As the sun came up and touched the top of the tree, a multitude of leaves dropped down upon me. Something within me broke and I began crying. I cried and cried and cried. Initially it was for my father. Then I wept for my own lot. This was a terrible grieving for what I felt was the loss of my future. I felt almost betrayed. Then it changed into a deep sadness. There was no part of me that assumed I would be around even to see the next leaf fall from the branches above my head and land on the ground at my feet. Everything appeared fragile and uncertain. As the *Diamond Sutra* says: "Thus shall you consider this world: like a star at dawn, a bubble in a stream, a flickering lamp, a flash of lightning in a summer cloud, an echo, a mirage, a dream."

There were times when I felt the deepest gratitude for the fact that I really knew I was going to die one day. I sat in the back of the meditation hall and looked at the heads of all the people sitting in front of me. I wondered how many of them were going to die before me without being shaken and woken up as I had been.

Around Thanksgiving, when the snow came, my mind started to quiet down. I began to experience a peace and a calm in the meditation practice that I had never known before. I saw that it was possible to be balanced and OK with the sadness, fear, and pain, and accept these as wholeheartedly as I did the rapture and happiness that were there also.

This was a time of great appreciation and gratitude. I felt deep reverence for each breath, for every moment, for life itself. I felt aglow with this radiance, and very protected. Not protected from dying, because I knew that I would die one day, but protected by the understanding that I was not a victim of this disease. All that had really happened was that I was consciously taking my place in the scheme of things.

"Letting go" had always been an easy phrase for me to say, yet this has been the hardest lesson of all. The phrase will never roll off my tongue as easily as it used to. Letting go of the idea of future, of good health, and of physical ability has been difficult for me. Some days it feels as if everything I experience is a reflection of what is no longer possible in my life. In the fire of this teaching, I realize that out of compassion and love for myself, I must die to the way things used to be—to Gavin the athlete, Gavin the tennis player, and Gavin the skier. I have let go of the way things were, so that these memories are no longer a yardstick against which I measure the present moment.

This feels like the ultimate act of inner compassion. And this is the challenge for all of us as we get older, as ill health comes our way or we experience other losses, such as deaths of close ones or even just changes in our accustomed way of life. Dying to our history and to the way things used to be would seem to be the biggest challenge and the greatest gift of all.

There are times when I feel gratitude for the AIDS virus. Not often, mind you, but there are times. There have been blessings. I live now with an unshakable resolve to inquire, to care, and to love. There is a strength and commitment to find the deepest meaning in this nightmare. I am thankful that it has been possible for me to have a rich and deep sense of purpose at this time in my life.

My refuge in community feels sure. There are people in my life who teach me great lessons of love. They guide me, help me, and support me in ways I never thought possible. Long before my own diagnosis, I believed that in the deep interconnection that links us all, when one person is HIV positive, we all have AIDS. Nobody is immune. I believe this more than ever now. The lessons of spiritual friendship have been profound.

Another blessing of this experience is that I've been taught precious lessons about loving myself. There is a tenderness and gentleness within me that was not there before. In all the difficulties and challenges, there is no time left for the inner violence and conflict and the lack of forgiveness that had existed in my life before.

When I reflect on what it has taken for me to wake up to what is really important in my life, I sometimes feel a deep sadness. But I guess that is the way we learn the hard lessons of life—through the fire of difficulty. I now understand why sacred traditions say that suffering is the first grace.

In the Tibetan Buddhist tradition, the development of an ever-present awareness that we will one day die is considered one of the most precious transformations a human being can undergo. It is taught that we will use our time on earth with real effectiveness only when we truly embrace the fact of our oncoming death. Only in the light of death will we truly treasure the uniqueness of each fleeting and irretrievable moment. Thus, meditators try very hard to internalize the fact that they too will die. When or how we cannot predict. Yet we can seek out evidence of the certainty and unpredictability of death, challenging ourselves to reflect on these truths as deeply as possible.

One simple way that we Westerners can reflect on death is by reading the obituary pages. We may be disappointed by the blandness of the language, but the pages do vividly demonstrate that people are dying, even if the disease and circumstances go unmentioned. One writer has made this telling observation:

> The obituary pages tell us of the news that we are dying away, while the birth announcements in finer print at the side of the same page inform us of our replacements.
>
> But we get no grasp from this of the enormity of the scale. There are five and a half billion of us on the earth, and all five and a half billion must be dead on schedule within this lifetime.
>
> The vast mortality involving something like 70 million each year takes place in relative secrecy. Less than half a century from now our replacements will have doubled the numbers.
>
> It's hard to see how we can continue to keep the secret with such multitudes doing the dying.
>
> We will have to give up the notion that death is a catastrophe, or detestable, or avoidable, or even strange. We will need to learn more about the cycling of life in the rest of the system and more about our connection to the whole of the process.

It is unusual in the West for anyone to want to see a corpse or witness an autopsy. If we try to arrange for time with a dead body, most people will question our mental health! We may instead ponder deeply the truth of mortality inherent in human life. In many spiritual traditions, reflection or contemplation on death is considered an important way to arrive at deep understanding and peace.

Obviously life is uncertain. Only our death is a certainty.

We observe that seasons come and go. Summer dies; the leaves slowly catch fire, winter approaches. We read about accidents in the newspaper and see powerful images of wars, famine, and disease on television, and we know that we are not exempt. At times we may wonder, when we say goodbye to a friend, whether we can summon all our love for that parting, as if we knew for sure that we would never be together again.

The purpose of these reflections is not to frighten ourselves, but to become more aware of what is true. The Yaqui sorceror Don Juan says to Carlos Castaneda in *Journey to Ixtlan:*

> Death is our eternal companion . . . It is always to our left, at an arm's length. . . . It has always been watching you. It always will, until the day it taps you. . . .
>
> The thing to do when you're impatient is . . . to turn to your left and ask advice from your death. An immense amount of pettiness is dropped if your death makes a gesture to you, or if you catch a glimpse of it, or if you just catch the feeling that your companion is there watching you.[10]

There are other ways to work with the fear of death. In Asia, Buddhist nuns, monks, and lay practitioners are often sent to cemeteries and charnel grounds where they can witness bodies being burned and buried. Watching these ordinary processes, people begin to dismantle the delusion of immortality, a delusion built on fear. Of course, in Asia these sights are easier to witness than in our own culture. I myself grew to adulthood before I ever saw a corpse. But when I was a Buddhist monk in California, one evening the monastery arranged for us to visit the anatomy department at a nearby medical school. Seeing a dead body for the first time was a sacred moment for me. These people were exactly like me, except that they were no longer breathing! I could never relate to myself in quite the same way as I had before. The shift was immediate and irrevocable.

There are specific exercises, too, that open the mind to the reality of life's end. A traditional Buddhist practice that we did at the monastery was to focus our attention on different parts of the body. For months we systematically visualized the body's fluids, hair, bones, and flesh—thirty-two parts all together. After a while the sense of solidity began to evaporate and we experienced the body as a dynamic energy system, changing from moment to moment. It is not necessary to spend months in meditation to experience this fact. If we bring a careful awareness to the body, immediately we experience it as a mass of changing sensations.

To experience the body directly, without mental imagery, is very freeing. When we begin to understand that we, as beings, have no real solidity, we stand at the threshold of freedom. We ask ourselves: Who is it that dies? If everything is changing, then who or what is doing the dying? Who am I?

In Buddhism it is stated that the only death that occurs is the death of an idea, the idea of a personal and fixed being who is going to endure. And when the illusion of immortality breaks apart, we experience a powerful groundswell of relief. We let go of the deepest fear and great inner compassion takes its place. An ancient Buddhist text states:

> Yes, there surely is suffering,
> But not somebody who suffers.
>
> Deeds indeed can be discovered,
> But not the doer of the deed.
>
> A quenching does in fact take place,
> But no person is extinguished.
>
> There is such a thing as the path,
> But no walker of it is found.[11]

Rumi, the great Sufi poet, sees the journey to the heart of life and death in this way:

. . . God's presence is there in front of me, a fire on the left, a
lovely stream on the right.
One group walks toward the fire, *into* the fire, another toward the
sweet flowing water.
No one knows which are blessed and which not.
Whoever walks into the fire appears suddenly in the stream.
A head goes under the water surface, that head pokes out of the
fire.
Most people guard against going into the fire, and so end up in it.
Those who love the water of pleasure and make it their devotion
are cheated with this reversal.
The trickery goes further.
The voice in the fire tells the *truth*, saying, *I am not fire. I am
fountainhead. Come into me and don't mind the sparks.*

If you are a friend of God, fire is your water.
You should wish to have a hundred thousand sets of mothwings,
So you could burn them away, one set a night.
The moth sees light and goes into fire. You should see fire and go
toward light. Fire is what of God is world-consuming.
Water, world-protecting.
Somehow each gives the appearance of the other. To these eyes
you have now
what looks like water, burns. What looks like fire is a great relief
to be inside.

. . . . 12

FEAR OF DEATH

All of us have been deeply conditioned by a value system based on solidity and security. Our society values careers, wealth, physical perfection, goals, achievements, and rewards. We are required to be strong, invulnerable, and victorious. It is not surprising that most of us carry a deep-seated fear of insecurity. The fact that our moods and feelings change, often against our will, is a big problem for many people. As we open in meditation to the change that is occurring on every level of life, we feel terrified. We desperately yearn for solid ground under our feet. However, in truth, everything is shifting. And of course fear arises when we feel insecure.

We feel insecure in myriad ways. We are afraid of being unloved. We are scared of being alone and vulnerable. We are terrified of being rejected, of not being accepted and recognized in ways that are important to us. Within the grip of this fear, we may turn toward others for validation. We become yes-men and yes-women. We sell our souls for a smile of approval. If, in reaching outside of ourselves for attention, we disconnect from our inner references, we also open ourselves to the possibility of being used, hurt, and disappointed by others. We may over time feel increasingly reluctant to trust the people around us.

The biggest fear of insecurity is the fear of death. Many people are terrified of dying, and expend vast amounts of energy avoiding any thought or indication of what is absolutely inevitable for each one of us. The degree to which we are caught in the fear of death is the extent to which our life cannot be really whole. Nor can we be deeply and truly happy, for the fear of death separates us from the fullness of life. Whenever we resist change, that resistance is a fear of death in disguise. As long as we hold on to the body or to any idea of a separate self, we will always be afraid of death.

In meditation, we experience that the body is constantly dissolving. Wherever our examination takes us, we find change, with no one controlling it. We see also that our emotional states and thoughts arise and pass away. Nothing is solid. This is a terrifying insight. It is a time of great challenge when we let go of the idea of solidity and allow the truth of who we are to emerge.

How do we engage our fear of death? This is a huge undertaking. We sense that this fear is very deeply conditioned, as though it were built into our cells. We may even feel that this fear protects our life itself. How can we ever come to grips with it? And yet somehow we must make peace with our mortality, or else live in dread of our eventual demise.

Meditation offers a full response to the fear of death. When we look closely into our experience, we see that evanescence and dissolution are everywhere. Seeing, feeling, and knowing the movement of each unrepeatable breath, we sense the truth of change. We observe the birth and death of sounds and smells, the arising and passing away of emotions, and the beginning and end of thoughts. We begin to understand that every passage between moments involves the end of something. No phenomenon ever returns in exactly the same form. We begin to deeply know that our own passage out of life must happen just as swiftly and surely someday. When we take refuge in the arising and dissolution of phenomena, on a momentary level, we begin to dance with the truth of our finality instead of struggling with it. We live *with* our mortality, not just in spite of it.

Reflections on Transience and Death

- Be aware of the sensations of the breath. Notice how the sensations change. Once a sensation disappears, it never returns. Be aware of the fleetingness and rapidity with which these sensations arise and pass away.

- Reflect on your life since childhood. When you were young, you looked forward to being older, and now you are. There is no way that you can turn back the stream of time, as every moment, you grow closer to death. Life is an arrow that was shot at birth and will never return to the bow.

- Think of everyone who has gone before you on this planet. Socrates, the Buddha, Jesus, Muhammad . . . Steven Biko, Arthur Ashe . . . your own ancestors, your great-grandparents, people close to you who have passed away. Where are they now?

- Reflect on the inexorability of the progress of all living beings, including yourself, toward death. Does this moment seem more precious and alive when held within the light of mortality?

⋮

WORKING WITH ANGER

ONE DAY THE Buddha addressed a gathering of monks who had been squabbling among themselves:

"If a person speaks or acts with evil intention, pain follows like a wheel following a beast of burden.

"If a person speaks or acts with pure and kind intention, happiness follows like a shadow in the sunlight.

"Hatred never ceases with hatred," the Buddha emphasized.

"Hatred only ceases with love. This is the law, ancient and eternal."

The monks felt ashamed of themselves. The Buddha continued:

"Let no one deceive another.

"Let no one scorn another.

"Let no one wish another harm.

"As a mother watches over her child with dilligence, care, and love, so too let all beings cultivate boundless love toward all creatures everywhere."

———————

Once upon a time there was a hermit who lived in a cave in the hills above a village in India. Some of the old people still remembered when he first came to the village as a holy mendicant and took up residence in the cave to perform religious practices and meditations. He remained in the cave day and night. No one ever saw him, though some villagers left him offerings of food. At night a faint glow was visible at the mouth of the cave, and the village would congratulate itself upon the progress of its holy man.

Finally, one day, after thirty years, a great light glowed at the mouth of the cave, defying the brightness of the sun. The eyes of the villagers were drawn to the miraculous sight. They saw their hermit stepping out of the cave, blinking. The children rushed up the slopes, and the adults scrambled after them. They met the hermit, who was walking down, his eyes modestly downcast and his face and body radiant. The children cast flower petals on the ground before him. He was so holy, it seemed, that his feet touched neither the flowers nor the ground beneath him.

Awed by the presence of so accomplished a being, the people eagerly asked the holy man, "What is it that you have accomplished after all these years of spiritual practice?"

The holy man lifted his eyes, beamed a glorious smile, and replied: "I have overcome anger."

The villagers clapped and danced and threw flowers at his feet. Then somebody asked, "And what else have you achieved after all these years? What have you learned? Please tell us."

The hermit coughed and said, "Well, I have accomplished much. I have conquered my anger."

The people were still excited and joyful. Then somebody else said, "There must be something else you've learned after thirty years! Please share your wisdom with us."

A cloud passed over the eyes of the holy man. He clenched his fists and growled, "Idiots! Fools! Is it not enough that I have laid down my anger?"

It is said in the Buddhist texts that anger is permanently uprooted in the third stage of enlightenment, just before the fourth and final stage when one is fully enlightened. In this light, it would seem that most of us will be dealing with anger for some time yet.

Anger is one of the three root causes of suffering, the other two being greed and ignorance or delusion. These roots obscure the nature of reality, and, enmeshed in them, we are likely to manifest these qualities in our actions, speech, and thoughts.

True awareness has the power to neutralize these roots of suffering. It is possible to be completely freed from the grip of the three roots and all of the painful emotions that stem from them.

In meditation we slowly open to the fullness of who we are. Each of us is like an exquisite flower bud, opening into fullness and wholeness. We open to the beauty, the wonder, and the truth of who we are. We open to our capacity to love, to care, to share, to nurture, and to understand. We open to spaces of joy, calm, silence, and emptiness within ourselves. At the same time, we open to our so-called dark side, to the shadow. We come to know our capacity to hate and rage, to fear, clutch, and hold on. We open to forces of guilt, attachment, confusion, doubt, and chaos within ourselves. When meditation is wholehearted and true, it must call forth the entire range of what it means to be human.

We must eventually open to everything if we are to understand and be freed from all suffering.

Like the hermit in that Indian village, most of us carry images of ourselves that are somewhat lofty, very well defended, and rather partial. Meditation gently forces us to recognize the painful disparity between these self-images and the emerging truth of who we are. The process can be hard, and it calls for great compassion toward ourselves. Our resources of patience and endurance can be deeply challenged as we begin to see that we are indeed only human. We are sometimes angry, sad, fearful, greedy, deluded, and selfish.

It is utterly human to have anger arise in one's mind. Yet, for most of us, anger is usually taboo. I remember how once, in the middle of an argument, a friend suddenly looked at me and said, with a mixture of shock and triumph, "You are really angry, aren't you?" She had found a trace of the dreadful defilement, and because I was angry, I had lost my right to be taken seriously!

Anger terrifies us so much that we are even afraid to admit its presence, in ourselves and in others. We are afraid that if we get angry, others will disapprove of us. Very often, too, the arising of anger signals a need for change, and change can be scary.

Our society has a special bias when it comes to women dealing with anger or manifesting it in any way. Angry women are labeled unladylike, unfeminine, strident, shrill, witches, nags, and shrews. There seem to be no corresponding derogatory terms for angry men. In fact, it seems largely acceptable, noble, patriotic, just, and brave for angry men to wage vicious and bloody wars all over the planet, murdering, raping, mutilating, and leaving children homeless and hungry.

Considering all this confusion about anger, it is no wonder that we have difficulty accepting the feeling in ourselves or in others. The extent to which we deny its presence is the extent to which anger remains unexplored and unknown. Yet if our quest for self-knowledge is serious and our wish for wholeness sincere, we must integrate any and all cut-off emotions that there might be. To open into the fullness of who we are, we must reclaim all that we and others have deemed unacceptable.

Of course, reclaiming the anger does not mean that we give ourselves the right to act harmfully toward others. As our sensitivity deepens, we identify in others the same vulnerability of heart that we ourselves know. As we become more honest, we no longer deny that we are so much like other people. We are capable of being vindictive and hurtful. In fact, our willingness to acknowledge and feel the anger is a direct expression of compassion for ourselves, and for others. Genuine awareness is inextricably linked with compassion.

In our culture, anger is usually dealt with in two ways, both of them are regarded as unskillful from a Buddhist perspective. "Unskillful" is a term used to describe actions and thoughts that perpetuate rather than alleviate suffering. The first unskillful method of dealing with anger is to suppress it, and the second is to vent it. Suppression adds clinging and fear to the original feeling of anger. We contract and hold the anger closely within ourselves. Afraid to let our anger show, we don't let go of it either.

Venting anger is a largely aversive reaction. Anger hurts us, so we spit it out into the world, as if this will free us of what is so painful. There is often a sense of revenge and a wish to inflict harm as we make sure that the other person gets a genuine, high-quality piece of our mind!

Clearly, neither venting nor suppression moves us away from suffering in any direct way. Rather, each reaction only re-conditions, solidifies, and maintains the underlying patterns that precipitated the anger in the first place.

Let us examine suppression more closely. Why is anger so often hidden? One reason is that people deeply fear that their rage will spill out, destroying relationships and causing others to abandon them. Sadly, this is just what can happen if anger is suppressed for a long time. It can emerge in jagged, neurotic, and painful ways.

Therefore we often keep anger to ourselves to avoid conflict and keep the peace. A great deal of energy is then devoted to protecting others from our anger and preserving relationships. Over time, we lose all sense of our own needs, priorities, and perceptions. This is painfully self-defeating and self-denying. We become Pollyannas of one sort or another. Ah, what nice ladies and nice men we are, sporting our radiant smiles while seething and raging inside with resentment! Sometimes the anger is suppressed so deeply that it feels as though it is buried under rock. This is blocked energy, and the effects of this can be dangerously unhealthy. Suppressed anger clearly has the ability to cause disease and discomfort in the body. Deep and long suppression can have profound psychological consequences, too.

A while ago I was in a difficult conflict with someone, and for several weeks I grew more and more angry. Yet I suppressed my feelings and lost all touch with the degree of anger that was there. One morning I woke up in a paralyzing depression. I lay in bed, unable to move. This is very uncharacteristic of me. My spirit was completely gone. I called a friend, who suggested I close all the doors and windows and scream and shout for a while. Perhaps this would move some energy, I thought. I began roaring like a lion. Suddenly, as if a switch had been thrown, a huge column of energy roared through my body. The listlessness and depression instantly vanished. It was immediately clear to me that the buried rage had caused the paralysis and depression.

For me, what was most important was not the yelling, but the understanding and clarity that came with it. First of all, I understood the danger of suppressing the anger and losing touch with the truth of what was happening. Furthermore, once I became aware of the depth of the feelings, I was able to look at the situation realistically and respond in an appropriate way.

Sometimes if anger is deeply suppressed, skillful techniques can help lift the energy to the surface so that healing and insight may occur. This process should be undertaken cautiously, perhaps with the support of an accomplished therapist. Releasing suppressed anger must be done with great care and skill, without perpetuating any identification with and attachment to the emotion. If we become attached to the intensity, power, and feeling of release that come with yelling and screaming, this will only create further suffering. Venting and releasing anger do provide momentary relief in cases where there is suppression, but they are not ends in themselves.

Let us look more closely at the venting of anger. There are two kinds of behaviors called venting. The first entails expressing anger at the person who made you angry, or displacing it onto some other person, the dog, or whatever else is around. The second kind of venting is the release of anger by shouting, hitting a pillow, or going out and playing a vigorous game; no other person is involved, and one is simply trying to let off steam. Both are considered potentially unskillful from a Buddhist perspective, although the former is certainly more dangerous. How often have well-intentioned friends advised us to let our anger out or get it off our chest as a prescription for mental and physical health? You'd think human beings were dangerous volcanoes, with lava seething constantly in the dark nether regions of the abdomen and chest! In truth there are no reservoirs of anger within ourselves that we need to tap or empty.

In meditation we see that everything that arises passes away. Things arise because of causes and conditions. When the causes and conditions change, the situation changes too. Nothing is permanent, not even anger. Anger arises because of causes and conditions. When these are removed, the anger must fall away or change in some way. If we believe that we must vent our anger, we create patterns of conditioning in the depths of our consciousness. Our belief conditions further anger and predisposes us to react in unskillful ways in the future.

The strategies of venting, releasing, or acting out our anger tend to involve a great deal of identification. We hear ourselves yelling and screaming and in the background we think: "I'm an angry person. I am furious. I'm really getting my anger out!" It's always *my* anger, *my* rage. We may even believe that it is our nature to be angry. If we identify with anger to the point where we believe that the emotion truly defines who we are, we create a prison rather than the possibility of freedom within ourselves.

Venting can feel very satisfying. In this age of psychology, anger has been ennobled and honored. How often do we witness righteous anger in the world? We hear people choking with indignation about this or that. Righteous prophets, foaming at the mouth, allow their anger to splash out all over the place. Often this leaves them feeling very proud of themselves.

Thich Nhat Hanh, a Vietnamese Zen monk, poet, and activist, has seen some of the worst suffering our world has known. He has carried the bodies of friends across fields of fire, and he has seen war destroy his homeland. One might think he would be angry and bitter about all that has happened. Instead his activism is filled with love and tolerance. He speaks often about anger, in a gentle and often humorous way:

> Some of us may prefer to go into our room, lock the door, and punch a pillow. We call this getting in touch with our anger. But I don't think it is getting in touch with our anger at all. In fact, I don't think it is even getting in touch with our pillow. If we are really in touch with the pillow, we know what a pillow is and we won't hit it. Still, this technique may work temporarily, because while pounding the pillow, we expend a lot of energy, and after a while we are exhausted and we feel better. But the roots of our anger are still intact, and if we go out and eat some nourishing food, our energy will be renewed. If the seeds of our anger are watered again, our anger will be reborn, and we will have to pound the pillow again. Pillow-pounding may provide some relief, but it is not very long-lasting. In order to have a real transformation, we have to deal with the roots of our anger—looking deeply into its causes. If we don't, the seeds of anger will grow again. If we practice mindful living, planting, new, healthy, wholesome seeds, they will take care of our anger, and they may transform it without our asking them to do so.
>
> Our mindfulness will take care of everything, as the sunshine takes care of the vegetation. The sunshine does not seem to do much, it just shines on the vegetation, but it transforms

everything. Poppies close up every time it gets dark, but when the sun shines on them for one or two hours, they open. The sun penetrates into the flowers, and at some point, the flowers cannot resist, they just have to open up. In the same way, mindfulness, if practiced continuously, will provide a kind of transformation within the flower of our anger, and it will open and show us its own nature. When we understand the nature, the roots, of our anger, we will be freed from it.[13]

How do we follow this advice and get to the true nature of anger, to its very roots? This is the third way, the way of meditation and awareness. Here the challenge is to simply allow the anger to be present. Neither denied nor indulged, the anger is allowed to come fully and wholeheartedly into the mind and into awareness, so that it can be met, investigated, seen as empty, and seen as changing.

The way of meditation is the way of acceptance and patience. Where anger strikes and lashes out, acceptance and patience welcome and invite. These attitudes contradict the anger and open up the possibility of relating to the anger rather than from it.

In no way does meditation ask that we become docile, wishy-washy, or passive. With a clear comprehension of the anger, we respond to the emotion forcefully when it arises. With discrimination and wisdom we see clearly into the situation that caused the anger. This is a powerful shift, which results in healing both inwardly and outwardly. We may choose to speak or we may keep silent. We examine all aspects of the situation and consider the probable outcomes. We then choose a response that is balanced, appropriate, and true. If we choose to forgive, we stand behind our decision. We are not victims. Whether we choose action or forgiveness, our timely and clear awareness short-circuits the murky escalation of blame and hurt that so often spirals out of control when we act out of anger.

True awareness dispels anger, for awareness is an expression of love. Our wish to know the truth of things is a gesture of the deepest self-love and compassion. We may choose to generate lovingkindness as an antidote to anger. (See part 4, "Meditations of the Heart.") If it feels appropriate, we may choose to direct loving qualities of heart toward people we are angry with or people who bear us ill will. Lovingkindness eases the mind and enables it to return to a state of balance and clarity.

The way of meditation requires that we come close to anger and see it directly. We accept anger with patience and respect. We come to know it fully, as if it were an old, cranky friend, with all its quirks, edges, idiosyncrasies, and its great power. We take tea with the anger again and again . . . and patiently again.

Getting to know anger, we see that it manifests in the body. We feel it perhaps in the face and neck, in the throat, in the chest, in the gut, in the bowel, or in the lower back. We become aware of how anger affects our breathing and body temperature.

How does the mind feel when anger is present? Rigid, stiff, tight, rough, tense, contracted? We feel our mental state with clarity and sensitivity. This is the way of meditation.

We may feel frustration as we try to meet anger with clarity and compassion. At such times, when we find our mental state unworkable, this is often a clue that we are feeling impatience with or aversion to the anger. Within ourselves, anger can seethe on and on behind an almost invisible screen of impatience and self-judgment. This secondary anger—aversion to the aversion— often arises as a wish that our anger would go away. However, recognizing anger and bringing true awareness to the emotion does not mean it necessarily disappears. Patience is a great friend when grappling with anger. Patience allows people and situations to be just as they are, in every moment, including whatever anger may be involved. Far from being a passive and submissive attitude, true patience has a core of great strength and resolve.

In spite of our sincerity, patience and resoluteness, we may find that the anger itself is difficult to recognize. This is true for many of us, particularly if there has been a history of great suppression. Personally it took eleven years of "wild patience," in the words of the poet Adrienne Rich, before I was able to engage anger directly.

For me, much of the anger relates to a deep pattern of conditioning, the legacy of sexual abuse in my infancy. When I touch the depth of the pain, it seems reasonable for this anger to have taken so long to emerge into the light of day. I believe my heart and mind needed to mature to some degree before opening to the powerful, strong, and deeply buried patterns of anger that are there.

If we are feeling overwhelmed by anger, it is important to honor this. We do not always have to go right to the core of things. Sometimes it is skillful to back off. If we find ourselves in a situation where anger feels out of control, random, or freewheeling, it can be advisable to step back. This is an expression of discriminating wisdom in a difficult situation. We might choose to return to the situation later, when we are clearer and more balanced. This is true of both inner and outer situations.

The practice of awareness calls us to be present with the truth of what is happening. When there is true awareness, the present moment is always sufficient. It is all there is! Can we trust this moment? Do we believe that everything that needs to arise will do so in its own time, like a flower blooming in its season?

For many of us, the befriending of anger is a long, slow, and gradual process. Perhaps the anger has been hidden for a long time, and for good reason. If our work is slow, it will teach us great patience and tolerance for both ourselves and for others. We learn to love ourselves just as we are, in each moment.

We start by learning how to stop. There is one simple resolve I have found very useful over the years. I allow myself to stop and pay careful attention to what is happening anytime I begin to feel unbalanced, tight, or uncomfortable within myself.

We give ourselves permission to stop, any time of day, in any situation, and simply ask:

- What is happening?
- What is this feeling?
- Where do I feel it?
- In the mind?
- In the body?
- Is it anger?
- Is it sadness?
- Is it grief?

We explore, inquire and look at ourselves honestly. This is the essence of meditation practice. This attitude of openness and questioning is ripe with possibility.

It is most desirable to recognize anger right when it arises, before it evolves into a raging monster. When we notice that anger has arisen, we simply acknowledge it, name it, and feel it. We may say softly to ourselves: "Anger, anger." The mental label keeps us in place so that we can feel the emotion clearly and steadily. As we do so, we observe the relationship of anger to other emotions, such as fear, desire, shame, and boredom. The clouds of the mind are rarely simple! With resolution we open to the anger, again and again and again. Over time, slowly and gradually, the full energy of anger emerges into the open, to be befriended, respected, and made workable.

Anger contains a great potential for transformation. It is

said that the high and direct energy of anger can be like a sword that slices through delusion to a place of complete freedom. The powerful energy of anger can motivate us to say no to all the ways we are defined by others, and yes to the dictates of our hearts. In our commitment to true awareness, anger can be a signal for us to turn inward. Rather than staying involved in outer distractions such as blame and mental analysis, we turn inward to understand what is true for us. Here we grapple with the issues of reality, freedom, and release rather than being trapped in a cycle of reaction and retribution.

The task of fully opening to ourselves requires courage and conviction. It is not easy. Genuine effort is involved. Painful emotions are often tenacious. They can rapidly overwhelm a situation before we realize all that is happening.

The Zen master Shunryu Suzuki Roshi refers to painful emotions as "the weeds of the mind." He says, "We pull the weeds and bury them near the plant to give it nourishment. So even though you have some difficulty in your practice . . . you should not be bothered by your mind. You should rather be grateful for the weeds, because eventually they will enrich your practice. If you have some experience of how the weeds in your mind change into mental nourishment, your practice will make remarkable progress."[14]

What do we see when we engage anger? In my practice over the years, I have found a number of characteristics that seem important. First, the experience of anger is unpleasant. This seems to be its most outstanding and obvious characteristic. The popular description of "burning up" with anger can be painfully accurate. Raging anger is a real hell, especially if fueled with lots of blaming and judgmental thoughts. The fire burns on and on as long as it is fed. I have spent days with a forest fire of anger raging through my mind!

Second, anger also has a way of being icy-cold. It concentrates the mind coldly on whatever object is precipitating the anger. Perhaps you have noticed that when angry with someone, we usually fixate very sharply on their clothes, facial expressions, and tiny mannerisms. We are probably not very generous in our evaluation either! We are certainly very focused, though. This concentration can intensify the experience of anger.

This sharp focus can be useful in meditation. Though we sometimes believe that meditative concentration is available only at elevated levels of peace and saintliness, this is not necessarily so. When anger erupts in the mind, we can react as if a burglar were breaking into the house. The mind jumps to attention instantaneously, totally focused and clear, watching the movements of the intruder. This intense attention can shine to the roots of anger.

Third, as we observe anger, we see that it arises in association with causes. It does not randomly flare up on its own. Neither does it burst forth from some internal reservoir. If we don't get what we want, anger arises. If we get what we don't want, anger comes up. Whenever anger arises, we can be sure that we are at an edge, a place where the opportunity for freedom and understanding is enormous. Anger arises when there is attachment. Where there is attachment, there is also the opportunity to let go.

Fourth, we see that even if we don't let go of anger, it will go away eventually anyhow. Anger, like everything else, is impermanent. As soon as we are distracted, or the conditions that precipitated the anger change, the anger itself falls away too. This insight into the impermanence of anger is important. When anger arises, it appears fixed and interminable, as if it were going to last forever. We may feel that we are going to be angry for the rest of our days. Having seen anger arise and pass away many times, we tell ourselves, "This anger will pass; this too shall pass." This may seem a small shift, but in reality it is an enormous transformation. Acknowledging the impermanence of anger changes the fundamental tone of our relationship with it.

Most important, we come to see that not only is anger impermanent, it is also devoid of any owner or abiding essence. This subtle but vital truth loosens the grip of anger. Recognizng the interaction of cause and effect also helps us to see that anger has no owner. It is impersonal. It arises out of causes and passes away when circumstances change.

Finally, we see the role of thoughts in fueling anger. When we are aware and present, we see a familiar sequence: we have a thought, we get angry. The anger then tends to generate further thoughts. "He did this. She said that. I felt bad. They retaliated. They are always like that!" Before we know it, the mind is spinning out of control, blaming, analyzing, and plotting revenge. It is almost laughable at times. We create imaginary situations and then get angry about them. Through all of this fiery thinking, who in the end is hurting? Who is the one in pain?

Being truly aware of the fundamental emptiness of thoughts is a soothing balm when dealing with anger. Thoughts are no more personal than the clouds in the sky. Like clouds, thoughts float through the mind. Angry thoughts. Loving thoughts. Not me, not mine—just thoughts. Just anger.

When anger arises, I often recall the poetic words of the Buddha:

> Anger, with its poisoned source and fevered climax
> murderously sweet, that must you slay to weep no more.

SELF-HATRED AND
SELF-LOVE

Over time, as we engage anger, we find that it no longer shuts us out of our heart. Rather, it becomes a reminder to release awareness, mercy, compassion, and kindness. It becomes a stimulus to self-love rather than self-hatred. We see clearly that the capacity of our hearts and minds is much vaster than the greatest rage that might blow through. We no longer live in fear of anger. Rather it becomes a full part of the beauty of who we are, and our flower has opened that much further.

With a commitment to take full responsibility for our anger, we wage peace within ourselves and so too in the world. We do not allow our rage to overflow into a world already overwhelmed and reeling under the impact of conflict, violence, and hatred.

As we both open to and take responsibility for anger, we see that the energy moves in two directions. On the one hand, ungoverned, it lashes out and strikes out at the world, people, situations, and even objects. On the other hand, unchecked, anger manifests as self-hatred and a lack of inner forgiveness and love. The internal voices of anger and rage can be crippling, vicious, and relentless. As we hear these voices clearly, we realize a shattering and heartbreaking truth: we often treat ourselves in ways that we would never treat anybody else.

At the time of the Buddha, many seekers of the truth engaged in severe practices of self-mortification. People starved themselves and in many other ways pushed their physical bodies to the most extreme limits of deprivation and pain in the hope that they could transcend the body and be free of its limitations. The Buddha himself engaged in austerities and came to understand that punishing the body was not a doorway to liberation from suffering. In his enlightenment he understood that the way to freedom ran midway between punishing and indulging the body. Thus the path of the Buddha has become known as the Middle Way.

Today in the West, physical self-torture is uncommon. However, self-hatred and inner violence rage within the hearts and minds of many people. For most of us today this inner torture seems to have supplanted the physical torture of long ago, and it is this habitual behavior that we need to move away from, in order to find our own Middle Way to liberation.

Many of us have known this for a long, long time. Now the tyranny of these voices of judgment and violence must be gathered into the light of our awareness. In meditation, we open to negative patterns turned inward against ourselves. We draw on both the heart of compassion and the eye of wisdom as we grapple with anger. The Indian sage and master Nisargadatta Maharaj said: "Love tells me that I am everything. Wisdom tells me that I am nothing, and between these two my life flows."[15]

We open to anger with love and wisdom. Into the brightness of awareness we bring the high and impossible self-images we have of ourselves. We come to know the grandiose ideas that we have of being perfect, always kind and never angry or ungenerous. We see, too, how we use these impossibly inhuman ideals as the yardstick against which we measure ourselves. And we always fall short! We open our broken hearts to the pain of all this cruelty. We see how we lacerate ourselves by comparing these heartbreaking models of who we and others think we should be with the reality of who we truly are.

It is as if in each moment of the day, we ask these questions:

Who shall I be now?
The one my mother wants me to be?

The one my father hopes I'll be?
The one my schoolteachers believed I could have been?
The one my partner thinks I am?
The one my children expect me to be?
The one I want myself to be?

For so many of us these barely perceptible yet very debilitating questions of self-crucifixion go on all the time, removing us from a healthy sense of our true selves. We feel empty, barren, and dry. There is often great rage, too, for all the self-denial and pain.

Yet it is our birthright that we be fully open, bright, and completely free of all the inner violence and conflict that has kept our flower bud tightly closed and contracted for so long. I would like to share with you my process of opening to the voices of self-hatred, and share with you some of the lessons I have learned.

I have been aware of the inner war for a very long time. I came to spiritual practice crushed by the weight of the division within myself. Over years of meditation, I observed anger and its associated thoughts again and again. I felt the suffering of all this violence and conflict within myself.

Some time ago I was in a very complicated relationship. There was great pain and much disappointment. There was considerable anger and a lack of reconciliation for quite some time. What was most shattering about the situation was the relentless barrage of self-criticism and judgment that the situation unleashed within me. Fueled by the strong emotions of the time, the onslaught of these inner voices did not abate for months. I could not sleep. Interpersonal wrangling and difficult decisions fueled the fire. I was in hell, and no one was doing it to me but myself. I had never before seen this aspect of myself so vividly and clearly.

At first I endeavored to bargain with the tormenting

thoughts. I tried repeating words of affirmation to contradict them. I reminded myself that what I had said and done in the situation was neither wrong nor inappropriate, but that effort too was of no avail. The self-hatred poured on.

It was obvious that I was experiencing the painful reality of the inner wiring I'd lived with all my life. I learned a further interesting lesson. Emotions are not rational, and neither are the thoughts that arise out of them.

I took this nightmare into a two-month meditation retreat. In the silence and the quiet, the full extent of the inner conflict blossomed and revealed itself. I decided to give a special label to these relentless thoughts. I named them "the Voice." When they started their barrage, I would say, "the Voice, the Voice." I pitched my label deep and low, as if I were narrating my own horror film.

A label is very useful when dealing with recurring thoughts in meditation. If there are obsessive, repeating thoughts associated with planning, fantasizing, plotting, or analyzing, give these thoughts a simple label. Labeling similar thoughts has a way of cutting through their tape-loop quality. "Obsessing, obsessing. Plotting, plotting. Fantasizing, fantasizing." The label allows for a detached, objective, and impersonal awareness to be present. As one observes the thoughts, one begins to see how repetitious and tenacious they are.

I began to see how the Voice featured in every aspect of my day. The Voice criticized me if I ate too much or too little. The Voice had something to say if I meditated too much, not at all, or not enough. If I walked too much, or too little, or not at all, there was a judgment. It was incredible. I began to see that I could not win. The Voice was there, criticizing all the time. I felt bereft as the truth revealed itself. At the same time I felt grateful and relieved that I was finally able to see it so clearly.

Recognition is really the crucial first stage in opening and healing. If we choose to open candidly to the truth of ourselves, it can be immensely difficult. As we see what is truly going on within us, it often takes great strength and courage to stay open and awake, for we cannot heal what has not first been recognized. This time of recognition calls for immense care, tenderness, and skill. While it may feel that our noses are being rubbed in self-understandings that are neither pleasant nor desirable, we must be careful that we do not use this difficult information as a further weapon against ourselves.

This wonderful piece of advice was offered by a Hindu monk named Kirpal Venanji:

> Break your heart no longer. Each time you judge yourself, you break your heart. You stop feeding on the love that is the wellspring of your vitality, but now the time has come, your time, to live, to celebrate and to see the goodness that you are. There is no evil, no wrong in you or in any other. There is only the thought of it, and the thought has no substance. You are dear, divine, and very, very pure. Let no one, no thing, no idea or ideal obstruct you. If one comes even in the name of truth, forgive the thought for its unknowing. Do not fight it, just let go and breathe into the goodness that you are.

The lovingkindness meditation is a powerful practice at times like this (see page 79). During my retreat, I began alternating lovingkindness meditation with awareness meditation. I alternated the two meditations through the day. I did lovingkindness meditation while eating, walking, and washing. It was very helpful. It softened the inner turmoil. Each phrase of lovingkindness seemed to calm the Voice, leaving a feeling of warmth, protection, and love.

This scenario involved physical pain also. At times it felt as though every muscle in my body were screaming and tightening and every nerve were on fire. When the pain was most intense,

I switched to compassion meditation. I repeated one single phrase: "I care about this pain." I touched the area of pain with tenderness, acceptance, and compassion, saying to myself, "I care about my pain."

At first I felt browbeaten and humbled as I realized for the first time that most of my life had been lived under the weight of the Voice. Slowly the situation began to change. With time a sweet calm set in. Lovingkindness and compassion began to pervade my days, and I began to feel less and less affected by what the Voice was saying. This movement took me out of the content of my thoughts and into the deeper process of what was happening. Thoughts are like trains in the mind. Sometimes we catch them long after they have begun their journey. Other times it is possible to see thoughts soon after they begin. It really does not matter which we do. The willingness to be truly aware of thoughts without judgment or comment is what is most important. The mental labels I used sounded sometimes like this: "In, out . . . Voice, Voice . . . in, out . . . thinking, thinking . . . out . . . Voice, Voice . . . anger . . . in . . . disappointment . . . Voice, Voice, Voice!"

Thankfully a sense of humor began to emerge. Because awareness is sometimes difficult work, keeping the practice as light as possible is vital, particularly when the content is heavy. It is so easy for there to be a sense of struggle and aversion to thoughts. This aversion exacerbates the situation and creates further tension, complexity, and contraction. If there is aversion to the thoughts, we need to open to the aversion.

It is vital that we also open to the emotions that condition the thoughts. If there are a succession of angry or revengeful thoughts, there is certainly anger fueling them. We then open to the anger. This may seem obvious, but on the level of inner process, we often listen to the thoughts with great fascination without being conscious of what is conditioning them.

For me, as the Voice and the anger became more and more OK, things got lighter, joyful, and even playful. I was seeing the Voice everywhere, but the reaction was minimal or even nonexistent. Once, out walking in the woods, instead of making a mental label when the Voice came up, I put my thumb on my nose and wagged my fingers at the Voice. It felt great to play with this thing that had hurt so much.

Then one night I had a very clear dream: I was with the man who had abused me when I was an infant.* In the dream I realized that in the future I would coexist with this person without any trouble. There was a deep sense of knowing this truth. Awareness was strong throughout the dream. My abuser opened his mouth to speak to me in the dream. His voice was the Voice! His words were uncannily deep and gruff. I got such a fright, I woke up! But it was a time of great enthusiasm to look, understand and know more and more.

After recognition, the second stage is acceptance. After we have slowly recognized and felt the suffering, we must accept the cause of the suffering before real genuine healing is possible. Both of these processes call for patience, courage, and commitment. We accept the self-hatred, self-anger, and conflict and the thoughts that go along with them. We accept the pain of the struggle too. This is not easy.

Why is it so difficult to accept these thoughts? First of all,

---

*Although I am fully aware of who it was who abused me in my infancy, I have decided not to divulge his identity in this book. He is now dead. He died before my recollection of what happened. All those who need to know have been told the full facts of the abuse. As I now live ten thousand miles away from South Africa, I feel disinclined to identify my abuser when I will not be present to deal with the repercussions of the disclosure. In this decision, no part of me wishes to protect the perpetrator.

identification with thoughts is one of the primary ways in which we create a sense of ourselves. This has been going on for a long time. It is a deeply conditioned pattern. We see the thoughts as "me" and "mine," and if the thoughts are charged with emotion and pain, it is not easy to see them as empty and changing. But it is possible. In a moment of true awareness, the thought usually falls away. The moment we see it, it is over. We return to the sensations of breathing.

A further problem arises for many meditators. We develop the idea that thinking is wrong. Many experience this, though it is not a part of the instructions. We fight the presence of thoughts. We somehow believe that the end of thinking is the goal of meditation practice. This is frustrating, since thoughts are a natural part of being human. They will, as I understand, always be around. The challenge is to come to know the true nature of thoughts rather than try to obliterate them.

As we recognize the true nature of thoughts, we reach the third stage of healing, the stage of process. With awareness we see thoughts as no more personal than the clouds passing across an open sky, or the sound of rain on the ground. We see thoughts as utterly empty of selfhood. Thoughts are just another empty phenomenon alongside the sounds, sights, sensations in the body, and so forth. Seeing thoughts in this way brings great joy and a sense of space and freedom to the mind. Thoughts become less sticky. They are no longer a source of difficulty. There is no longer a struggle. We glimpse the possibility of letting go at this fundamental level. In a very powerful and succinct teaching on the nature of reality, the Buddha said:

> . . . among those things
> that can be seen, heard, felt, or known,
> in the seen there will be just what is seen,
> in the heard there will be just what is heard,

in the felt there will be just what is felt,
in the known there will be just what is known.[16]

That is all there is in any moment: what is seen, felt, or known.
By "felt," the Buddha is referring to what is smelled, tasted,
and touched.

In times of subtle practice, there can be a further awareness
of the process of knowing or consciousness. This happens simultaneously with the arising of what is seen, thought, tasted,
heard, and so forth. We see two parallel processes: the object and
the knowing of the object arising and passing away, from moment to moment. That is all there is! No me. No you. Just ap-
pearances and the knowing of them.

Of course, from this perspective, the Voice became just another empty phenomenon. In the voicing, there is just what is
voiced—no Gavin, no struggle. Utterly empty.

Throughout this book, I have emphaszied the importance
of our relationship with the process of thinking. This Buddhist
aphorism succinctly addresses the vital influence of thoughts in
our lives:

> The thought manifests as the word.
> The word manifests as the deed.
> The deed develops into a habit,
> And habit hardens into character.
> So watch the thought and its ways with care,
> And let it spring from love,
> Out of respect for all beings.

Our belief systems, which are the product of thoughts, have
immense power in our lives. If I believe the AIDS virus will kill
me, if I believe I have no choices, if I believe I am helpless,
hopeless, victimized, and doomed by the circumstances of my
life, I suspect that these thoughts can become a self-fulfilling
prophecy. If, on the other hand, I "watch the thought and its

ways with care," I see the thoughts as empty, impersonal, and cloudlike, and I allow them to move on, without response or repercussion. A clear and balanced relationship with the process of thinking is pivotal to the deep freedom that is possible for all of us.

What are the ramifications of opening deeply to the inner judging, self-hatred, and condemnation? First, I suspect that the Voice, and all the other voices, will probably remain around for some time. But as I give them less power, by not identifying with them, they very gradually will lay themselves to rest. Perhaps they continue to speak, but they become less of a bother. When they start talking, I can say, "Thank you for sharing, and good-bye."

As inner conflict dies down, there is also more space for healthy individuation to happen: that process whereby we evolve more fully than ever into the truth of who we are. Our flower at last opens into fullness and loveliness. Our eyes, which have been downcast with embarrassment, shame, and self-denial, can be uplifted. The forces of lovingkindness, compassion, forgiveness, and tenderness become the foundation upon which we live our lives. These forces now define the way in which we care for ourselves and for others. We are participating in the deepest healing so that we might know in our lives a peace that passes all understanding.

TRANSFORMING THE LEGACY OF ABUSE

In previous chapters I emphasized the nonconceptual nature of meditation. Instead of focusing awareness on stories, words, and concepts, in meditation we drop down to the level of process and energy. We explore the nature of every aspect of our experience free from ideas and intellectuality. We come to know that the complexity of life is in the end reduced to the six ways in which we ultimately experience the world:

> by seeing with our eyes,
> by hearing with our ears,
> by tasting with our tongue,
> by smelling with our nose,
> by touching with our skin,
> and through our minds, with thoughts, emotions, etc.

Nothing more than this.

A part of the discipline of meditation practice is the development of our ability to return constantly to this level of reality. When we think, judge, conceptualize, and plan, or when we get lost in our stories and our drama in meditation, we simply acknowledge what has happened and return to the bare experience of what is occurring. When we are called away again into words and thoughts, we return yet again to the experience of life beyond the concepts.

For many people, one of the most common fruits of meditation is an opening to the reverberations of their personal history. This can happen in many ways. Memories that were suppressed suddenly bubble to the surface with astonishing clarity. Hidden emotions pour forth as the mechanisms of repression loosen up.

The difficulties in our infancy, childhood, and youth suddenly feel immediate, compelling, and very strong as we reexperience the emotions and images of those times.

How do we work with all of this? It would seem as though the storyline has tumbled into the lap of meditation.

The power of meditation practice is always served by returning to the bare experience of what is happening. We let go of the story. This does not mean we suppress what is emerging. With true awareness we acknowledge all the memories, images, thoughts, emotions, and sensations that have arisen. We bring awareness to all the elements of the situation, but we do not indulge the story. We may find it skillful to engage in psychotherapy, bodywork, or energy therapies that directly address what has emerged, but this is separate from the process of meditation. Of course the story is important, but must be clearly seen as a focus very different from that of meditation practice.

For me, when history emerges, it is most often related to the history of abuse. The dance between not indulging the drama in meditation and at the same time responding appropriately to what is coming up is an ongoing challenge. Over the years I have learned many lessons in this dance.

In recent years, I have left my home in New England during the cold winter months to spend time in South Africa with my mother. While there, I recently celebrated my forty-third birthday. During the visit, my mother and I had a lot of free time together. This gave me a rare and precious opportunity to learn more about my early life.

I asked my mother about her pregnancy, giving birth to me, my infancy, and my youth. These were wonderful conversations. Adelaide is seventy-four years old now, high-spirited and gutsy. As we spoke, I began to feel that those months within her womb must have been a time of very special interconnection for us both.

For many people the nine months of gestation must be a time of the greatest intimacy they ever experience. Although only some of us have had the privilege of being mothers, all of us have had the experience of feeling supported, caressed, deliciously warmed and nourished by our mother's body. We have known the comfortable sound of her heart beating close by: regular, ever-present, and dependable. Our mother's protectiveness, love, care, and joyful expectation communicated themselves to us in a myriad of ways. Perhaps we even felt the hands of others on her belly, and sensed their excitement as we kicked and played in our contentment and happiness.

And then abruptly, it's over and we are pushed out into the world. We are tender, vulnerable, completely dependent, and obviously shocked by the painful movement through the birth canal. The umbilical cord is severed, and we know the terror and the confusion of being hung upside down and whacked on the backside by some stranger, as was standard procedure at my birth. There are suddenly so many changes—the brightness, harsh sounds, and new sensations. Obviously, we need great affection and care from our mother, and perhaps also our father and others, to sustain us through all this newness and upheaval.

Infants must have immense trust. I suspect that deeply embedded in their cells is the assumption that all their needs will be taken care of. Wide-eyed, utterly open in body and mind, a baby seems ready to receive everything that will support his or her movement into wholeness and growth.

For some of us this trust was shattered by deprivation, betrayal, neglect, or abuse. Often there is little time between birth and the beginning of abuse. The ways in which infants and children are damaged are too numerous and odious to mention. Because so much sexual abuse goes undisclosed and official statistics are widely regarded as unreliable, many researchers believe that the best picture of the scope of the problem is obtained by asking adults about their childhood experiences. The percentage of adults disclosing histories of sexual abuse range from 6% to 62% for females and 3% to 31% for males.[17] Abuse is clearly not selective. It occurs among people of every class, nation, race, belief, and sexual orientation. Yet it is mostly kept secret.

It is of course true that whether loved or abused, a baby is born into an existence where there will be suffering. We are all born crying, in a process that is unavoidably painful for both mother and infant. Once born we all suffer diaper rash, moments of hunger, colds, bumps, and upsets of many kinds. It is obviously very difficult for parents to witness this suffering and pain. Most mothers and fathers instinctively try to protect and soothe the child. Yet, no matter how much love a child receives, suffering does touch each human life from its very beginning. Parents cannot eliminate their child's human susceptibility to suffering. The pain of a child offers adults an opportunity to reflect upon the inevitability of suffering in all our lives. No matter how dear and near someone may be to us, we cannot protect them entirely. Suffering is universal and indiscriminate.

Still, it is patently clear that the experience of abuse is utterly different from the normal jolts of early life. It differs both in its nature and in the magnitude of its effect. Abuse may be sexual, physical, or verbal. It may consist of overstimulation or of neglect and deprivation. It may involve physical touch, or it may not. All abuse is betrayal, however, by trusted adults, or by people who are more powerful than the child. Abuse leaves the child with a legacy that is crippling, insidious, and deeply shattering to the body, psyche, and spirit. The surest way to prevent a child from discovering the capacity for self-love and dignity is to abuse him or her physically, sexually, or emotionally. Denied the capacity for self-love, the individual may find it difficult to form loving and trusting relationships with others. Her or his whole life can be stunted and marked by deprivation and intense suffering. Early childhood sexual abuse is commonly a factor in suicidal behavior, drug addiction, and other serious problems in adulthood.

The direct abuse of children is perhaps the greatest violence that human beings do to one another. The power imbalance is extreme. Not only are infants and childen physically defenseless and unable to escape or to survive without their parents, but emotionally they lack the means of coping with the treatment they receive. A child has no reference for what is happening in her or his immediate environment. The sense of self and of life is built from the available material. When love, trust, care, and respect for the child are jettisoned in favor of the satisfaction, titillation, sickness, or confusion of the adult, the effects are devastating.

Many people know and sense the profound impact of abuse in their lives. Perhaps the only force equal to or greater than the effects of the abuse is our instinct to grow, heal, and love.

I was sexually abused from a very young age. The pattern of sexual and physical abuse continued well into adolescence and my teenage years. For some years now, I have devoted an enormous effort toward transforming the legacy of what happened. Meditation practice has been invaluable in dealing with the crippling aftereffects of the violence. The process of awareness, of opening up and letting go, brings a healing as deep as the pain goes. While meditation certainly is not the only tool I have chosen, it has nonetheless opened up possibilities for healing and understanding that I might not have otherwise had.

I was sent to an all-boys' boarding school in Kimberly,

South Africa, from the ages of nine to sixteen. The years I spent there were very difficult. Corporal punishment was a part of the fabric of school life. Like many other boys, I was frequently caned or strapped. There was one teacher in particular who used to beat me quite regularly. He used a hose pipe or a leather strap on my backside or on my lower back. I remember vividly the bruised welts there. This teacher would also humiliate me when we were alone and ridicule me in front of the other boys. Furthermore, I was sexually bullied by older boys who forced me to masturbate them. Once in a while I was forced to engage in other sexual activity with them also. I was not popular with my peers. They teased and humiliated me. I was largely ostracized.

Although many survivors of abuse repress their memories, I've always remembered nearly everything that happened at that school. It was the emotions that were repressed. On my first long meditation retreat, in a maelstrom of fear and confusion, I realized that all that had happened was deeply wrong. It was as though a movie of those years began playing and I saw the violence and abuse in an entirely new light, from a completely different perspective. Even though elements of what happened had been titillating and satisfying, I was not to blame. I had been betrayed and subjected to immense violence.

This recognition was a huge relief. The burden of emotional cover-up and denial was beginning to disintegrate. Until that retreat, I had been convinced that I was fully to blame for my punishments and humiliations, especially since I had felt some pleasure during some of the forced sexual experiences. Consequently I had never spoken to anyone about my time at school.

Ten years later, in the middle of another retreat, I gained access to the fact of much earlier abuse. Over weeks it became clear that the abuse had begun in my infancy. A pattern of sexual violence started in my first months and lasted a number of years.

The memory of this is not visual, but is undisputable in its clarity. I experience these memories primarily as sensations of smell and touch.

For some, memories of abuse are clear and always have been. Others have a sense that an abusive history has occurred, but have no direct or clear memories of exactly what happened. For yet others, memories surface in the process of healing. We need not blame ourselves if we cannot remember. We have already suffered enough. What is at stake is the quality of life right now. We can become obsessed and desperate in our efforts and determination to recoup memories that have been occluded. We may feel a terrible need for our emotions to be validated and grounded in some kind of reality that feels genuine. In fact, as I discuss later, the shape of our suffering in the present can provide ample evidence that trauma of some sort has indeed happened in our life.

As we strain for memories, we may squander the opportunity to deal with and engage the present affects of the abuse. In fact, very often it is when we wholeheartedly engage the present reality that memories begin to surface. For me the memories arose in the natural unfolding of the meditation process. Along with meditation I have found psychotherapy, hypnotherapy, group work, and movement therapy to be helpful. Slowly, we grow to trust our healing instincts wherever the path takes us.

Some people may decide to put life on hold as they desperately quest to remember what happened. They try to force a process that would perhaps be better left to its own rhythm. Trusting this rhythm of process requires great faith. For many, the ability to trust and have faith has been stunted by the abuse itself. Yet in the end, what alternative is there? We can fight and struggle to remember, or we can trust and have faith that all we do is enough for now. I believe that in our willingness to remain open and honest, great and deep healing emerges in its own time, with all the recollections and memories we need.

Even if we have no memories, certain attitudes can be strong evidence that abuse of some sort probably occurred. Within myself, these attitudes to life are very clear. I see that it is easy to feel victimized by the circumstances of life. I have often received life as threatening and malevolent rather than as an opportunity for growth and happiness. Fear of physical and emotional intimacy and closeness is part of the legacy, too. The feeling tone of difficult emotions like fear, anger, or sadness sometimes seems very young, indicating a link to trauma in the early years. Many who have been abused feel out of control, helpless, hopeless, and worthless at times.

To engage these attitudes, and the emotions that support and surround them, opens us to the possibility of freedom and relief. In meditation we open to the full spectrum of emotional life, without exclusion or denial. It is a brave and courageous act for the abused person to open the door to all aspects of the legacy of history.

One of the most freeing aspects of the meditation is its non-conceptual nature. To relate to our experience increasingly free of the overlay of ideas, words, theories, and opinions is a great relief. It is also a movement toward simplicity and truth. The way we conceptualize the history of abuse and hold the fact in our minds is very important. If the past evolves into something solid, rigid, and unchanging in our minds, this may preclude change, healing, and evolution.

For example, if I constantly relate and refer to myself as a sexually abused man, and if I invest the label with great emotion, perhaps even status, I am assuming a fixed identity into which I am feeding much energy and investment. The word *abused* is intensely charged. If I used this word to define my existence, it can become a straitjacket that hampers me in my efforts to be free.

If the abuse evolves into something solid, it may become a familiar place from which I can relate in a threatening and sometimes precarious world. Furthermore, this place of security, hellish though it might be, can become a refuge when so much of life feels unstable, undependable, and perilous. Keeping the abuse solid may give one a sense of identity: the abused man or woman, the wronged one, the victim. While what happened was unquestionably wrong, solidifying it perpetuates the struggle rather than alleviating the suffering.

There are passages in healing from abuse that require extreme delicacy. Trusting ourselves does not require that we develop an identity based on the abuse. Our willingness to feel our feelings does not mean that those feelings define who we are and who we want to become. Nor does it mean using the intensity of emotions to brutalize others. Engaging the aftereffects of abuse does not mean that we take up permanent residence in a landscape of fractured emotions. If we do not solidify and gridlock around the abuse, we open to the possibility of relating to what happened in a way that is true and potentially freeing.

What is the truth of abuse?

Meditation practice gives us insight into the transitoriness of all phenomena. No matter how deeply we look, we find change. When we deny this change, we contradict what is true. If we were abused, we have not been left with a fixed quota of rage, terror, grief, or pain. Nor have we been given some specific mantle in which we must now cloak ourselves. Rather, the experience leaves us with a specific pattern of conditioning. It is almost as if we were wired in a way that brings forth certain responses. We have buttons, and these buttons get pushed!

In meditation, we work with this pattern of conditioning.

Moment by moment, we see the body and mind interact with each other in a causal fashion. Here is an example of one causal chain: a physical sensation leads to a memory, which is a thought in the mind. The memory leads to an emotion. The emotion leads to a movement, which is composed of physical sensations. Body–mind–mind–body.

If we are aware, moment by moment, we see these chains at work. We see how circumstances of intimacy condition the arising of fear. We see that certain people, images, or memories tend to condition rage or terror. We know how being touched in inappropriate ways causes anger or panic or nausea to arise. Having one's sense of boundary and autonomy violated brings forth rage and fear. All of these are patterns of conditioning. The violence of abuse left us with a pattern of conditioned responses that is alive and active in our lives now. As we observe the cause and effect and as we understand the wiring, our relationship with history becomes more malleable. We see the separate links of the chain more clearly. The patterns become more and more workable, and this dissolves the inevitability of the linkages. We see that no matter how loaded or compelling a thought might be, it is just a thought, another cloud passing through the mind. We are no longer convinced and bound by its content. We watch our inner life go by, like a show. This delivers us from victimhood. Slowly, the suffering and heartbreak of abuse becomes more workable and fluid.

In conversations with people, I try not to use the word *abused* if possible. This is not a denial of what happened, but an effort to inwardly distance myself from a word that is, for me, charged and fixed. If I speak about my life, I try to be specific about what actually happened. If it is appropriate, I acknowledge this aspect of my history and let go of the rest. I know many people (including myself at one time) who wield their abuse like a weapon against themselves and the world. I do not believe this attitude directs one toward healing and freedom. It can, conversely, become its own prison.

When we know and understand the patterns related to abuse, we can make choices in our lives based on wisdom and compassion. We can avoid situations that are too overwhelming. We can choose to walk through our fears, slowly and gently. We soften and slow down. We allow rigid, knee-jerk reactions to become less automatic. Our conditioning gradually becomes more and more workable in relationship to other people, to physical and emotional intimacy, and to situations that are difficult.

Fear is central to the experience of abuse. For those who have known enormous terror as a child, fear is deeply dyed into the fabric of life. Often, we find it easier to trust fear and gloom rather than joy and love. (This is a huge topic. Please see the chapter "Beyond the Grip of Fear.")

In meditation we bring a loving acceptance and patience to the fear, terror, and panic wherever and whenever they arise. We become friends with fear. During the moments of abuse, we contracted and armored ourselves in terror and fear. Because of this armoring, we survived to do our healing now. Can we befriend the fear rather than banish and reject it? By banishing the fear, we are repeating the treatment we received long ago, when we ourselves were marginalized and ostracized in the same way.

Often, fear is camouflaged, lying just beyond our sleepiness, physical pain, or depression. As we shine the light of true awareness on what presents itself, we open to the full reality of fear.

I recently have come to realize that I have lived almost all my life with an ever-present sense of fear. I never saw this before, because the fear was as familiar to me as breathing. Recently I've known interludes when this fear has subsided, and this has enabled me to acknowledge the fact that what happened all those years ago conditioned me to a life of fear and withdrawal that has endured in a subtle way. Can our awareness be sufficiently sensitive that we come to know even the most subtle shadings of fear within our mind?

Over the years, I have come to understand that the terror associated with the abuse in my infancy has a very specific quality and tone. Because the violence happened before I could talk, I was unable to verbalize or conceptualize what was happening to me at the time. The associated fear had definite tones of annihilation and extreme panic, and it is this emotion that comes forward at times in my life now. As I open to these feelings of annihilation, I realize that any movement toward this fear feels violent and invasive. Instead I bow respectfully to the terror, I acknowledge it, I bear witness, without agenda, without manipulation or penetration in any way. The healing of this preverbal fear is in its revelation, in its coming forward, at last, into the light of awareness now.

Upon this journey of recovery, we are called upon to explore many aspects of our woundedness. In my experience, meditation practice can suffuse awareness with a sense of love, acceptance, patience, and wisdom that help to heal these difficult areas. To be simply present is a priceless gift of self-love and compassion. To touch the surges of self-loathing and self-flagellation with tenderness and mercy is an act of immeasurable healing.

Many and varied emotions arise along the path of healing. Fortunately, the ways of opening to emotions do not fundamentally vary. Opening to sadness and loss must also be a part of the journey. In the experience of abuse, we lose innocence, virginity, self-worth, a trust of others, and a sense of safety. We probably need to mourn the loss of time and all the opportunities that passed us by. There could also be feelings of guilt, shame, and betrayal. Furthermore, we open to any feelings of pleasure associated with what happened. We slowly open to the full legacy of history in our lives now, bringing the greatest tenderness and care to every facet of our woundedness.

The meditation instructions given in chapter 2 show the value of bringing awareness to the process of breathing. This is a useful tool for cultivating the factors of calm and concentration. However, for some people, one of the ways in which trauma registers in the body is its effect on the cycle of breathing. For me, any awareness given to the sensations of the movement of the breath can immediately evoke terror and panic. My chest heaves and tightens, and my breathing becomes complicated and difficult. I end up gasping for air.

When awareness of breathing is not possible, the use of touchpoints around the body is an alternative. In meditation I bring awareness to the physical sensation of my lips touching each other. I then move to the sensations of touch where my hands rest in my lap. Next I open to sensations of touch thoughout the body, before returning to the lips again.

When the factors of equanimity, concentration, and tranquility are strong, I do sometimes observe my breathing. However, using the touchpoints serves the same purpose, and there is no reason to believe that one method is preferable to the other. After all, making our experience workable is the fundamental challenge in meditation. Nothing else is more important.

Recently I have come to see that one of the ways in which I most strongly separate myself from life and collude with the legacy of the abuse is in my relationship with struggle. Because so much of life has been difficult and challenging, the presence of struggle has become one of the most powerful ways in which I have defined myself. In relationship with struggle I have developed a sense of self and an inner identity. At times this struggle falls away, and I am then left with the heartbreaking realization that it is fundamentally difficult for me to simply enjoy the easier times, to revel in the lack of struggle and enjoy the holiday. The mind seems to panic in the unfamiliarity of ease and often tries to create some kind of struggle with which it can then grapple in old familiar ways.

For me one of the most difficult aspects of the abuse was accepting that it truly happened. Vivid memories notwithstanding, for a long time I could not believe it had occurred. I sensed that if I did, I would open to deep feelings of betrayal, abandonment, rage, and sadness. I would uncover the pain of all the ways I had been hurt.

This was indeed the case. Not believing it had happened can be a mechanism for holding back the full impact of history. Acceptance may well be the greatest challenge on the road to recovery. Here again, we need not push the river. If we live with honesty and compassion, we create the space within which acceptance can flower in its own time and way.

It is not possible to cover comprehensively every aspect of abuse as it relates to meditation. The ramifications of history are as variable as we are unique. However, I would like to share a few further lessons I have learned over the years.

In times of confusion, struggle, chaos, physical pain, and difficult emotion, I try to remember to give this pain a love and respect I did not always receive long ago. Those who abused me probably did not know much about these feelings in their lives either.

I have also learned deep appreciation for difficulty in meditation. Difficulty and challenge are the compost out of which healing can grow and flower. I love this image, and try to bring it to mind whenever I feel overwhelmed and stuck. People who've been abused have survived an immense wounding. To heal the effects of what happened requires great effort and limitless patience.

Recently I have come to engage a part of myself which believes that someone will rescue me from the suffering of abuse. This hope originates in the desperation of the infant who yearned for deliverance from the nightmare. The wish for rescue, the belief that it would come, was a survival mechanism and a protection from hopelessness. As I engage the legacy of abuse, and take more and more responsibility for healing, the idea of a rescuer dies and falls away. This death is fundamentally empowering. As we release the expectation that someone or something outside of us will remove the suffering, we begin to take full responsibility for life and healing.

Nowadays there are interludes when I feel free from the effects of abuse. This is a new experience. I love these tastes of freedom, and as I savor them, the impetus for healing escalates. There is a powerful motivation never again to subject myself to what I suffered before. I move ever more deeply from life as struggle to life as celebration. In my experience, celebration is the birthchild of contentment and acceptance: acceptance of how things are now and how they were, so long ago.

Seeing the connection between a history and current behaviors is often very difficult. It is a real challenge to recognize and admit that one's interpersonal relationships may reflect the distorting effects of history. Recalling how helpless and hurt we once were can remind us to be patient and forgiving when we see ourselves needing control and power over others. Can we forgive ourselves for instinctively needing to have vast amounts of space of all kinds in our life? When we see that we are capable of hurting others in the same way that we were hurt, can we be compassionate and loving rather than angry and unforgiving?

More and more, I am learning to accept my life exactly as it is—patterns, wiring, buttons, and all. I endeavor with all my heart never again to act out the conditioning that leads to suffering for myself and others. Can we accept and work with the truth of all parts of ourselves, letting go of self-recrimination and self-hatred? These are important challenges in the movement toward wholeness and recovery.

In this movement, we often find it difficult to maintain workable boundaries in our lives. We may feel the conflicting impulses to say yes to everything, including violation, because that is what we were forced to do long ago. At the same time we feel a reactive impulse to say no to everything, to make up for all the no's we have perhaps never said. The sensitivity that comes with meditation practice helps us stay alert to what is true and appropriate for us. As we live with clearer parameters and perimeters, this can be threatening to others. Perhaps they have difficulty setting their own boundaries, and thus feel threatened. Perhaps we no longer fit into the mold in which they would like to hold us.

Setting clear boundaries, however, is a powerful ritual of compassion, both for ourselves and for others. Clarity and compassion are rare in our world. Anytime we act from these feelings, we are an important model for those around us. When the abused person sets clear limits, this has the potential to heal the fundamental transgression that happened so long ago.

Meditation practice enables us to be acutely sensitive to our edges, and awareness helps us respond in ways that are appropriate, loving, and supportive. For me, initially, I set boundaries with a lot of fear, sometimes anger, and certainly a degree of charge. Slowly it becomes possible to do this more and more clearly, feeling an alignment of purpose, a clear comprehension of the circumstances, and a forcefulness appropriate to the situation. Perhaps in defining boundaries, I've been called more fully to inner compassion and patience than ever before.

It is my strong sense that ultimately we must, as adults, again leave home, in a deeper, more complete way than we did in our earlier lives. Wayne Muller, a psychotherapist and mediator from California, says:

> In leaving home, we leave behind the limited understandings that our family teachings gave us about life, joy, abundance, compassion and grace. These teachings were not limited because our parents were bad or evil; our parents were simply human, and could never be more than they were. The story is told of Jesus sitting in front of a crowd, teaching. His mother and brothers arrived to beg him to come home. Because of the size of the crowd they could not reach him, so they sent someone to give Jesus a message that his family was waiting for him. Jesus turned to the messenger and said: "I have no family. I have no mother and brothers. These who are with me, these are my family, and my mother, and my brothers."
>
> To some, this may seem like an act of cruelty. Yet in many ways it was a gesture of great compassion, for in that moment, Jesus set both parent and child free, liberating each to seek the path of their own heart. Jesus was honoring the tremendous shift we must make to allow our biological family to fall away as we begin our own path to God. Not out of anger or rage, not as punishment for what they did to us; rather, out of love for who we all are, to set each of us free from the limitations of our family drama.[18]

The words of Jesus were echoed earlier by the Buddha, who said, "I was never born, nor had I parents," and by the fourteenth-century samurai who wrote:

> I have no parents.
> I make the heaven and earth my parents.
> I have no home.
> I make awareness my home.[19]

Our world is terribly difficult for many human beings. When we reflect, explore, and examine ourselves and the people around us, we sense that many people live their days from a foundation of deep hurt and trauma. All the ways in which life has refined itself into activities of distraction and avoidance speak of the pain that is there. Many adult men and women devote enormous energy and time to covering up the effects of the hurt and violence that happened in their earlier lives. Many of these abused boys and girls have grown up to perpetrate further violence. Whenever I perceive this cycle, I feel the deepest gratitude for the meditation practice, which unquestionably helps break this cycle in my life.

When I began meditation, I had no idea what lay ahead. As I look back, I now see how natural the process has been. In the willingness to let the sunshine of true awareness fall equally upon every aspect of our lives, so much healing is possible. I believe that everything that needs to arise will do so in its own way and time. The process is perfectly orderly.

Our willingness to be present is all the faith we need. As we open to the truth of every discernible aspect of our being, the confused and the clear, the pleasant and the painful, healing happens in its own unique way for every one of us.

This poem by Ina J. Hughes is titled "A Prayer for Children."

We pray for children
who put chocolate fingers everywhere,
who like to be tickled,
who stomp in puddles and ruin their new pants,
who sneak Popsicles before supper,
who erase holes in math workbooks,
who can never find their shoes.

And we pray for those
who stare at photographs from behind barbed wire,
who can't bound down the street in a new pair of
    sneakers,
who never "counted potatoes,"
who are born in places we wouldn't be caught dead,
who never go to the circus,
who live in an X-rated world.
We pray for children
who bring us sticky kisses and fistfuls of dandelions,
who sleep with the dog and bury goldfish,
who hug us in a hurry and forget their lunch money,
who cover themselves with Band-Aids and sing off key,
who squeeze toothpaste all over the sink,
who slurp their soup.
And we pray for those
who never get dessert,
who have no safe blanket to drag behind them,
who watch their parents watch them die,
who can't find any bread to steal,
who don't have any rooms to clean up,
whose pictures aren't on anybody's dresser,
whose monsters are real.
We pray for children
who spend all their allowance before Tuesday,
who throw tantrums in the grocery store and pick at
    their food,
who like ghost stories,
who shove dirty clothes under the bed, and never rinse
    out the tub,
who get visits from the tooth fairy,
who don't like to be kissed in front of the carpool,

who squirm in church and scream in the phone,
whose tears we sometimes laugh at and whose smiles can
    make us cry.
And we pray for those
whose nightmares come in the daytime,
who will eat anything,
who have never seen a dentist,
who aren't spoiled by anybody,
who go to bed hungry and cry themselves to sleep,
who live and move, but have no being.
We pray for children who want to be carried and for
    those who must,
For those we never give up on and for those who don't
    get a second chance.
For those we smother . . . and for those who will grab
    the hand of anyone kind enough to offer it.[20]

4

Meditations of the Heart

THE DIVINE ABODES

ONE DAY A monk named Purma came to the Buddha and asked if he could teach and spread the Dharma in the land of the Sronaparantakas.

"The Sronaparantakas are a hot-tempered people," responded the Buddha. "In all likelihood they will curse and insult you with angry, abusive, words. How would this be for you, Purma?"

"Even if they do all these things, I shall think them a good and kind people. After all, they did not strike me or hurl objects at me!"

"What if they do strike you and throw rocks at you?"

Purma replied, "I shall nevertheless think them good, for they did not club me. And even if they go on to club me, they still will not have killed me."

"What if they kill you, Purma?" asked the Buddha.

"Then I shall think of them kindly, for they will have delivered me from this suffering world."

"Very well, Purma, I give you permission to dwell and teach in the land of the Sronaparantakas."

One day soon after his arrival there, Purma met a hunter. The man saw the shaven monk and decided to kill him right away. Purma opened his robe in order that the hunter could accurately aim his arrow and said, "Dear sir, I am here in your country on a difficult mission. Aim here!"

"This man has no fear of death," thought the flabbergasted hunter. "I cannot kill such a brave and kind man." The man was so moved that he sat down and listened to Purma's teachings.

Over the next months thousands of fiery Sronaparantakas were won over by the lovingkindness, compassion, and extraordinary fearlessness of the monk named Purma who had come to live among them.

———————

A life of awareness is a journey into the landscape of our hearts and minds. If our way is honest and true, we must come upon vistas of great joy, happiness, and calm. So, too, we may come upon sharp and unexpected turns, descents into valleys of pain and confusion where we feel heartbroken and alone. This is natural. Born human on this exquisite planet, our truth unfolds through both joy and sorrow.

To be awake and present in each moment is all that is necessary to open us to the deepest truths of life. Certain qualities of heart support us on our journey. These qualities serve both the deepening of our understanding and help heal our inner wounds. While these factors of the heart are inherent within each of us, we can strengthen them with specific meditation practices. The Buddhist tradition offers four such practices, known as the divine abodes of the Buddha: lovingkindness, compassion, sympathetic joy (joy in the happiness of others), and equanimity. They are called abodes because they encourage our hearts to dwell and stabilize in these places. They are called divine because they are limitless and blissful.

As we develop these qualities of heart, we are more and more able to bring them strongly to our lives in times of difficulty, pain, and challenge. Meditation on the divine abodes does not look directly at reality. Rather it is based on wishing and affirming the best that is within oneself and others. Thus, it is not a substitute for insight or awareness meditation, but it most certainly supports and befriends the process of insight.

What could be more important than holding ourselves within an embrace of deep compassion? Should we become aware of an area of painful self-hatred within ourselves, the force of our compassion could enable us to hold this conflict with forgiveness and care. We learn that our hearts are always bigger than the problem that threatens to overwhelm us. At another time we may come upon great anger or fear that threatens to separate us from another person. What a gift of healing, when we shift out of our sense of injury and instead surround ourselves and the other with an atmosphere of lovingkindness and well-wishing! Meditating on sympathetic joy brings forth that irrepressible beauty of the heart in which we celebrate the success and happiness of another without feeling diminished or envious by comparison. A by-product of sympathetic joy is an enormous and loving sense of self-sufficiency and contentment. The meditation on equanimity opens us to the possibility of remaining balanced and present within all the joys and the sorrows of life.

Practicing the divine abodes not only softens the way of awareness meditation, but can directly support that process of meditation as well. Sometimes in meditation, when the factors of the heart are strong, an old wound may reveal itself, or a hidden memory could emerge into the light. When lovingkindness and compassion are present, there is likely to be a feeling of trust, strength, and openness of mind too. The energy it takes to generate these boundless positive emotions also helps us feel more powerful and less victimized by people and situations. When we experience our capacity to love, our boundaries and definitions amplify, soften, and change, and we are able to experience life more clearly.

It is not unusual for people to meditate exclusively on lovingkindness for days, months, or even years, and later practice the other three divine abodes. To the instructions for these meditations, I have added another guided meditation, on forgiveness. Although forgiveness is not one of the traditional divine abodes, it is often used as a preliminary practice to periods of meditation. You may wish to experiment with any or all of the meditations of the heart. They provide a wonderful atmosphere within which to begin or end periods of awareness meditation. They can be helpful in times of physical or mental pain, by softening resistance, gladdening the heart, and lubricating the processes of acceptance and surrender.

The divine abodes expand the circuit of the heart and mind and soften the edges between ourselves and others. They connect us with powerful and creative sources of positive energy. They can shift and loosen the grip of difficult mental states like obsession, vengefulness, antipathy, and confusion. While cooking, cleaning, walking, or driving, one can softly repeat the words of these meditations. The divine abodes help create an atmosphere that is healing, nourishing, and loving.

These meditation practices work in a way that may seem surprising. In the meditations we repeat certain phrases over and over, either in the mind or out loud. The phrases express a benevolent wish toward ourselves and others. Simply repeat the phrases again and again. Stay connected also with the power of your positive wishes. There is no need to worry about whether your wishes will come true or what the mechanism might be that grants them. The meditation practice unfolds in its own way and time.

Most people who have practiced the divine abodes have commented, usually at the beginning, "How can this work? They're just wishes, just words!" Before the heart takes hold of these beautiful qualities, the meditations may seem rather dry and empty. Over time, with faith, trust, and patience, our heart eventually pours forth all its beauty.

TO BEGIN

For each of the guided meditations that follow, take a position that is comfortable for you. You may wish to lie down, although sitting upright tends to help the mind stay more alert. You may find it helpful to recite the instructions onto a tape and then play them back to yourself to guide your practice. Alternatively you may read and then repeat the phrases. Let the words move gently through your heart.

Lovingkindness

- Allow the eyes gently to close.
- Give attention to the breathing.
- Be aware of each breath as it enters and leaves the body.
- When the mind feels calm, allow the attention to drop to the heart center. This is the point in the middle of the chest, the emotional center.
- Repeat the following phrases.

> "May I be happy."
> "May I be peaceful."
> "May I be filled with love and kindness."
> "May I have ease of well-being."
> "May love fill and heal my body and being."

- Direct feelings of love and kindness to yourself as you repeat these phrases for a while.
- Be aware of any feeling or stirring that there might be.
- If there is no lovingkindness, that is OK. To direct lovingkindness to a heart that is closed is a central part of the practice also.
- Continue repeating the phrases. Or you may wish to use personal phrases that have meaning for you.
- Bring to mind the image or sense of someone you love. It may be someone close, someone already deep within your heart. Direct the phrases of lovingkindness to this person:

> "May you be happy."
> "May you have ease of well-being."
> "May you be satisfied, loving, and joyous."

- Bring to mind further images of people whom you hold dear—perhaps a benefactor, someone who has been kind to you, a teacher, a family member, or a group of family members. (If no images come, a sense of their presence is sufficient.)

- Repeat the phrases.
- Bring to mind a neutral person, someone of whom you are aware but do not know in any way.
- Continue directing the phrases.
- Bring to mind the image or sense of someone with whom you have had some difficulty. It may be someone who has hurt you or with whom you have had a conflict or disagreement.
- Extend feelings of lovingkindness to this person:

> "May you too be happy."
> "May you be free from suffering."
> "May love fill and heal your body and being."
> "May you be happy."
> "May you have everything you wish for."
> "May your life be easy."
> "May you be filled with love, kindness, sensitivity, and joy."
> "May you be free."
> "May you be happy."

- Use whatever phrases have meaning for you.
- Expand your great heart of lovingkindness and allow the wish that all beings be happy and peaceful to radiate outward into the world.
- Include all creatures in your loving wishes.

> "May all beings know joy, kindness, and love in their lives."
> "May all beings be free from anger and fear."
> "May all beings be mentally and physically healthy."
> "May all beings have everything they need."

- Allow the feelings of lovingkindness to shine outward, all over the world and to all the universe.

Compassion

There is an important distinction between lovingkindness and compassion. In both meditations there is the aim of addressing the problem of suffering, but in lovingkindness we seek to bring happiness to others, whereas in compassion we direct this wish specifically at their suffering.

- Think of the aspects of difficulty in your life. Be willing to love yourself even as you struggle and suffer.
- Direct these phrases to yourself:

  "May I be free from suffering."
  "May my pain be resolved."
  "I care deeply about myself."
  "I hold myself with softness and care."

- Repeat these phrases for a while. Or use your own phrases of compassion if you wish.
- Now think of someone who is impoverished, either spiritually or materially.
- Consider the pain and struggle in his or her life and direct compassion toward these difficulties, using either specific words or general ones.
- Bring to mind a sense or image of all beings who suffer in so many different ways. Extend the same love and compassion to them.

  "May you be free from suffering."
  "I care about your pain."

- Include all beings within your great compassion.

  "May all those who suffer be free from their pain."
  "May all of us be free from suffering."

- If you wish, consider beings who live under conditions of specific hardship and extend your compassion to them.

  "May you too be released from pain."

"May you be free from suffering."

- Continue to expand the compassion to include different life forms, every being that lives in your city, your country, the hemisphere, the world, and all the universes.
- Extend compassion to all beings.
- Wish them freedom from suffering.
- Wish that their minds be free from anger, terror, and insufficiency.
- Send compassion to all beings who live in conditions of great suffering:

    "May the hungry be fed, may the unloved be loved, may the imprisoned be freed. May all beings be free from suffering."

Sympathetic Joy

The meditation on sympathetic joy cultivates a heart that celebrates the happiness of others. The salient characteristic of sympathetic joy is gladness. Its opposite is envy and jealousy. The success, happiness, and accomplishments of others are what cause sympathetic joy to arise in us.

- Bring to mind the image or sense of a friend who is experiencing happiness in any or all areas of life. Direct these phrases toward that person:

    "May your happiness and good fortune continue."
    "May prosperity and success not leave you."

- Use whatever phrases communicate to your heart this generous wish.
- Next, choose someone whom you envy.
- Wish for them to continue to enjoy pleasure and happiness.

    "May your happiness and good fortune continue."

- Send sympathetic joy to other individuals, to groups, and to all beings, known or unknown to you.

Equanimity

The equanimity meditation cultivates a mind that is balanced and calm within all the changing circumstances of life.

- Direct the phrases toward an image or sense of a person whom you do not know well and toward whom your feelings are neutral.
- Reflect on phrases such as these:

  "All beings are the owners or heirs of their karma."
  "Good actions lead to good results; bad actions to bad results."
  "Everyone must face his or her own situation."
  "Although I wish only the best for you, I also know that your happiness or unhappiness depends upon your actions, not upon my wishes for you."

- Use whichever phrases have meaning for you.
- As with other meditations, move through the different categories of people, ending with yourself.

To Conclude

After completing the meditation on one or several of the divine abodes, be aware for a few minutes of any feelings that have arisen within your mind and heart. Rest in your experience of the divine abodes. They are a priceless blessing that you bring to yourself and the world. "May all beings be happy and at peace with themselves and with the world."

Slowly open your eyes.

Sometimes it is not possible to feel lovingkindness, compassion, sympathetic joy, or equanimity. This is OK. Opening to a heart that is closed becomes the meditation practice. Do not fight what is true. Feel the pain of constriction and tightness. Being OK with all things as they are is the essence of equanimity and love.

FORGIVENESS

AT ONE TIME there was great dissension in the community of monks and nuns. A certain monk had violated an important rule of discipline. This rule was obligatory for all who lived in the community. Because the monk refused to admit the offense, he had been expelled. The community was deeply fragmented and divided. Some felt he had deserved explusion, while others felt the treatment was too harsh.

Much heated argument arose. Laypeople became involved in the squabble. The Buddha sought to prevent this rift in the community, but no one wanted to heed his advice. After reflecting upon the situation, the next morning the Buddha departed, alone, for the woods. He took up his abode at the foot of a lovely tree. It was blessedly peaceful, away from the fighting and consternation.

Three months later, the repentant monks came to the Buddha, apologetic for their careless behavior. The Buddha offered his forgiveness:

"Monks, there two kinds of people who store up great demerit for themselves. The first kind are those who do not ask for forgiveness after doing wrong. The second kind are those who do not forgive after wrongdoing is confessed and forgiveness is asked for."

One of the most inspiring aspects of awareness meditation is its utter simplicity. As we bring a true and simple awareness to our bodies, minds, and hearts, healing naturally unfolds on many different levels. Perhaps one of the most important dimensions of this healing is the movement from insensitivity into a sensitivity that can be deeply freeing.

With the unfolding of meditation, we become more and more aware of our bodily responses, needs, and limitations. We have the choice to respond ever more appropriately and carefully to what we find. Our body deserves great care, for it has important work to do. The Buddha said: "The body is the temple of the spirit, the raft by which we cross to the other shore"—that is, to liberation. Living less in conflict and more in harmony and balance with the truth of the body is a profound gesture of compassion for ourselves.

In meditation we also become increasingly sensitive to the shadows and clouds in our hearts and minds. Often we become conscious of feelings and emotions whose existence we were unaware of before. We hear the muffled whispers playing below the surface of our worldly persona. In this knowing great freedom is possible.

We may hear what somebody once called the unfinished symphony—the symphony of unfulfilled desires, uncompleted parts of our lives, shattered hopes, perhaps, and dreams that never came true. We hear and feel the pain of all that is unapproached and unresolved in our lives. We may feel the cramped sensations of grief, loss, and incompletion holding tight around the heart.

Some of us may also come to feel a heaviness of spirit and a protectiveness of heart that we, as young children, designed in our determination never, ever to be wounded again. This heaviness can be so tight that the great light of our hearts is not able to shine through, nor is the voice of our heart able to be heard.

The question then becomes: Can we listen more closely to this symphony? Can we approach the heaviness of heart? Can we say yes to the fear, rage, grief, and sadness? The path of awareness brings us into the domain of the heart where these feelings may be waiting to be healed. Very often it is the practice of forgiveness that eases our way gently into the center.

True forgiveness is not on any level a condoning of events

that should never have happened. How could we say yes to torture, abuse, or rape? To do so would be unthinkable. Rather,
forgiveness is a strength, a power and maturity of heart, that
brings profound healing on many levels.

My parents were born and grew up in South Africa, both
of poor families. When they were married, it was with the understanding that they probably would never be able to have children. So it was a great surprise for them when, exactly nine
months after they were married, I arrived! They told me many
times of their determination that I would never want for any of
the things that they had been deprived of in their youth. As I
have mentioned, when I was young I was sent to an all-boys'
boarding school three hundred miles away. No doubt my parents intended this to benefit me, yet at that school I was sexually
and physically abused over many years.

Much of what has been unworkable in my life has to do
with the shadow of those years. Yet I have learned important
lessons of forgiveness in relationship to my parents for sending
me to that school. I have also come to know a healing forgiveness
toward the older boys and the master for what they did to me
there.

On my first long meditation retreat, I reexperienced the
loneliness, the overwhelming friendlessness, and all the terror
and shame of that time. It was really difficult. I experienced immense rage, fear, and a sense of betrayal, all of a magnitude that I
had never considered possible. These recollections and emotions
continued for many months during the course of this long retreat. At this time, a letter arrived from my mother in South
Africa. She wrote that she could not understand why I had given
up my career as a financial consultant, nor why I was doing in-
tensive meditation practice. She and my father were bewildered.

She added that, nonetheless, I could be absolutely sure that they loved me and would be there for me in every way possible.

Her loving words cut through the internal storm like a lightning bolt. Reading my mother's letter, I had my first pure experience of forgiveness. It felt wonderfully warm and a great relief. Immediately my mind came in and said, "Hmm, now I've forgiven my parents, I can go back to business as usual." I felt quite pleased with myself, really.

Of course, the sense of completion that I had in that moment was only relative. There was a great deal more healing work in store for me after that. In fact, the deeper lesson that I learned from the letter was that forgiveness is a process rather than a one-time event. Healing on one level often opens up another level where healing needs to happen. I also learned how important it is not to have models for how forgiveness should unfold. There really are no "shoulds" in the process. Forgiveness is a slow, gradual, and very individual process.

The willingness and intention to forgive are of primary importance. It is not always possible for our hearts to forgive everything all at once. However, with genuine willingness and sincere intention, much forgiving is possible over time. Like a flower, forgiveness will open when ready. If our wounds are deep, the process of forgiveness probably needs to go deep also. Yet not every situation requires a long and protracted forgiveness process. Some flowers open quickly! Each is a unique blossom that will bloom in its season and in its own special and beautiful way.

When my period of retreat ended, I decided to return to South Africa. While staying with my parents, I told them everything that had happened at the boarding school. They had no idea I had been abused, and it was really difficult for them. They both cried deeply. It was wonderful to allow them to share my pain. A barrier that had divided us fell away in the truth-telling.

I had taken refuge in honest communication more fully than ever before.

Next I went to my old boarding school and asked them to arrange three meetings for me: one with the headmaster, one with the staff, and one with the students. When I arrived at the headmaster's office, others who had been there during my years at the school were present also. The headmaster leaned back in his chair, pointed to photographs behind him, and said. "This is the hockey team and this is the rugby team. Our rugby team is at the top of the league this year."

I said to him, "Stop. I have come a long way for this moment. I really don't care at all about the sports teams. All I ask of you is that you listen wholeheartedly to what I have to say."

For the next hour I told them everything that had happened during my years at the school. I assured them that there was no doubt about the accuracy of what I was telling them. I spoke about meditation practice and related how, in the process of meditation, it is sometimes possible to go back in time to events that were very painful and reexperience them, free of the old fear that had forced one to shut down long before. I reflected on how our suppression of what happened is a way we protect ourselves when the pain is too great. I told him that my memories of what had happend at the school were clearer to me than the books on his table.

The headmaster and teachers were obviously very shaken and uncomfortable with what I had told them. They asked me why I didn't want to tell them who did those things to me. "Who was the master? Who were the boys? We will follow up."

I said, "I am not here to blame. Neither am I here to point a finger. I've come here today for three reasons. The first is to unburden myself. The second is to speak the truth, as I was unable to do all those years ago. The third is my hope that this will never happen again at the school."

When I met with the students, we spoke of AIDS, about being gay at an all boys' school, and about apartheid. These were all issues that were not discussed at the school. For me this was a precious ritual of speaking the unspoken in a place where so much of my early life had been silenced and suppressed. When I left the school I felt exhilarated, freer, and much lighter.

As a result of the communication with my parents and the school, I discovered the importance of getting the truth out into the open. It seemed to matter far less whether the actual people involved were present than that what happened be fully revealed. Insofar as telling my parents is concerned, some people felt strongly that I was selfish to force this unsettling information on these two elderly people. However, I know that for all three of us the truth-telling has been very important. In the careful relating of what happened, immense healing occurred in my family. No longer did we have to protect one another from what is difficult. Rather, we learned to live with a deep trust that the truth, no matter how challenging, will be brought forward and shared. This is a world apart from the way things used to be.

The meditation practice has enabled me to be carefully aware of my motivation and intention in speaking out and confronting others. If we do this truth-telling in a way that is hurtful, unkind, vengeful, and uncompassionate, we keep the cycle of violence turning. But with discriminating wisdom and a clear comprehension of the situation, born of awareness and care, we can speak truth powerfully and forcefully in a way that is both healing and appropriate and which, in the end, removes us from the orbit of someone else's nightmare. Even though the others involved may choose to continue living the lie about what happened, or may continue to hold on to their delusions about the relationship, through the practice of forgiveness we can open to the possibility of disengaging ourselves from both the relationship and the aftermath of the experience.

It has been many years since my abuse memories surfaced. The emotions stemming from that period of my life are no longer as intense and omnipresent as when they first emerged. However, sometimes an event or a conversation can still restimulate the full force of old feelings. My dreams are often populated by characters from those times. I tell myself that this is the way it needs to be for me right now. It is vital to have a long-enduring mind. Patience is great friend along the way.

Some days there is no calm, peace, patience, or forgiveness. Even though turmoil and inner conflict do not feel OK, accepting these clouds is part of the meditation practice. By marginalizing and rejecting what is difficult, we do violence to ourselves. We come to the heartbreaking realization that we often treat ourselves far worse than we treat others. At those times I remind myself of the Buddha's kind words: "If we looked all over the world, we would not find anyone more deserving of our love and compassion than ourselves."

When our hearts are closed, the pain can be hellish. It is difficult to remain open to the conflict and turmoil raging within ourselves. This is the great challenge in meditation: opening to what feels closed. Yet what an act of inner mercy this is. We remind ourselves again and again that there are no "shoulds" in the healing process. We do not have to reach perfection on any schedule. This attitude is a gesture of immense forgiveness itself and a doorway back into our hearts. Nisargadatta Maharaj says:

> All you need is already inside you, only you must approach yourself with reverence and with love. Self-hatred and self-distrust are grievous errors. Your constant flight from pain and search for pleasure is a sign of love you bear for yourself. All I

plead with you is this: make love of yourself perfect. Deny yourself nothing. Give yourself infinity and eternity, and discover that you do not need them. You are beyond.[1]

When I returned to America, I assembled a great pile of literature about sexual abuse and mailed it off to the school. Childhood sexual abuse is not openly addressed in South African schools, and I wanted to support the administration in dealing with the issue.

The school has never acknowledged receiving that literature, nor did they ever contact me after my visit. Months later I received a copy of the school magazine. There was news, again, of the wonderful victories of the rugby team, but not a word about my visit or my meetings with the administration and students.

At first I felt hurt and angry. Then I recalled the feeling of relief and empowerment at having had the opportunity to speak the truth when I did. Regrounded in my experience, I clearly understood a further important lesson on the path of forgiveness. Forgiveness is an act of self-love. The outer results of the act of forgiving—that is, any effects it may have on the other person or people involved—are secondary. Forgiveness is a powerful choice to free ourselves from the repercussions of the past. When we forgive, we cease to be victims of somebody else's pain and confusion.

Several years ago, Pope John Paul II was shot and wounded by a would-be assassinator. He chose to forgive his attacker. A writer in *Time* magazine remarked:

> Not to forgive is to be imprisoned by the past, by old grievances that do not permit life to proceed with new business. Not to forgive is to yield oneself to another's control. If one does not forgive, then one is controlled by the other's initiatives and is locked into a sequence of act and response, of out-

rage and revenge, tit for tat, escalating always. The present is endlessly overwhelmed and devoured by the past. Forgiveness frees the forgiver. It extracts the forgiver from someone else's nightmare. "Unless there is a breach with the evil past," says Donald Shriver [president of Union Theological Seminary], "all we get is the stuttering repetition of evil."[2]

As we practice awareness meditation, we see clearly the changes within our minds and hearts. In one moment we may have the mind and heart of Saint Teresa, and in the next, the mind and heart of a devil. To the degree that we are able to accept these movements of heart and mind, we are potentially able to bring the power of forgiveness into our lives and into our relationships with others.

Though we all look quite angelic as we sit quietly in meditation, every one of us knows how it feels to be embroiled in inner turmoil, seething with anger, jealousy, and conflict. Our minds may be tortured by images of people who are living their lives happily elsewhere, or who are perhaps even dead. When we realize what is happening, we may ask ourselves: "Who is in pain? Who is suffering? Is it the person receiving our animosity, or is it we ourselves?"

When I read accounts in newspapers of injustice, atrocity, and crime, I often wonder what would have become of me, had I been born under the same circumstances, conditions, and influences as the jailers, torturers, and abusers of this world. Would I have acted any differently?

Here is a poem by Thich Nhat Hanh:

> Promise me,
> promise me this day
> while the sun is just overhead
> even as they strike you down
> with a mountain of hate and violence,

remember, brother,
man is not our enemy.

Just your pity,
just your hate
invincible, limitless,
hatred will never let you face
the beast in man.
And one day, when you face this
beast alone, your courage intact, your eyes kind,
out of your smile
will bloom a flower
and those who love you
will behold you
across 10,000 worlds of birth and dying.

Alone again
I'll go on with bent head
but knowing the immortality of love.
And on the long, rough road
both sun and moon will shine,
lighting my way.[3]

With the deepening of meditation practice, we come to see that the world in which we live is profoundly ordered. There is nothing haphazard about what is going on, either within us or without. Our happiness and unhappiness depend not on our wishes or fears, but on our actions and intentions. As this perspective deepens and we observe people acting in a way that is hurtful to themselves or to others, we do not respond with vengeful glee or self-satisfaction. We are far more likely to respond with compassion. We realize that karmic seeds of future pain and destruction are being sown. From this perspective, the imperative for forgiveness is overwhelming. In the words of Mahatma Gandhi: "What is true of individuals is true of nations. One cannot forgive enough. The weak can never forgive. Forgiveness is an attitude of the strong."[4]

Remember when I thought I had forgiven my mother? Some years ago my mother came from South Africa to visit me in the United States, and one afternoon while we were together, I was able to share and express feelings with her which originated from a very young place, feelings that I'd thought had been lost to me. I cried and was very angry. She was shattered and several times reached out and asked me to stop. She said, "Please forgive me! I am so sorry."

I said to her, "This is my time. I must be heard." I continued until I had said everything and every tear had fallen. When I had finished and it was her opportunity to speak, she told me truths of her childhood and her life that I had not known before. She had never voiced these truths to anybody! This wonderful seventy-year-old woman had not shared the facts of her own very difficult childhood with my father or with any of her friends. When she had finished her story, I was deeply shaken and touched by her anguish. My heart felt it would break with the great love I felt for her. I appreciated, in a whole new way, how well she had mothered me. When I reached out to her and we held each other, it was with a feeling of forgiveness and love that went far beyond anything I had ever known before.

This was a further lesson I learned. If possible, it is important to open to the pain of those who have hurt us, whether they have done so deliberately or inadvertently. This act of opening is precious beyond words. In doing so, we recognize that all of us are human beings. All of us want desperately to be happy, but we sometimes have no idea how to create that happiness. Sometimes our efforts backfire, upon ourselves and on others.

The process of forgiveness has been like a flower opening in the morning sun, each petal making space for the next petal to open. The willingness to be tender with myself as I enter places of woundedness and pain brings forth whatever is needed to deepen the healing.

On a more recent retreat, my own flower opened further as new memories of sexual assault surfaced, from earlier years. It was as if more pieces in an old, old puzzle were falling into place. When I shared these images and recollections with a friend, she said to me, "Oh, now you have to go through colossal rage and shame and terror. This is going to be another long and protracted process."

At once a voice spoke up within me: "I will allow this process to unfold in its own way. No assumptions, no expectations, no preconceptions!" The voice of forgiveness can be a fierce one too!

In fact, the impact of the new information was far different from what I might have expected. I feel peaceful, calm, and able to rest gratefully within this further understanding of my life— an understanding that often feels quite workable now. Certainly there have been strong emotions related to the new memories, but there is also a great deal of joy and relinquishment. In fact, the most pervasive sensations have been ones of gratitude and relief that I now have this information. The process of healing and forgiveness continues.

May the practice of forgiveness open us to all that is needed for the completion of the healing that is the birthright of every one of us.

Forgiveness Meditation

- Take a comfortable position.
- Close your eyes if you wish.
- Breathe and allow yourself to relax.
- Reflect on forgiveness and what forgiveness means to you.

It may be an image. It may be an energy, a sense, or a
feeling in the body.

- Dwell on the meaning of forgiveness in your life. What is
forgiveness? Have you ever forgiven someone? How did
that feel? Consider how it would feel to live with a sense
of forgiveness in your life now.
- Rest the attention at the heart center, at the middle of
the chest.
- Allow these words to move through you:

> "I forgive myself."
> "I forgive myself for any pain, suffering, or hurt I may
> have caused myself by my words, my thoughts, or my ac-
> tions."
> "Whether I intended or didn't intend the suffering, I for-
> give myself."
> "I forgive myself."

- Within your heart, silently forgive yourself.
- Continue to repeat these phrases for a while.
- Shift now to the pain you may have caused others.

> "I forgive myself for any pain or suffering I may have
> caused you, by my words, thoughts, or deeds, whether
> intentional or unintentional."
> "I forgive myself."

- Hold yourself in the embrace of a forgiving heart.
- Wipe the slate as clean as possible and move on.

> "I forgive myself."

- Repeat the phrases for a while.
- Now turn outward, asking for forgiveness.
- Bring to mind an image or sense of someone whom you
have hurt.

> "Please forgive me."
> "Please forgive me for the pain and heartbreak I may have
> caused you by my words, thoughts, or deeds."

"I ask for your forgiveness."

"I ask you to let me back into your heart."

"Please forgive me for any way I may have hurt you."

- And now, as you sit, feel that forgiveness coming to you, for the ways you might have caused pain or suffering through confusion, doubt, ignorance, or carelessness.

  "Please forgive me."

- Repeat the phrases, directing them toward others whom you may have hurt.
- Now bring to mind the image or the sense of someone who has hurt you—someone who has caused you pain, sadness, suffering, or heartbreak.
- Extend feelings of forgiveness to this person:

  "I am willing to forgive you."

  "I forgive you for what you did."

- Keep breathing.

  "I forgive you."

- You may wish to use the name of the person.

  "I forgive you for what happened."

  "I forgive you."

- Allow forgiveness to crumble the walls that stand between you and the person who caused you pain and suffering.
- Touch the person with forgiveness and mercy.
- Repeat the phrases, and direct them toward others who may have hurt you.
- Now open the heart and allow feelings of forgiveness to spill out to include anyone who may have hurt you in small or big ways.
- From there include all beings, all over the planet. Allow the feelings of forgiveness and mercy to encompass and

embrace all who live and breath in this beautiful world of ours.

"May our planet and all who walk, crawl, swim, and fly be free from suffering."

- Return awareness to the breathing for a few minutes.
- Slowly open your eyes.

If, during this meditation, you find that you reach the limit of your ability to forgive, remember that forgiveness is a practice that unfolds in its own time. That you were willing to undertake the forgiveness meditation demonstrates your sincere intention to forgive. This is important. Forgiveness arises in its own time and way.

Consider the pain of one who hurt you. Reflect upon their suffering. You may wish to offer the phrases of forgiveness again. If you still feel no openness, that is OK. Forgive this also. You are perhaps at your limit for now. Or it may feel as though extending forgiveness beyond yourself is a stretch for now. It may be too much. This is fine too. Many of us have lived lives of immense self-sacrifice, a lack of balance between care of ourselves and care of others. We may now feel resistance to shifting the focus of forgiveness from ourselves. Honor this feeling. Experiment with the balance. There may be good reason right now for embracing only ourselves within our great loving hearts. The rest will unfold in its own rhythm. We need to address our aching hearts first, and this pain will surely change with time.

5

Questioning

FAITH, DOUBT, AND
SELF-ACCEPTANCE

THE VENERABLE SHARIPUTRA was one of the most senior and dearly respected monks in the community. One day, when the Buddha was staying in the mango grove near Nalanda, Shariputra visited him in his dwelling.

"I have the deepest faith in you, dear teacher," said Shariputra. "There has never been a buddha like you, nor will there ever be one to compare with you. Furthermore at this time there is no man or woman more exalted in enlightenment than you are."

The Buddha considered Shariputra's words and then replied: "Lofty indeed is this speech of yours. A bold utterance. A veritable sounding of the lion's roar! But how is it that you say this, Shariputra? Have you full knowledge of the buddhas of the past, how they conducted themselves, how they meditated, how they lived their lives? Were they deeply free? Do you know these things?"

"No, sir, I do not know these things."

"Have you the self-same knowledge of the buddhas to come, Shariputra?"

"No, sir."

"Have you full and direct knowledge of how I conduct myself, how I meditate, how I live my life, and how free I truly am?"

"No again, sir."

"How, then, can you so boldly make a statement of faith involving understandings you do not have?"

Heeding the call to a life of wakefulness, honesty, and a love free of attachment is, perhaps, the most courageous and noble challenge facing any human being. This challenge calls into question every assumption that we have about ourselves, every idea about who or what we are, and every preconceived notion we hold about the nature of the world. We are called to step into the unexplored and unknown. This is a movement into the great mystery of life. On this journey we must die. We die to all attachment, delusion, and sense of security.

This is a powerful call to spiritual warriorship, and this path of purification and freedom is not always easy. As we open to the depths of who we are, and as the true nature of the world in which we live begins to reveal itself, there come times of shattering heartbreak, profound sadness and grief. Probably there will be interludes of enormous pain, both in the body and mind. So, too, there must also come times of great joy, happiness, and calm.

All things considered, this call to warriorship is a powerful challenge to our spirits and our sense of commitment. Where do we get the resources to stick with it, to start over again and again? In my experience it is the force of faith, trust, and confidence that strengthens the ability, the willingness, and the sheer guts it takes to continue. Faith, trust, and confidence are deeply interconnected and interrelated, so that it is impossible to explore one without embracing the others to some degree.

Faith is a deep sense of conviction in a reality or a truth which underlies all experience but which cannot be pinned down or understood with the ordinary mind. Spiritual life begins with some degree of faith. This faith is not tangible, nor can it be expressed in words. It is not an intellectual belief. Rather, true faith is intuitive, beyond words, beyond the mind. It is crucially important, for without this inexpressible faith, we would never seek the freedom and peace that lie beyond the limits of our current experiences. We would not meditate, we'd never make a single effort, let alone the great and enduring effort necessary to transform ourselves. The Buddhist texts say that faith is the doorway through which all positive qualities manifest.

There are three kinds of faith. The first is what is known as blind faith. This is a belief in something outside of ourselves. If we have blind faith in someone, and she or he turns out to be good and trustworthy, then we are lucky. If that person turns out to be misleading or hurtful, however, the consequences can be devastating. An extreme example of blind faith would be the religious fanaticism that prevails in our world, with all the accompanying dangers of intolerance, cultism, and indoctrination. The characteristics of blind faith are rigidity, closedness, and defensiveness. Blind faith avoids possibilities that might lead to questions. Blind faith is easily threatened by difference. An important truth about blind faith is that it is not verified by our experience in any way but is merely accepted without contemplation, questioning, or testing.

The next kind of faith is known as bright faith. The texts say that this faith brightens and gladdens the heart and mind. For many of us, bright faith shines out when we first set foot on the spiritual path. Often, on hearing the Dharma for the first time, there is an arising of bright faith and enthusiasm. For others this bright faith might arise upon meeting an inspiring person, seeing a religious image, or witnessing a beautiful sunset. There sometimes is an element of devotion too. Bright faith is important, for it inspires confidence and energy. It gets us going at the beginning, inspiring us to set forth and heed our own particular call to destiny. Yet an important characteristic of bright faith is that it lacks knowledge or wisdom. With bright faith we can still be fooled. We do not yet question the object of our faith.

The third kind of faith is verified faith. For me, the arising of verified faith is one of the greatest happinesses in the unfolding of the meditation practice. As we see the truths of the Dharma for ourselves, in our experience, we have in effect verified the Dharma. Our faith has been confirmed. We have checked out, and verified to some degree, what we have heard or read. What inspired us in the beginning turns out to be true for us. As mindfulness gets stronger and insight deepens, we see more and our verified faith grows. The Buddha said, "You, too, come see." He directed his statement to each one of us. Each of us can heed this call to faith.

The question of suffering is important when considering faith, for it is suffering that provides the impetus to examine life further and to continue our quest. If there were no suffering, we might never think of looking below the surface of things. Suffering is a conditioning factor for faith; it really awakens us to faith. The Buddha said that suffering either ripens as confusion or ripens as search. Our contact with suffering, and the despair that results, energizes the faith and trust that liberation from suffering is possible.

Each insight deepends our faith until it becomes unshakable. We cannot be swayed by the opinions of others or the prevailing views of society. We become sure. We trust in the spirit of our inquiry. At the same time, the direct experience that we derive from meditation and observation gives depth and power to our faith.

Ultimately, meditation practice calls us to have faith in each moment. We relinquish the past and the future in favor of the present. We surrender even the most minuscule resistance to life. In this surrender, we feel the pain of how strongly we want things to be stable and reliable. We open to our yearning to feel a firmer ground beneath our feet, even while we discover that this ground does not exist. It takes huge faith to let go of the deep existential yearning for stability and to let go into the insecurity of life. Jae Jah Noh speaks of this faith as a form of "radical acceptance," which he defines as radical acknowledgement of the presence of truth in this very moment. The only thing to do is to do nothing but accept truth in all ways, as all things, at all times, in all forms, in all ways. To let go, to accept, it is necessary only to give up your concerns and your fears. It's not a matter of whether or not faith is present in your life. It is. It's only a question of whether you place your faith in truth and reality or in your considerations, your abstractions and thoughts about it. Do not doubt whether or not you are practicing faith. Consider only where it is placed. Radical acceptance is the practice of faith.[1]

I have been both humbled and strengthened in my own grappling and wrangling with faith. The period surrounding my HIV-positive diagnosis felt very dire. It was a time of despair and hopelessness. My mind seemed to focus obsessively on every possible terrifying eventuality of living with the virus. So many friends had died of AIDS, and I could not free my mind from the ghastly memories of what some of them had to go through in the course of the disease. I cast about for meaning in all of this, searching for some reason to continue, some faith. At first I tried to strike a bargain with the virus. I vowed that if I got better, then I would have faith and trust. Soon enough, however, I found myself stumbling over the agreement, for I just didn't get any better!

Now I understand that there can be no conditions when it comes to faith. Trusting the process by surrendering to the unknown, to the insecurity, and to each moment, feels to me to be a true expression of faith. Chögyam Trungpa writes:

> The result of letting go is that you discover a bank of self-existing energy that is always available to you—beyond any circumstance. It actually comes from nowhere, but is always there. It is the energy of basic goodness.
>
> This self-existing energy is called *windhorse* in the Shambhala teachings. The *wind* principle is that the energy of basic goodness is strong and exuberant and brilliant. It can actually

radiate tremendous power in your life. But at the same time, basic goodness can be ridden, which is the principle of the *horse*. By following the diciplines of warriorship, particularly the discipline of letting go, you can harness the wind of goodness. In some sense the horse is never tamed—basic goodness never becomes your personal possession. But you can invoke and provoke the uplifted energy of basic goodness in your life. You begin to see how you can create basic goodness for yourself and others on the spot, fully and ideally, not only on a philosophical level, but on a concrete, physical level. When you contact the energy of windhorse, you can naturally let go of worrying about your own state of mind and you can begin to think of others. You feel a longing to share your discovery of goodness with your brothers and sisters, your mother and father, friends of all kinds who would also benefit from the message of basic goodness. So discovering windhorse is, first of all, acknowledging the strength of basic goodness in yourself and then fearlessly projecting that state of mind to others.[2]

I used to spend a great deal of time going to healers and doctors and having interminable blood tests and treatments. I became exhausted from seeing all these people. I worried about all the others whom I didn't have time to see and all the tests and therapies I didn't have the money to pay for. Now I see that the question of faith is important here too. I come more deeply to trust that everything that I do is sufficient in each moment. Living with the virus is unworkable if I bring into this moment every ghastly projection, fear, and possibility that the future might hold. I do what I can now, and then let go, in faith. Thus, faith is centered on this immediate moment—this breath, this heartbeat, this landscape. We live as fully as we can right now and trust that the next landscape will take care of itself.

The arising and maturing of faith manifest very clearly in the meditation practice. In my experience a very important shift happens at some point, a change that is simple and sweet. We come to have a deep gratitude for presence in each moment. Gratitude and balance replace the older patterns of confusion, heaviness, judgment, frustration, and the constant focusing on negativity. With faith there arises a wonder, awe, and gratitude for being simply present. This shift gives birth to deeper faith and happiness. There arises a fuller commitment to meditation and true awareness. When there is confusion and distraction, the memory of times of presence and alertness rekindles our faith and provides the strength to continue.

Our world today is experiencing a deep crisis of faith. Humanity seems to have lost all faith in itself. Why is a sure faith so difficult to develop and so hard to find? It seems that the lack of self-acceptance and an inability to trust are often an integral part of the reason for this. Within the individual, the roots of the situation invariably go back to childhood. Perhaps our parents had problems and difficulties that prevented them from loving us in ways that were healthy. The child was perhaps not considered, accepted, or validated. Perhaps the child was abused in some way. What love there was may have been conditional, intermittent, and confusing. All of this makes a healthy trust both difficult and unlikely to arise easily later in life.

At the collective level, we are bombarded by natural and human-made disasters in the news, violence and alienation in films and on television, and the conflicting pronouncements of various political, religious, and scientific groups. Surrounded by these forces we learn to doubt our own ability to look, listen, and discover the truth of life for ourselves. Because society puts us under great pressure to "improve" our circumstances, we can rarely relax. The gadgets and technologies designed to save us time and labor increase the speed at which we live and only make us more anxious in the end. Our environment is on the brink of catastrophe. All of the suffering produced by this predicament is compounded by a fundamental lack of faith. Will we be able to save ourselves before it's too late? Humanity's lack of faith in its own potential and in nature itself is reflected in this anxious question asked by so many people. We lack faith in the orderliness and interconnectedness of the universe.

Healthy children seem to have an intuitive and instinctive trust in the rhythms of life and of nature, and often we as adults have to search to find this trust again. As adults, many of us live our lives as victims of circumstance. We fight, struggle, and feel blown around by the winds that rage about us. The way of faith is different. In every situation of difficulty and challenge, men and women of faith ask this same question: what can I learn from this?

Faith is the trust that no matter what is happening in our lives, we are exactly where we need to be, in the circumstances best designed for our individual spiritual journey.

This view shifts our focus from punishment to opportunity. We no longer try to bear up under the crushing weight of circumstances, we use those circumstances for growth. This shift is radical. Faith gives meaning to the challenges that come. It opens up profound possibilities in life. With faith we go forward and move mountains.

For many people, grappling with faith is a great part of the spiritual journey. Sometimes we feel spontaneously inspired and dream great dreams, but at other times faith seems to have deserted us. We may also discover that faith is conditioned and impermanent. Can we cultivate a long-enduring mind that will allow even our faith to come and go?

When considering the lack of faith, what we find in the end, is fear. Fear is the opposite of faith. If we are engulfed by fear, there can be no faith. In our movement toward faith we must get to know all the masks of fear, such as fear of pain, death, loneliness, insecurity, confusion—and the fear of fear itself. Faith and trust take us to our edges, and it is at these same edges that faith and trust thrive.

To live fully means to take risks, sometimes going right to our limits. This takes a lot of guts. Fear dictates that we must hold on, while faith allows us to move beyond the limitations of fear into the deepest dimensions of love.

In a letter to a fellow poet, Rainer Maria Rilke gave this reassurance:

> We have no reason to harbor any mistrust against our world, for it is not against *us*. If it has terrors, they are our terrors; if it has abysses, these abysses belong to us, if there are dangers, we must try to love them. And if only we arrange our life in accordance with the principle which tells us that we must always trust in the difficult, then what now appears to us as the most alien will become our most intimate and trusted experience. How could we forget those ancient myths that stand at the beginning of all races, the myths about dragons that at the last moment are transformed into princesses? Perhaps all the dragons in our lives are princesses who are only waiting to see us act, just once, with beauty and courage. Perhaps everything that frightens us is, in its deepest essence, something helpless that wants our love.
>
> So you mustn't be frightened . . . if a sadness rises in front of you, larger than any you have ever seen; if an anxiety, like light and cloud-shadows, moves over your hands and over everything you do. You must realize that something is happening to you, that life has not forgotten you, that it holds you in its hand and will not let you fall. Why do you want to shut out of your life any uneasiness, any misery, any depression, since after all you don't know what work these conditions are doing inside of you?[3]

DOUBT

In grappling with faith, it seems vital that we know the darkness too, for when we see our shadow, we at the same time behold the light. One of the shadows that we are shown in the course of the spiritual journey is doubt.

What exactly is doubt? In my experience, it is a mixture of ingredients. Take a little fear, a touch of discontent, add a dash of boredom and sleepiness, and let it all stew in an atmosphere of unmindfulness. The concoction will soon ripen into paralysis, exhaustion, hesitancy, and unwillingness to commit. Under the influence of such a brew, we very often turn against outselves. Our thoughts proliferate in harsh and unforgiving ways. The usual ones may be familiar to you:

> "I can't do the meditation."
> "I'll never get it."
> "I'm failing at the practice."
> "I'm not working hard enough."
> "I'm working too hard."
> "Everyone else can do it, but I can't."
> "I hate myself."

What is truly happening is that anger and frustration are being turned inward, against ourselves. We then identify with the whole process and feel stuck and paralyzed.

Doubt has further voices, ones that say:

> "The meditation practice doesn't work."
> "There is just too much noise."
> "There is too little noise."
> "The teachings are not right."
> "The teachers are awful."

Here again there is boredom, anger, and frustration turned outward. We then identify with these doubtful thoughts. In neither case do we see the truth of what is happening.

A further danger arises when doubt is really strong. We may in desperation shift the responsibility for freedom outside of ourselves. The danger of relying on outward things is enormous. We cling to opinions and beliefs, perhaps even to the Dharma, instead of having a faith born of our own experience and understanding.

Perhaps the greatest tragedy occurs when a spiritual practice that is potentially freeing becomes a prison instead. When we believe and strongly identify with the voices of doubt, we may end up using the meditation practice as a weapon against ourselves. The mind may even convince itself that freedom is impossible. We thus kill the very heart of the practice.

In dealing with doubt, it is pivotal to clarify our relationship with thoughts. As the practice deepens, thoughts become less and less burdensome. They do not stop, of course; they will always be there, coming and going. Yet, as practice deepens, with true awareness, we see their real nature. We know their limitations. We perceive their emptiness. No one is thinking. Rather than identifying with thoughts and believing them, we focus more on the ground from which the thoughts come. We trust the stillness rather than the chatter. We move from the mind into the heart.

Peter Matthiessen writes vividly of his experience of doubt during a Zen meditation retreat:

> . . . after six long days of pain, hurling myself to no avail against iron cliffs, I began to wonder why I'd come, why I'd persisted year after year with this frustrating practice. . . . I gave up struggling and settled calmly into moment-by-moment quiet, breath after breath. Soon I was light and taut, at one with pain as I was with breathing, with incense, far crows, and autumn wind. Small, silver breaths, further and further apart, scoured the last patches of thought and emotion from the inside of my skull. Now a silent bell. Very suddenly on an inhaled breath this earthbound body-mind in great hush began to swell and fragment and dissolve in light, expanding outward into a fresh universe and the very process of creation. At the

bell ending this period, this perspective ended, yet those clear moments had been an experience that everything was here, now, contained in me. I mourned that bell, that came so swiftly, and tried to cheer myself during the walking meditation. "Who, me?" I murmured right out loud and began to laugh. The laughter quickly turned to weeping and with the tears came a sudden rush of love for everyone and everything without distinction. This feeling was instantly followed by a rush of doubt. Had I really perceived something? All this damned soggy weeping. Had my mind gone soft? The doubt came sweeping back again. Perhaps I was wanting such experiences too badly. Perhaps I was exaggerating everything. I was filled with gratitude and at the same time felt frustrated and aborted. This experience, valid or otherwise, had scarcely started before being cut off by that bell, which, had it come even a few minutes later, might have rung these cliffs of iron down around my head.[4]

At one point in my own meditation practice, there was a lot of what I had referred to as "great difficulty with the practice." On retreat, I was dealing with physical pain, fear, confusion, and exhaustion. There was also a profusion of thoughts relating to insecurity. I felt unsure of my ability to deal with the relentlessness of that pain. I felt insecure in my ability to find balance with the vastness of the suffering. Furthermore, my health felt very unpredictable. Compounding all of this, I was experiencing a strong chemical withdrawal reaction after moving off a year of drug therapy. I was also unable to sleep at the time.

Altogether, I felt deep despair and hopelessness. Suddenly, like thunderbolts of challenge cutting through the storm, these questions rang out within me:

> Is what is happening now perfectly OK?
> Do I truly believe all this to be OK? As it is?
> Am I in any way a victim of what is going on?

When I confronted the question of victimhood, there was an immediate release. The gridlock of tightness that had annexed my spirit and body shifted and disintegrated. It felt as though a light had come on, and awareness was able to move to places that had been formerly in the shadows. It was clear that I had allowed myself to be victimized by the doubt that had arisen. Now I saw the doubt as no more than a series of paralyzing thoughts born of fear and giving birth to more fear. The resistance to fear, the aversion to thought, the denial and avoidance of the pain and sadness, and the identification with the whole process—all had come together into an overwhelming mass of doubt. Yet how easily that mass dissolved when I saw it for what it was.

When I saw the true face of the doubt, great joy, buoyancy, and happiness arose. A huge resurgence of faith brightened my heart and mind, followed by a deep feeling of renewal and commitment. I felt deep gratitude and great happiness.

Thomas Merton has written that "faith is not the suppression of doubt, it is the overcoming of doubt, and you overcome doubt by going through it." Yet it must be acknowledged that going through doubt, struggling to the depths of what Merton calls the big doubt, which calls into question the very meaning of life, can bring us to unexpected depths of suffering within ourselves. Times of great difficulty and pain are often times of great doubt as well. We may find ourselves unable to cope. We perhaps feel that we have really reached our limit and cannot go on. Such a crisis has been called the dark night of the soul. We feel that we are unable to open to the suffering we are experiencing. It is all just too painful.

Within this difficulty, can we give ourselves permission to back off and shut down for a time, if necessary—whether in meditation or in our life at large? Often, when suffering is too great, doubt arises also. Lacking confidence in ourselves, we give up. However, if we do give ourselves permission to withdraw a little from what is happening, we can perhaps still maintain our sense of commitment. It is always possible to return to the edge again, sometime later, feeling rested, stronger, and renewed. This shutting down and renewal end up strengthening faith rather than feeding doubt.

Can we welcome doubt as fully as any other aspect of our experience in this ever-shifting present moment? Can we see doubt as just the next landscape, just the next friend, the next cloud, the next bubble—all empty and changing?

SELF-ACCEPTANCE

Our faith deepens as we heal from what may be a lifelong pattern of self-rejection. In order to cultivate self-acceptance, we do not need to build up anything new inside ourselves. We do not replace the old, bad messages with new, good, nice ones. All we need is to see clearly.

Habits of self-criticism, guilt, unworthiness, and self-condemnation are composed of emotions and the thoughts born of them. They are like transparent mirages that convince us of their solidity and truth. Meditation practice brings greater acceptance and allowance toward all that arises, including all the negative feelings we might have about ourselves. We open to, feel, and accept all that we are ashamed to admit and all that seems too painful to be felt. Slowly, as we accept the truth of the inner violence and conflict, our heart may eventually one day whisper, "No more," and let go.

Letting go is the purest expression of faith. As Jae Jah Noh says, "Try everything, and then faith."

The degree to which there is a consolidation of self-acceptance and inner faith is the degree to which we can know an outer faith, a faith in humankind and our world. The luminosity and the brightness of our faith can illuminate the path of others, guiding them toward their own resources of faithfulness, trust, and confidence. In a world deeply lacking in trust, our faith-filled spirit is precious and vital.

I will never forget the words of Nelson Mandela soon after he was released from prison in South Africa after twenty years. Somebody said to him, "How can you now sit down with those who jailed you for all those years? How can you negotiate the freedom of your people with those who kept you in prison?" He said, "Ultimately, we are a forgiving people." What a statement of faith in humanity.

I have also been struck by the words of Dr. Sheila Cassidy, who was arrested and tortured in Chile for treating a man hunted by the secret police there. Now the medical director of St. Luke's Hospice in Plymouth, England, she said in an interview with Christopher Titmuss:

> What reinforces my faith is the selflessness that can be elicited out of very ordinary people. I find that to be a very holy thing. I see so many people who are totally giving. One of the nice things about being here [in the hospice] is that you meet people stripped of pretense and in the raw. Some of them are very selfish, but you also see so many people who are so lovely. I find that miraculous.
>
> I think the world is bloody marvelous, and people are lovely. And it's not that I don't know that people are wounded and fragile, but I believe they are fundamentally good.[5]

KARMA: "WHY ME?"

ONE DAY, A student by the name of Subha came to the Buddha with the following question:

"Why are there differences between human beings? Some are handsome and beautiful, others are ugly and distasteful. Some are clever, others, stupid. Some take high births, others are born in the lower castes."

The Buddha replied: "All beings are the heirs of their karma. Karma determines appearance, birth, health, intelligence, and so forth. This is why beings vary one from another.

"A man or woman can never hide from the effects of an unskillful deed. Not in the highest cave nor in the depths of the sea can one sidestep the laws of karma.

"Beings are the masters of their destiny. Happiness follows goodness. Unhappiness follows evil actions. No one can purify another. None can escape the consequences of their own actions."

After his enlightenment, with the great power of his mind, the Buddha reviewed the countless births and deaths of human beings, past, present, and future. He saw that one thing was true for everybody: all yearn for happiness, yet the great majority live in ways that make true happiness impossible.

Happiness and sorrow are ruled by the laws of karma. Though karma is enormously complicated, its basic principle is simply that of cause and effect. Our actions and thoughts have consequences in our lives, in the lives of others, and in the universe.

Although cause and effect is a simple principle, the link between a single action and its result is subject to many influences. We cannot begin to disentangle them all. The Buddha named karma among what he called the four imponderables. These are four topics on which thinking flounders.

> Do not try to think about the mind of a buddha. Nobody can really understand that, except another buddha.
> Do not think too much about the power of a highly concentrated mind unless you have one yourself. Only a concentrated mind can understand itself.
> Do not waste too much time thinking about the beginning of existence. This will drive you crazy!
> Do not try to fully understand the laws of karma, since this is impossible. Only a fully enlightened being, someone whose mental powers are completely developed, can really understand the complex, subtle, and all-pervasive ramifications of these laws.

It is possible, nonetheless, for us to observe karma at work moment to moment. This is important, since we can choose options that cultivate joy and protect us from sorrow. If we observe the present moment, we see how our thoughts, attitudes, and behavior condition the atmosphere of our lives.

If we act out of genuine generosity, compassion, and loving-kindness, how does this feel? If our words, actions, or thoughts are vindictive, angry, or divisive, what is the resultant feeling in the mind and body? Personally, whenever I act or think in ways that are open and loving, I notice bodily ease and a sense of mental receptivity and connection. When I act out of anger or vindictiveness, the body and mind both tighten. There will probably be constriction in the small of my back, chest, shoulders, or throat also. In my mind there is likely to be a feeling of closure, complexity, separation, and confusion.

Padmasambhava, one of the founders of Tibetan Buddhism in the eighth century, said, "If you want to know your past, look at the present. If you want to know your future, look at the present." In the light of true awareness, cause and effect can be seen directly in the present moment. We see that there is a direct relationship between behavior, mental states, and bodily well-being. Mind and body condition each other. As our sensitivity deepens, we become acutely aware of the inner and outer effects of our actions. We come to know whether the consequences of our actions are pleasant, painful, or neutral, beneficial or harmful.

In meditation, we observe the chainlike succession of causes and effects. For example: first there may be a thought, perhaps about the future. "This cough is going to get worse." In the next moment, fear arises. Next, the belly tightens followed by an image of severe illness. All causes and effects. The first thought conditions fear. The fear conditions physical sensation. The sensation conditions emotions and images.

Our lives are not haphazard or chaotic. The processes of nature are profoundly ordered. However, we are not the controllers of the process. Once we begin to understand the concept of karma, we use this understanding to serve our happiness.

It's extremely important to understand how one aspect of our experience conditions another. For this, it is not necessary to be sitting with our eyes closed. Say we are walking outside and see somebody go by with an ice-cream cone. The thought arises: "Ice cream." This gives rise to craving. After the craving comes another thought: "I must have ice cream." The next thought is, "Kitchen freezer." There arises an intention to change direction. Now we move in the direction of our house. We pick our feet up. We put them down. We reach for the freezer door handle.

This is a sequence of causes and effects: the mind conditioning the body, which is conditioning the mind. When we see our behavior broken down into its components, it is much simpler to understand. With mindfulness we find that we no longer arrive in the kitchen without quite knowing how we got there!

How did we end up in this particular city, with this partner, this car, and this job? Understanding the increments of karma can help us feel less estranged and victimized by the circumstances of our lives. Appreciating karma, we become more careful in our decision-making.

As meditation practice deepens, the growing insight into orderliness becomes one of the most liberating understandings we have. Direct observation of the arising and passing away of phenomena, seeing clearly the cause and effect within that process, is potentially very freeing.

One recent fall, I sat a three-month meditation retreat. The first thing I noticed at the start of the retreat was that my abdomen felt like lead. In fact, my entire body felt heavy. Each hour of sitting seemed to last for weeks. The mind felt solid, immutable, and congealed. It was extremely painful. As best I could, I tried not to hate what was happening. I sat with leadenness, keeping the awareness as clear and detached as possible.

Lead meditation!

Day in and day out—it seemed to last forever. The only thing moving was the imperceptible growth of my willingness to sit with the leadenness. One day, the hardness changed a tiny bit. It felt a little alive, like the hardness of a flower bud, still young, green, and very tightly closed.

Opening began to slowly happen. As the bud shifted a tentative petal, a huge wave of fear poured through me. As the tightness and heaviness gradually released, further fear was released, in powerful torrents.

There was nothing to do but sit with the fear. It felt as though a faucet had been turned on. As the intense feelings rushed through me, I gradually came to notice that there was constriction around the fear itself, as if someone were putting a finger over the end of the faucet.

The awareness moved to this resistance. It felt as though the musculature automatically closed down around the strong feelings that had arisen. I stayed with the feeling of contraction in the body. Over time, it, too, slowly started to dissolve. The rushes of fear grew weaker, until there was nothing left except a tiny little bubbling energy, way down in the bottom of my heart. It was not hard to stay with the tiny bubbles of fear. Presently they disappeared. There was nothing left.

Peace.

For me this sequence of causes and effects demonstrated vividly how layers of suffering are built up. Awareness revealed and reversed the process. As the layers unfolded, it was possible to see how aversion to fear had conditioned the leadenness. Each component of the experience conditioned another component. This exploration taught me a great deal. It demystified some of my bodily tensions. It reaffirmed my faith in the power of awareness and patience.

It is vital that we also observe these patterns of conditioning outside of meditation. Ordinary activities like doing laundry, going to the dentist, contending with traffic, or watching a film all fall within the dominion of karma. We observe cause and effect at work here too. Karma governs all we do and think, including the consequences. To understand the past, look in the present. To know the future, look in the present.

Two aspects of awareness are especially important when considering the working of karma in our lives. The first one is a quality of mind called clear comprehension, the mental faculty that enables us to clearly understand what is happening in each moment of time. This means that when we are walking, we clearly comprehend that we are walking. When we are sitting, we clearly understand that we are sitting. We are clearly aware of our motivations and our mental atmosphere.

The second aspect of awareness is called suitability of purpose. This means responding to whatever is happening in an appropriate and skillful way. Suitability of purpose follows upon clear comprehension. First, with clear comprehension, we go to the heart of a situation. Next, with suitability of purpose, we are able to respond with wisdom and compassion.

These two qualities help bring harmony to situations. We make choices that create happiness for ourselves and others. As we open to deeper levels of feeling, our comprehension deepens and our responses become more honest and appropriate. These possibilities do not arise if awareness is not true and strong. If awareness is weak or absent, one moment of anger simply conditions further anger. A moment of fear conditions more fear. If we are not clear within ourselves, we cannot respond suitably and wisely.

With a deeper understanding of karma we see that our personalities are not fixed irrevocably. Any moment carries the most profound opportunity for change. Just as fear can condition more fear, so, too, can one moment of fearlessness condition further fearlessness in our lives. We take full responsibility for our lives and for how we live. This is the great spiritual imperative.

Some time ago, I had a dream whose clarity and message have not dimmed. I was inside a house with a large group of friends and loved ones who had gathered to support and care for me as I grappled with AIDS. I was furious and ran outside brandishing a pistol in each hand, firing shots randomly into the ground and up into the air. Meanwhile, I screamed out for help and understanding. I begged to be rescued. People came running out, gasping and flustered. I felt alone and embarrassed. Even my mother came out, dressed in her white bowling outfit. In spite of her obvious love and devotion, I realized that even she did not fully understand my situation and really could not save me. A long, full moment followed in which I felt utterly alone.

I awoke from this dream feeling exhilarated and filled with conviction and certainty. The dream told me that an illusion was disintegrating. No savior was going to gallop into my life, scoop me into his arms, and remove all of my pain. I could finally stop looking outside myself for solutions that would never come.

Of course, this dream was directly related to HIV, but the fantasy of being saved is related to the trauma of sexual abuse. It originates in the yearning of a baby and a child for the protection, care, and attention that he did not always receive. The fantasy was also born of a yearning for deliverance from a nightmare that at times was unendurable. Clearly my unconscious was beginning to release these frozen yearnings.

After the dream I felt more fully responsible for my own freedom from suffering then ever before. No one else could do it for me. This was an exhilarating realization.

On his deathbed, the Buddha categorically directed those who gathered around him to take responsibility for their liberation from suffering. He clearly stated that no one else can do the work for us. We must accept no other authority. This is a radical injunction, especially for those of us who have known much codependency and unhealthy reliance in our lives.

It is profoundly challenging to remind myself that there is no divine being out there poised to rescue me from my diagnosis and other suffering. No external redeemer, no savior, no mother, no rescuer can enter into the center of the suffering and take charge. Yet I myself can take responsibility for living in a way that offers a very real possibility for freedom from suffering.

In meditation practice we see more and more clearly that

happiness or unhappiness depends on our actions, not on our wishes. We feel the utter aloneness of birth and death, and within that solitude, we come to feel both a contentment and an intimacy with our resolve to take deep responsibility. We sense that holding the idea of a savior tilts us away from our center. If we depend on others, we cannot see what is true within. If we reach outside of ourselves, we are unable to tap the strengths and the resources of energy, compassion, and wisdom that potentially exist within each of us.

Meditation practice eventually brings us home to ourselves. We listen carefully to the voice and movement of our heart and respond accordingly. Access to self-reference allows the wisdom of our being to emerge. As we apply continuous, nonjudging awareness to the movements of body and mind, we ground ourselves more and more powerfully in the truth of who we are. We are aware of our limits, boundaries, and emotions and can then reach out to others in ways that are healthy, healing, and wholehearted.

Philip Kapleau, a Zen master in Rochester, New York, recommends that we train ourselves to see that even the minutest events in our life have karmic significance. The benefits of this training are that our horizons expand and our lives take on fresh meaning. We gain a new awareness of our power and dignity as we see our influence on all that surrounds us. At the same time, Kapleau continues, we become more humble, for we realize that we are not isolated fragments thrown into a universe by random and capricious fate, but one vast ocean in which all currents intermingle. Wonder and joy replace boredom and frustration.

The Buddha said that karma is determined by volition. Volition is a mental urge, the moment of intention or motivation that precedes action. This means that if I am driving along a road and inadvertently run over a squirrel, no karmic energy is released, because I had no intention to harm that animal. On the other hand, if I am irritated by a mosquito and try to kill it, even if I slap at the mosquito and miss it, the fact that I missed really does not matter. There was a clear intention to harm, and that intention releases a karmic consequence. The effect will certainly be lessened, however, since the mosquito was spared to live another day!

As meditation practice deepens, we become aware of the quality of our intentions. With awareness of the impulse before each action come possibilities for great freedom. Our intentions define the nature of our presence in the world. For example, an expensive gift can be given without love. Our intention could be to shame or embarrass the recipient. The gift may carry some form of vengefulness. If we watch intentions carefully, we can learn a great deal about ourselves and how we live.

There are various types of karma, classified according to the way the laws operate. Some karma is fixed and cannot change in this life. Some of us are born women; others are born men. Some are born black, and some are born white. Our parents are fixed for the duration of this lifetime.

Next, there is variable karma. Two people are imprisoned in identical cells. One person uses the time to embark on spiritual practice, while the other plots revenge. After two years, one prisoner emerges with a more beautiful heart and mind. The other perpetuates the cycle of violence out in the world. Variable karma means that in the same situation, the karma can vary, depending on motivation and intention.

A definition that I like is: "Karma is a wind that is always blowing: what matters is how we pitch our sails."

Immediate karma consists of effects that are visible instantly. We put our hand in the fire, and it is burned. The cause-and-effect relationship is instantaneous.

Then there is delayed karma. Some of our actions and efforts are like seeds. We plant them now, and they bear fruit after many years. If we ill-treat our bodies now, symptoms may not manifest until decades later.

The Buddha enjoined us to believe in nothing outside of our experience. Nevertheless, when examining the issue of karma, it is important to address the question of rebirth and other realms of existance. Given that we in the West are clearly trained in skepticism and reasoning, can we stay open to the ideas of afterlives, of heavens and hells? Are there perhaps levels of understanding that lie beyond our present mental scope? Could we admit to the possibility of rebirth, or that heaven and hell realms may exist that are invisible and inaccessible to us now?

Sometimes people who have a rigid belief in past and future existences invoke karma without sensitivity or insight. During the time that I ordained as a Buddhist monk, I experienced considerable back pain and could not walk. One day as I lay in bed, another monk came to me. He leaned down, put a hand on each side of my head, looked into my eyes, and said, "You must have done something terrible in a past life to have deserved this!" My spirits withered. His comment not only was totally unhelpful, but made me feel even worse!

This kind of speculation about past lives is unskillful and useless. Karma is not punishment. Furthermore, as the Buddha emphasized, karma is imponderable. Needlessly invoking past lives tends to take us out of the present, which is the only place where the possibility of freedom is alive and available. If we blame our ill health, tragedies, crises, and losses on the irretrievable past, we are immobilized. We are filled with guilt and shame. We feel helpless and fatalistic. We are victims.

In this new age in which we live, doctrines that are classical, ancient, and complicated are sometimes revived and reinter-

preted in ways that can be hurtful and even dangerous. Karma
is a case in point. Perhaps one of the most hurtful philosophies
might be articulated this way: "Since we all create our own reality, and since our lives are reflective of our decisions and choices,
then we must also be able to reverse our sicknesses, our AIDS,
our cancer, our suffering. We are to blame for what has happened to us, for we created our illness in the first place." Furthermore, according to this viewpoint, "by making right and correct
choices and decisions now, we can undo the damage. If we don't
succeed, we've failed. We have not done it right."

The effect of this is that we can hold ourselves in unforgiving harshness. Others can hide behind these philosophies and
keep us at a distance as they hold us in their judgment. To mis-
construe the laws of karma in this twisted and cruel manner is
perhaps one of the harshest ways we can relate to people who
are suffering—or to ourselves.

If our bodies remain unhealed, if the pain increases and the
disease spreads, have we indeed failed? Some ways of thinking
would oppress us in this tragic and simplistic way.

Perhaps a life in which the body is unhealed can be a life of
great integration and healing, embracing the heart and spirit. In
all that remains unhealed, we feel our interconnection with what
is threatened and devastated on our planet. The edges blur, and
we feel interconnected with our suffering world. The pain of the
world manifests in our struggling bodies. If indeed we are a living part of this world, and none of us can fall outside this interconnection, how can anyone say, "I am healthy, and you are
sick, and therefore your illness is not my problem"?

In his book *Grace and Grit: Spirituality and Healing in the Life
and Death of Treya Killam Wilber*, psychologist Ken Wilber reflects
on traditional and New Age thinking relating to karma.

According to [Hinduism and Buddhism], your present circumstances are the results of thoughts and actions from a *previous* life, and your present thoughts and actions will affect, not your present life, but your *next* life, your next incarnation. The Buddhists say that in your present life you are simply reading a book that you wrote in the previous life; and what you are doing now will not come to fruition until your *next* life. In neither case does your present thought create your present reality.

Now I personally don't happen to believe that particular view of karma. It's a rather primitive notion subsequently refined (and largely abandoned) by the higher schools of Buddhism, where it was recognized that not *everything* that happens to us is the result of your own past actions. As Namkhai Norbu, master of Dzogchen Buddhism (generally regarded as the pinnacle of Buddhist teaching), explains: "There are illnesses produced due to karma, or the previous conditions of the individual. But there are also illnesses generated by energies that come from others, from the outside. And there are illnesses that are provoked by provisional causes, such as food or other combinations of circumstances. And there are illnesses generated by accident. Then there are all kinds of illnesses linked with the environment." My point is that *neither* the primitive version of karma nor the more evolved teachings lend any support to the new age notion.[6]

Is there a way in which our understanding of karma can help us know why things are the way they are? I learned a lesson about this at a gathering of people living with AIDS. There were 150 of us present. It was an enormous privilege to be there. My favorite time came every evening, when we'd sit around and listen to one another's stories. We spoke about our lives, our struggles, our ups and downs.

Berta was an African-American woman. She weighed seventy pounds and had just come out of the hospital after a five-month stay. Although her five children had been taken away from her, her spirit remained strong. My mind began spinning out questions. Then there was Bruce, a man in his early twenties with bright cheeks, who was dealing with excruciating pain in his body. He was so young! The same questions began ricocheting in my mind. Then there was Jackie. She first got sick in 1979, then very sick in 1984, and she was still very much alive eleven years later, exuberant and happy. She lived with severe physical pain. At the same time, she was a radiant being. The same question haunted me, again and again: Why? Why? Why?

There was so much pain in all these people, and so much beauty. As the storytelling went from person to person, I heard incredible testimonials of how people were living their lives as fully as possible in the face of so much difficulty. Gradually I realized that each time I got inextricably enmeshed in the "why" question, I was separating myself from the wisdom and heart of each person. Quite simply, there was no answer to my question.

It was only when I entered each moment fully and was present with the pain, suffering, and joys of each of these people that I was able to contribute a measure of compassion, lovingkindness, and care to the situation. This gathering was a wonderful teaching for me. I understood what the Buddha meant when he said that thinking about karma too much can drive you nuts.

Once again I realized that being present and aware is the greatest protection we have. Furthermore, according to the Buddhist texts, mindful awareness is the greatest protection any of us can have at the moment of death. When we die, all bodily sense of ourselves dissolves, yet our mental experience is said to continue. Without strong awareness, we could be overwhelmed. It is said that our mental state at the moment of death helps determine the realm and circumstances in which we will be reborn.

According to Buddhist cosmology, there are six realms of existence. The first three are lower realms, including the animal realm, which is the only realm besides our own that people can see. In the lower realms, life is extremely difficult, and beings suffer greatly. Their minds are unable to consider and grapple with the possibility of freedom from suffering. Next come two kinds of heaven realms, which are as pleasant as the hells are awful. In one of the heaven realms, bodies are composed of radiant light and color. Celestial music plays constantly. In the other heaven, beings have no bodies at all, but consist purely of subtle, blissful mental states that last for eons and eons.

Between heaven and hell lies the human realm, which is considered to be the best place for birth, superior even to the heaven realms. This may seem surprising. In the lower realms, no one can live a spiritual life because the struggle to survive is so intense. In the heaven realms, everyone is so distracted by pleasure that the idea of spiritual practice seems absurd. The human realm is a mixture of heavenly pleasure and hellish suffering. The Buddha said that our human birth is very precious and not to be wasted. It gives us both an opportunity and an incentive to free ourselves from suffering.

According to the texts, at the moment of death, four karmic forces come into play to determine where we will be reborn. The first is called weighty karma, which overrides all others. Weighty karma can be either wholesome or unwholesome. According to the scriptures, an action such as killing a buddha or one's own mother produces an unwholesome weighty karma that will activate immediately at the moment of death, to dispatch us down, down, down. However, if we generate wholesome weighty karma by practicing true awareness, and if we develop our mind in healthy and loving ways, then, according to the cosmology, we can only go up, up, up!

If there is no weighty karma, proximate karma comes into effect. Proximate karma is the force of karma arising out of the actions immediately prior to death. This is why the scriptures say that the time of dying is very important. If we can die with awareness, clarity, and lovingkindness, the karmic possibilities are great. It is because of proximate karma that many Buddhists do not wish to take painkillers or other substances that might cloud consciousness at this very precious time.

If there is no weighty or proximate karma, then habitual karma will determine the rebirth. This karma grows out of the habits of mind that predominated during one's life. If we have been generous in life, our ample mind will lead us to an existence where we will have much satisfaction. If we have been selfish and mean, we may be reborn in a lower realm.

Lastly, there is random karma, which works more or less by chance. Suppose we have lived a terrible and delinquent life, but we did do one good thing. If by chance we happen to recall this one good deed at the moment of death, then it is possible that this single memory could propel us into a heaven realm. Once there, we probably will look down and say, "Whew!"

An amusing story was told to me by a Western friend who was a Buddhist nun in Thailand at one time. At her monastery, there was one monk who was very difficult to be around. He was fastidious and proud. One day he went down to the local village and met with a man who had psychic powers. This seer told the monk that in his past lifetime, he had been a magnificent black stallion. The monk returned to the monastery, clearly very pleased with himself. Everybody asked what had happened. He responded, "I'm clearly on the up-and-up here. In my last lifetime I was a magnificent black stallion. Now I'm a Buddhist monk. I've shaved my head. I'm practicing meditation. The sky's the limit for me."

People said, "Well, why don't you go down to the village and ask this fellow what is going to happen in your next lifetime?" The monk returned to the seer. When he came back from the village, he immediately disappeared into his hut. His friends pursued him and eventually found out what had happened. The man in the village had said that next time around, the monk was going to be reborn as a tapeworm!

Perhaps it's better not to know these things.

A vital question flows from both this story and the entire issue of rebirth. In previous chapters we explored the issue of impermanence. The truth of change is evident wherever we look, both within ourselves and outside, on every level of existence. Consequentially, the idea of an unchanging soul or some other fixed and static aspect of ourselves is contrary to the truth of change. Nothing is permanent. Nothing is static. Nothing is unchanging.

This being so, what is it that endures from one lifetime to the next? If there is no fixed and static soul, what is carried forward into the next existence? According to the Buddha, it is the energetic force of our unexpired karma that moves forward into the next lifetime. This is the continuity. Thus, according to the laws of karma, what we do in this lifetime potentially impacts our subsequent lives also.

Just as our lives are not lived in complete isolation, so our karma is not exclusively personal. The vast laws of karma encompass the entire universe. Our actions affect both the inner and outer circumstances of our lives. We are subject to what is termed collective karma—the karma of group membership.

For example, if someone chooses to drink alcohol, and his or her consumption goes from the innocuous to the highly problematic, this substance abuse affects many people. Alcoholism is a disease from which an entire family suffers. The friends of that family are usually also affected. Alcohol abuse, which begins in the realm of individual karma, can evolve into a force of collective karma that touches all those around us. We are not divided and separate. What we do affects one another, in subtle and obvious ways.

In South Africa, apartheid has at last been dismantled. At the same time there is enormous violence and bloodshed across the country. Just when things look hopeful, all hell breaks loose. People have armed themselves against one another. Fighting is commonplace. Deaths are recorded in the hundreds each month. Perhaps the only level on which the violence makes any sense is on the level of what is known as national karma. For decades South Africans have suffered greatly under the burden of the apartheid system. It would seem that the karmic consequence of all those years of separation and oppression cannot be abruptly halted. The years of South Africa's past are vivid in the present reality.

An understanding of the laws of karma can be helpful for those of us who care deeply about the planet, about issues of pollution, division, conflict, violence, AIDS, discrimination, and abuse. When the global situation seems overwhelming and unworkable, we can remember that our small actions do inevitably make a difference.

If we understand the workings of karma, we develop what has been called a long-enduring mind, a patient mind. We know that every bottle recycled makes a difference. Every word of compassion in a moment of anger is a gift to our suffering world. Every tree saved is a universal blessing.

Yael Bethian, who lives with a crippling and debilitating illness, writes:

> If we are, as the theory goes, the consciousness or nerve cells of the Earth, how can any one person's struggle not affect everyone? And if the Earth is a living being that is hurting and polluted, would its nerve cells not be affected? I believe in

personal responsibility. I believe we must examine ourselves deeply and constantly and increase our ability to see causes and effects. But I also believe that we must expand our vision beyond our self-centeredness. Perhaps when one's back is hurting it is not that one lacks support, or cannot hold oneself up, or whatever the current reasoning is. Perhaps it is the Earth whose back is hurting. Perhaps it can no longer hold us up. We may be the symptoms of its disease. We may be part of the working out of a design greater than our individual destinies.

Bethian concludes:

> To be willing to hear the whisperings of a different truth in the lives of those who have not succeeded in healing themselves physically is to take a step toward healing the world. Out of our willingness to live with this mystery a new understanding can evolve. The message of the unhealed life is that it takes all of us, all of our caring to bring this about.[7]

6
Living with Love

A HEALTHY FOUNDATION
FOR MEDITATION

During the lifetime of the Buddha, holy renunciants were as familiar a sight in the Indian countryside as they are today. Then as now, householders would offer meals and support to these wanderers, hoping for spiritual instructions or perhaps some magical blessing to protect their children, home, and crops. The Buddha and his followers practiced accepting whatever food was given. In fact, they did not eat unless someone offered food to them. After a meal, the Buddha would usually offer a small discourse as a gift to those who had fed him.

On these occasions, he gave some of his most accessible and moving talks, describing a spirituality that could be practiced by anyone wishing to live a happy life. Spiritual life, he said, is firstly composed of the spirit and practice of giving or generosity. The second element of spiritual life is compassion, as expressed in nonharming, or ethical behavior. Meditation practice came third.

The order of this list is important. It emphasizes that the establishment of generosity and morality in one's life is a prerequisite for spiritual progress. This is still the way most people think in the East, and they take a great deal of joy in both practicing and cultivating these qualities. In the West, on the other hand, our sense of priority is different. Often, the first thing we do is head for a meditation center. As we see it, generosity is nice, but we hardly consider it a crucial trait. Rarely is it considered a quality that can be strengthened. Morality, furthermore, is practically a dirty word. We take meditation instruction in the hope of entering the lavender glow of enlightenment directly, without giving up any of our favorite habits.

We start meditating, and perhaps it is only after some time that we begin to look into how we treat others, or how our patterns of consumption affect our mental and physical health and the condition of the planet. Perhaps we make some adjustments. Maybe, at the end of a retreat, we might hear someone give a brief talk about generosity, usually in connection with supporting the teachers.

From the perspective of the Buddha's teaching, this is all rather backwards. Any sidestepping of generosity and morality does affect meditation practice. It is as if we were looking through the wrong end of a pair of binoculars. With a meditative awareness, perhaps the world appears more clear and precise, but in truth what we see is far more constrained than it would be if the meditation practice had been given a more generous and loving base.

Generosity opens the mind, allowing it to let go. Generosity also helps create a feeling of inner sufficiency. Morality, too, is a gift we give both to ourselves and others. A life that is ethical feels clear and clean. Elements of secrecy, turmoil, guilt, and fear are reduced. It is a life in which there might be a blessed calmness that supports our efforts to meditate. Furthermore, behaving ethically, we offer a sense of safety and trust to those around us.

The following chapters explore these foundation stones of meditation practice: generosity and morality or ethical conduct.

GENEROSITY AND
SELFLESSNESS

ONE DAY A wealthy businessman known as Anathapindada ("Giver to the Defenseless") visited the Buddha. He spoke to the Buddha of his work as an investor. Although he felt burdened by the pressure of his responsibilities, he did nevertheless enjoy his work. "Should I renounce this worldly life and give up my work?" he asked the Buddha.

The Buddha replied, "A person who possesses great wealth and abundance and who uses his resources wisely and skillfully is indeed a great blessing to society. There is no need for you to abandon your work. Continue your good and generous life."

Over the years Anathapindada became a devout supporter of the Buddha. He sincerely practiced meditation and helped the community of nuns and monks in every way possible.

Many years later he devoted all his wealth to purchasing a beautiful park, which he called the Jeta Grove. There he built a huge monastery with all manner of useful facilities for the Buddha and his community. In order to purchase this land, he had to cover every inch of ground with gold coins, for this was the price demanded by the owner. He did this willingly.

Anathapindada's generosity and kindness was so great that he gave up all his wealth in order that the holy people could have a decent place to live.

———————

Before his enlightenment, the Buddha devoted many previous lifetimes to the task of perfecting every facet of his virtue. The stories of his past lives appear in a collection of tales called the *Jatakas*, and they are often told to children. The future Buddha devoted countless lifetimes to generosity alone. Whether born a rabbit or a prince, he over and over gave his life and all his possessions to others who needed them.

One of the most moving Jataka tales concerns a time when the Bodhisattva (as a future buddha is called) was a human being. Walking in the forest one day, he heard anguished cries and looked over the edge of a cliff to see what was wrong. Lying on the rocks below was an emaciated tigress with her three cubs. Tired of sucking at their mother's empty dugs, the cubs were yowling piteously. Moved by compassion, the Bodhisattva threw himself over the cliff so that the tigress might eat his body and thus gain the strength to feed her starving young.

Perhaps we are shocked by this radical tale. Western society certainly conditions us to hang on to everything that we claim as our own—including our possessions, ideas, and opinions, not to mention our life itself. We are trained to be acquisitive, to accumulate, insure, protect, and hoard. Financial wealth and security are accorded enormous importance. Status and value accrue from the accumulation of houses, vehicles, valuables, mates, children, pets, educational qualifications, athletic skills, careers, experiences, and travels. We tend to grasp and hold on to everything we come across. At the same time, many of us yearn for simplicity. Chögyam Trungpa once remarked, "If one of our sweaters gets thrown into the dryer by mistake, we react as if it is we ourselves who have been forcibly shrunk and diminished."

The way of spirituality is fundamentally about letting go. This is the opposite of acquisition and accumulation. We let go of all that obscures our Buddha-nature. In spiritual life, there is nothing to achieve, acquire, or attain. Spirituality and meditation move against our tendencies toward grasping, holding, and accumulating. By actively practicing generosity in our lives, we counteract the selfishness and insularity that are so abundant in our world. Inwardly, letting go is the heart of spiritual practice. Letting go returns us to stillness and peace.

Clearly, generosity of spirit is the opposite of greed, which itself is one of the most powerful forces that condition our minds toward pain. Greed is the first of the three roots of suffering (the other two being aversion and ignorance). Generosity is a potent force of the heart that has the power to overcome greed and selfishness.

Generosity can be directed outwardly or inwardly. It can have an active and visible expression in our lives through deeds of generosity, service, and sharing. Inwardly, this spirit of generosity may manifest in attitudes of unselfishness, nonattachment, simplicity, and renunciation. Everyday examples might include a generosity of attention, a willingness to listen to others, to receive from them fully, a willingness to give others space to be who they are. This inner generosity might also mean at times resisting the impulse to "help" or "give" when it is born out of our own needs rather than serving the well-being of another. This attitude is not one of penance or self-denial. The experience of generosity is often one of freedom and release.

Living generously is a powerful and a joyous way to be. It is said that the force of generosity can purify the mind completely. When generosity is felt to its deepest extent and fullest implication, it includes a true understanding of things as they are. We give, not because we want to be a nice person, but out of an understanding that all living beings are interconnected. Generosity is an expression of the love that is innate within our hearts. We give while remaining wholly within the space of understanding that there is nothing we are truly able to hold on to in the first place.

How do we begin to cultivate a spirit of generosity in our lives? To live generously, we begin from where we are. In order to cultivate generosity there is no need to embark upon a frenzy of giving away. Those who do this often lose all sense of balance and end up hurting themselves. Excessive giving can be a form of violence, if we give that which we are not yet ready to let go of.

Some people may feel, consciously or unconsciously, that they have nothing worthwhile to give. Usually such thoughts originate from a sense of inner poverty and worthlessness. In the process of meditation we open to both the difficulty and the beauty of who we are. In this opening we must come to know that we are precious and unique, always having something of value to offer others and the world.

We start by applying a sensitive awareness to the giving and taking that happens in our lives. No one lives without some degree of give-and-take. For example, every time we eat food, there have been many people and perhaps animals involved in bringing the meal to us. At meals we may serve others, offer a slice of bread, or pass the salt. At intersections, we stop to allow others to cross. As we begin to notice these acts, we see that receiving is the other half of giving. We come perhaps to understand that when we are able to receive deeply, we give a very real gift to others at the same time.

Buddhist texts list three kinds of giving. The first is a tentative, hesitant kind of giving. We give with one hand while holding on with the other. This is also called beggarly giving, perhaps referring to the poverty in our minds, or to the fact that we usually do not offer very much to a beggar; instead we give something we don't need, or give the least of what we have.

The second is friendly giving. Here there is a wholeheartedness, and we give openly with both hands. We give what we have, with a clear mind and an open heart.

The third is queenly or kingly giving, where we give the

best of what we have, even if nothing remains for ourselves. We relate to our possessions as caretakers more than as proprietors. Our giving is instinctive and gracious.

We begin to practice generosity wherever we feel comfortable. When we give, we might ask two questions of ourselves.

- Is this giving an expression of love and interconnection?
- In this giving, am I being true to myself?

If the act fulfills both of these possibilities, it is unquestionably an expression of wholesome generosity.

Generosity born of love is an act of purification. Giving is the natural gesture of a heart filled with openness and lovingkindness. When we give in this spirit, we give with the wish, "With this gift may you be free from suffering. May you be peaceful and happy."

We may notice that a sincere impulse to give arises from a feeling of abundance. With the practice of giving, we develop a sense that we always have enough to share. Even the poor can often have a profound feeling of abundance, while wealthy people, unable sometimes to let go of their attachment to possessions, may feel a deep sense of poverty within. The Buddha said: "If beings knew as I knew the ripening of sharing of gifts, they would not enjoy the use of gifts without sharing them. Nor would the taint of stinginess obsess the heart and there remain. Even if it were their last possession or morsel of food, they would not enjoy its use without sharing it."

The inner repercussions of generosity depend on our intentions, rather than upon the size or nature of the gift. If we look closely at intentions or volition, we see that their quality strongly defines the nature of an action. It is quite possible to give out of fear of not being liked or of being seen as mean or stingy. We may feel obliged to give out of a sense of duty or responsibility, in which case our mental space will probably be more resentful and constricted than generous. Because of the importance of intentions, it is vital for us to be clearly aware of them.

There was once a merchant who offered a meal to a fully enlightened person. Offering a meal to such a person is considered a highly meritorious act. Afterward, however, the merchant regretted his gift. For five hundred lifetimes subsequently, that merchant was reborn with great wealth as a result of having given the meal. However, in each of those lifetimes he was so miserly by nature that it proved impossible for him to enjoy his abundance. We can read this story literally or metaphorically. What does seem clear is that the karmic consequences of giving depend on our intentions, our mental state before and after the act of giving.

Greed and regret may arise at any time during the process of giving a gift. If we keep our minds awake, we help to foster the continuity of our love and good intention. If we subsequently come to regret the gift, we will be able to evaluate the reasons for this change of heart. Is it purely greed? Or have we violated or ignored some aspect of ourselves in some way? Reflecting on the original intention to give, we may discover that there was something important that was hidden from us at the time of giving. With true awareness we examine our intentions and the place from which our generosity emerges.

Kahlil Gibran speaks of different kinds of givers:

> There are those who give little of the much which they have—and they give it for recognition and their hidden desire makes their gifts unwholesome.
> And there are those who have little and give it all.
> These are the believers in life and the bounty of life, and their coffer is never empty.
> There are those who give with joy, and that joy is their reward.

And there are those who give with pain, and that pain is their baptism.

And there are those who give and know not pain in giving, nor do they seek joy, nor give with mindfulness of virtue;

They give as in yonder valley the myrtle breathes its fragrance into space.

Through the hands of such as these God speaks, and from behind their eyes He smiles upon the earth.[1]

The Buddhist literature lists the many benefits of generosity. The generous person is beloved by many. Noble people approach him or her, thus increasing the donor's wisdom and understanding. A generous person's good name is spread far and wide, without any effort or intention on the part of the person. When a generous person goes to a gathering, he or she is not afraid of criticism. The generous are reborn in happy circumstances.

Misers, on the other hand, are said to be reborn as "hungry ghosts" (*pretas*). These unhappy beings apparently have pinhole mouths, tiny necks, and huge bellies the size of the universe. They are always hungry and can never be satisfied.

One does not have to believe the entire Buddhist cosmology in order to appreciate the repercussions of an open or a closed mind. Generosity boomerangs. When we really want to give, our generous spirit infuses the mind with joy, purpose, strength, and happiness. This is itself a taste of heaven. Yet, even if we give with attachment or resentment, it is a start. The very act of giving diminishes our aversion or clinging.

There are ways to refine and intensify the practice of giving. For example, when we hand over an object, it is nice to offer it personally, perhaps even using both hands so that the whole body is involved in the movement of giving. This is a wonderful way to give a gift, but it even works when offering someone a shovel or passing the ketchup at table. There does not have to be a transfer of ownership for us to feel the joy of assisting someone. It is helpful also to make eye contact. If possible, focus the mind clearly on the intention or will to give, and stay aware of that intention throughout the act.

Giving expresses love. It can be carried out with purposefulness. And it can become a complete and profound gesture of interconnection and care. If we hold the intention firm, in thought, in action, and in reflection afterward, it is said that this strengthens the impact and result of the act. To give with wisdom means that in giving we understand what it is to have a mind that is open, connected, and full of love. True giving reveals the mind in its natural state of love, care, and openness.

The role of the receiver is equally important in an exchange. To receive is difficult for many of us. Often it is a challenge to be present and awake in the act of receiving. In receiving, we acknowledge vulnerability, interdependence, and at times even a great need.

To support the act of receiving, we may wish to reflect as follows:

> In receiving this gift, my wish is that all beings have what they need, and be free from suffering.

We are all interdependent and interconnected. Can our wholehearted receiving reflect this truth? In receiving, can our mind be filled with lovingkindness and thankfulness? If we receive a gift beautifully and with gratitude, we offer joy to whoever gives it. If, however, we are emotionally confused or resistant, we may tarnish the joy of the givers in our life and cause them to regret what they have done for us. So our receiving is, in the end, an act of giving, too. When people offer us compliments, do we receive these wholeheartedly, gratefully, and clearly? Or do we feel shame, confusion, or disbelief?

When I review my life, it is clear that I have been mostly a giver and not a receiver. Receiving has always been enormously difficult for me. Since my diagnosis, there have been times when I have been unable to care for myself, and I have had no option but to reach out for help. This has not been easy. I wrangled painfully with my resistance before I could ask for assistance. Whenever a benefactor arrived at my doorstep with groceries or laundry, there was a storm of inadequacy, shame, and embarrassment within me. Slowly over time things have changed. I've learned precious lessons about receiving. Out there, beyond the encircling fire of resistance, embarrassment, and intransigence, and beyond the notion that I have to do everything myself, are a multitude of people willing and ready to help in a myriad of ways. I ask for and receive help a lot more easily now. Often, my willingness and ability to reach out have been a gift for someone who wishes to help and express care in some way. I see that my own degree of clarity and presence helps keep the exchange clear. How tragic and sad that some people go to their graves stoic, rigid, and proud, rejecting the abundance of support and care that surrounds them.

Traditionally there are three kinds of gifts. First is external giving, which is the gift of what is needed to whoever needs it. The gift itself can be one of words, actions, or objects. This external giving leads to the benefit of others.

The second is the gift of fearlessness. This is the gift of all people who behave in a loving and ethical way. The gift of fearlessness is rooted in love and compassion. We offer to others the gift of trustworthiness. All beings know they need not fear us.

The third is the gift of Dharma, or the gift of truth. It is the gift of our lives lived in honesty, love, and compassion. Our very lives are the gift and inspiration we give to others.

The Buddha encouraged his disciples to consciously reflect on good deeds done. They reflected upon their acts of generosity, kindness, and caring. This was not an invitation to conceit or self-congratulation, but rather intended to cultivate love and respect for oneself. As we reflect upon our skillful actions, we appreciate the joy of a life lived on spiritual principles! We counteract the tendency to dwell in guilt, pain, and a sense of inadequacy rather than in contentment, connection, and joy. Acknowledging our spiritual blessings encourages us to continue living in a kind and careful way.

Inner generosity manifests quite naturally in meditation. There is a stirring toward a life of greater simplicity and less attachment. We hear a call to an inner spirit of renunciation and restraint. These stirrings may express themselves in how we live, where we live, whom we live with, and how we relate to our environment. What do we really need, as opposed to what we think we need?

In his teaching, the Buddha details our four real physical needs. There is a need for food, clothing, shelter, and medicine. How simple! Do we express our generous love by living lightly on the earth? It is clear that our life choices directly affect humanity and our planet. Issues of recycling, biodegradable options, energy needs, and fuel consumption go to the heart of our interconnection with nature.

Robert Aitken, a Zen master based in Hawaii, speaks of the essence of generosity and simplicity:

> Our task . . . is to respond generously to others. We can take as our models not only [the Buddha] and our other great Dharma ancestors, but also such humble beings as bushes and grasses. With every fiber, beings of the plant world are guiding others, . . . conveying their vitality to soil, water, air, insects, animals, and people.

How do we actualize this oneness of all beings? Through
responsibility, the ability to respond—like that of the clover.
When clover is cut, its roots die and release their nitrogen, and
the soil is enriched. . . . New seeds fall, take root, mature, and
feed other organisms.

Clover does not think about responsibility, and neither
did [the Buddha]. He simply arose from his seat and went
looking for his friends. The clover simply puts down its roots,
and puts up its leaves and flowers. . . . The human being does
not become an angel, but rather finds affinity with the silent
clover.[2]

In the end, perhaps the greatest expression of generosity is
the offering of ourselves. We give ourselves wholeheartedly to
each moment of life, and then let it go. We relinquish all grasping
and clinging to a separate sense of "I," "my," and "mine"—my
possessions, my attainments, my Dharma. In the moments that
our minds are free of all selfhood, we have made the supreme
offering. Our generosity has evolved to its perfection. We have
released all selfishness, possessiveness, and attachment to those
forces which for so long have torn us and our life apart. Our life
becomes a generous expression of unconditional love. The late
Venerable Ajahn Buddhadasa expressed this beautifully: "When
the I-feeling has come to an end, then the mine-feeling will van-
ish by itself. At the moment that one has a mind empty of ego
consciousness, then one has made the highest offering, for when
even the self has been given up, what can there be left?"

INTRODUCING THE PRECEPTS

WHEN HIS SON, Rahula, was ten years old, the Buddha returned to his birthplace to visit his family. Yasodhara, his wife, said to their son, "Do you see that monk who is radiant like pure gold, attended by thousands of monks? He is a buddha. He is also your father, who would now be king had he not renounced both the throne and the worldly life."

Rahula followed his father like a shadow. "She sent me to request my inheritance, sir," he said. "I shall someday be king and will need the wealth I have come to ask of you."

The Buddha replied, "You ask of me an inheritance that is subject to change and decay and that leads to certain suffering. I am unable to bestow that inheritance. However, I will make you owner of an inheritance that is beyond this world and that no one can take away from you.

"Rahula, when you wish to do any deed of body, speech, or mind, you should first consider whether it would lead to harm for yourself or other people. If it does, then such a deed is unskillful. Refrain from doing it. If restraint is impossible, then disclose and confess the deed so that restraint will arise in the future.

"However, if a wish arises to do a deed of body, speech, or mind that is harmful neither to yourself nor another, and you know it to be a good deed, then do it. Skillful deeds bring joy and delight. Train yourself, day and night, to behave skillfully."

The objective of insight meditation is the cultivation of true awareness. We practice awareness in order that our lives might be lived with this selfsame quality of care, sensitivity, and wakefulness. Generosity, as we have seen, is a full expression of the meditative life. So too are other aspects of living, referred to

in Buddhism as the precepts, or tenets of moral conduct. Together, generosity and the precepts comprise the foundation
upon which a healthy meditative life is built.

All Buddhist morality is based on nonharming as well as its
active and positive aspect, compassionate lovingkindness. The
purpose of the precepts is to create happiness and eliminate unhappiness, not only within ourselves but in all the world. The
Buddha said, "Nonharming is the central practice."

Gandhi lived a life that exemplified this quality of nonharming. He said, "To come to the heart of truth, one most be able to
love the meanest creature as oneself. And those who think that
religion has nothing to do with politics do not know what religion really means."[3] Politics and religion have always been inter-
twined, but the link between them has generally not been based
on nonharming. Often in history, the expression of religion in
the political realm has been one of enormous intolerance and
bloodshed. Nor is nonharming the principal motivation domina-
ting politics. Each year, Amnesty International publishes lists of
the many countries that systematically inflict torture on their
own people. No sooner has a war or conflict died down in one
part of the globe than another flares up elsewhere. The images
and memories of suffering in Hiroshima, Cambodia, Vietnam,
Dachau, Bosnia, southern Africa, Central America, and other
places tear the human heart apart.

Would anyone deny that our world cries out for more heart?
To change governments and economic systems might help a little, although even a generous political philosophy is short-lived
if it is superimposed on greedy, selfish, and angry human hearts.
For the world to become a more peaceful place, it seems that a
fundamental transformation within human beings is an integral
part of the solution. Each of us needs less prejudice and hatred
in our lives and far more mercy, compassion, generosity, and

selflessness. Our hearts and lives bear the scars of deep division and separation.

Separativeness may simply show itself in a strong sense of "I," "me," and "mine." When I place my country, my resources, my rights, and my needs above the needs and rights of all other countries and all other beings, it is a short step to violence of some kind. If our sense of "I" is rigid and defended, it excludes the truth that we are all fundamentally interconnected. Any identity built on division and separation causes pain. Republicans separate themselves from Democrats, men from women, gays from straights, blacks from whites, humans from other life forms. We do not ignore our differences, for these are real and important, but when we lose touch with the fundamental web of interconnection that holds all of life, we court the possibility of hurting one another in tragic ways.

The Buddha addressed the issue of nonharming in a unique manner. For lay followers he advocated the five training precepts as a basis for spiritual life. These precepts are not absolute commandments or rules, so there is no penalty or punishment for breaking them.

When working with the precepts, we simply notice whether our behavior causes pain or happiness, inwardly and outwardly. If we have caused pain, we resolve to start anew, just as if we were coming back to the breath during meditation. This process of recognition, regret, and resolve is considered the only wholesome form of remorse. Guilt, self-recrimination, and penance are seen as forms of inner anger, often cruel and damaging to oneself.

The five training precepts direct us toward considering our behavior in relationship to the world. They focus on killing, stealing, sexual behavior, speech, and the use of drugs and intoxicants. In each of these vital and fundamental areas of our life, we are asked: "Does our action lead to happiness and unity among beings, or toward sorrow and division?"

In meditation, as our sensitivity deepens, so too does our understanding of the precepts. What is true for us becomes clearer and more refined over time. Our lives become an expression of our deeper care. The precepts evolve with the deepening of our understanding and compassion. The precepts are a dynamic and fully alive exploration of the question of nonharming in our life. As always in Buddhism, the challenge is to take full responsibility for our actions of body, speech, and mind—our deeds, words, and thoughts. In this way, the precepts are dynamic and alive, rather than rigidly static, pious, and dead.

The Buddha said that if we are deeply established in awareness, the precepts are not necessary. This is the reason they are called training precepts. If we were fully mindful and aware, we could not live with harmfulness and division; the need for the precepts would automatically fall away. For those of us whose awareness is still developing, the five training precepts help create a calm and stable atmosphere in the mind and heart. They nurture us and all who come in contact with us.

Don Juan gives this teaching on harmlessness in Carlos Castaneda's *Journey to Ixtlan*:

> The art of the hunter is to become inaccessible. . . . To be inaccessible means that you touch the world around you sparingly. You don't eat five quails; you eat one. You don't damage the plants just to make a barbecue pit. You don't expose yourself to the power of the wind unless it is mandatory. You don't use and squeeze people until they have shriveled to nothing.
>
> To be inaccessible does not mean to hide or be secretive. . . . It doesn't mean that you cannot deal with people either. A hunter uses his world sparingly and with tenderness, . . . and yet he is inaccessible to that same world. . . .
>
> He is inaccessible because he's not squeezing his world out of shape. He taps it lightly, stays for as long as he needs to, and then swiftly moves away leaving hardly a mark.[4]

:

THE FIRST PRECEPT
REFRAIN FROM HARMING

Nonharming is the first and most basic precept. In its grossest sense, it means that we do not murder other people. However, the precept goes further and deeper than this. We humans are an arrogant species who rarely think twice about taking the lives of nonhuman species. A survey of the aisle in the supermarket where many brands of mousetraps and insecticides are displayed is instructive: killing "pests" is a lucrative business. One wonders how many people who use these products stop to ponder how they feel about killing another living being—even an ant or a fly or a mouse. Is there pleasure or fear or anger in the mind at the moment of setting the trap or spraying poison at the bug? Is the intention to kill fully felt, fully conscious? Does it feel comfortable?

The heart of the nonharming precept is the ability to identify with the point of view of the cockroach and the mouse, as well as the point of view of other human beings. Like us, every living creature wants to be safe, happy, and free from suffering. We are one in this sense. To live from this identification is to live the truth of our interconnection.

Decisions about nonharming are not always simple, easy, or obvious. We are challenged to listen carefully and deeply within ourselves and then to respond with courage.

Recently, I was picnicking on a lakeshore in Vermont. All of a sudden, a huge orange cloud came through the water towards me. I realized it was an enormous school of goldfish. I put my feet in the water and the goldfish nibbled at them. I was delighted. Soon a woman came down from her house and we began to talk. I marveled at the goldfish, and she replied that they were a big problem. A couple of years before, somebody had set free a couple of pet goldfish in the dam, and they had multiplied prolifically. Since they fed at the bottom of the lake, they were bringing to the surface much bacteria and poison. The whole lake had become toxic. In fact, the lake was about to be drained. The U.S. Department of Agriculture had announced that the draining would have to be carefully monitored so that not a single goldfish swam into the river, to ruin the waters downstream.

The effects of one person's ignorance and carelessness had proliferated wildly. Hundreds of thousands of fish were now going to die. Draining the lake was going to be expensive, too. In this world of invisible interconnections, we have to tread very softly and carefully.

Often, when there is a discussion of nonharming, the issue of vegetarianism arises. Should one eat meat? In the time of the Buddha, the community of monks and nuns ate meat. They lived as mendicants, eating only the food that others put into their begging bowls. He admonished his monks and nuns to receive with gratitude whatever was given to them. However, he asked them not to accept the flesh of any animal slaughtered specifically for their consumption. Other than that, he said, they should eat whatever they received.

Times have changed. We are not mendicants. Meat is still the body of another creature. So it is a perfectly understandable expression of compassion if we choose not to eat meat, or even milk and eggs. So much suffering is inflicted in the cruel methods of the factory farms and slaughterhouses.

Yet, again, these issues are not simple. Some of us who were vegetarians for many years may have been advised to eat meat again by health-care professionals. Some of us may feel comfortable eating only fish and not other kinds of flesh. Diet is an individual question, and we have to discover what feels right for us.

In the early years of my meditation practice in South Africa, I was a vegetarian zealot. Once, I went out to dinner with my parents, my brother, and my brother's partner. They all ordered crayfish, which in South Africa are enormous. These huge beasts arrived at the table, their feelers and claws hanging over the edges of the plates. For me, there was a petite bowl of cheese cannelloni. As the family began cracking and sucking the bodies of all those crayfish, I sat there with self-righteous distress and indignation. My brother's partner asked me to step outside with her. A forthright woman, she said, "You are such a sanctimonious vegetarian! You are spoiling this meal for everybody." She was absolutely right. I went back in, sat down, and let go of the whole situation. I enjoyed the meal with them, and they with me. Overattached to my ideas about nonharming, I had been causing harm of another kind, creating negative feelings and spoiling the atmosphere for others.

In practice, each of the training precepts has a restraining quality and an active quality. The restraining quality may ask us to be careful not to harm others. The active portion encourages us to generate connection, compassion, and love. In order to see what we are actually generating, it is important to examine our motivations with great honesty. The effect of our behavior depends on our motivation. Examining these motivations may be especially helpful for those of us who are politically active. Political action can be a wonderful expression of compassion and nonharming. But as activists, we need be carefully aware of the inner atmosphere within our hearts and minds when we do our political work. Are we angry and self-righteous, separating ourselves from the evil perpetrators of whatever situation we are trying to correct? Or do we go into our political work in the spirit of connection and love?

Gandhi said, "I cultivate in my soldiers the courage of dying without killing. I believe that nonviolence is infinitely superior to violence, forgiveness more manly than punishment, dignity more precious than indignation, and silent defiance more powerful than blustering force."[5]

To make a difference in the world, we don't have to adopt a new career or different eating habits. Every day is ripe with the opportunity to avoid harming others. Each day we can foster love and connection within ourselves. Parents who bring up their children in a home that is respectful of life, and who practice nonviolence and nurturing, are, by their example, doing work as important as any political crusader.

Practicing the precepts almost always requires stretching one's limits. Of course, the most fundamental method of practicing the precepts is to become increasingly aware of the effects of our behavior. Is what we do harmful to others, or are our actions an expression of compassion and lovingkindness?

THE SECOND PRECEPT
REFRAIN FROM STEALING

The second precept asks us to refrain from taking what is not given. In addition to not stealing, this precept addresses situations where we might rationalize:

"Oh, it's okay to appropriate this or that."
"I don't know whose it is, it's just sitting there."
"She doesn't really need that object. She has many others just like it."

When I ordained as a monk, I lived by 227 precepts. For me it was this precept that provided the greatest challenge. As monks, we interpreted the second precept in an extremely rigorous way. We were not allowed to take anything that had not been offered to us, and we were not allowed to ask for anything either. We were in a monastery where the laypeople around us understood, appreciated, and respected what we were doing, so we did not starve to death. They supported us. What we had was based entirely on what others were willing to give us. Our clothing, food, medicines, and shelter were all kindly offered. We took nothing. My relationship to what I felt I needed changed a lot. I was able to be content with a great deal less than I'd ever imagined possible. This is a trait I have tried to carry back to the world. It helps me appreciate all that I have, no matter what my material circumstances are.

Most of us, at some time, have taken things that were not directly given to us. We might have lifted a chocolate from the corner store or helped ourselves to the shampoo when we were house guests or taken a towel from a hotel. We have rationalized and interpreted the rules in our favor. At the very least, we probably know how it feels to covet another's possessions, qualities, or circumstances. If we have stolen an object, we may remember enjoying its use, even triumphing over adversaries and obstacles, real or imagined. However, if we are honest, we will admit that our pleasure was probably laced with fear, paranoia, complexity, and guilt.

We read that there are enough resources for all of us on this planet of five and a half billion people. Nonetheless, many people starve, most of them children. An active application of the second precept leads us to look beyond our own needs and give some thought to a personal ethic of sharing. Perhaps we might consider a life of greater simplicity, a life whose joys do not come from mass consumption of goods. A decision like this has nothing to do with guilt. We are guardians and custodians of this planet for future generations. We need to live in a way that is careful and respectful of our responsibility to them. The Buddha emphasized this again and again. He called his path the Middle Way because it avoids the extremes of asceticism and indulgence. We keep to the Middle Way by living with care and walking lightly on the face of our delicate and fragile planet.

With time, as the process of meditation deepens, we may come to understand why we are tempted to take something that is not given or why we may want to get something for nothing. We might discover within us strong feelings of deprivation or an anxiety that we will not get what we need. The feelings may be related to actual deprivation and abuse in childhood. Understanding the origins of our unskillful actions enables us to disentangle ourselves from any related compulsive behavior in the present.

The precept of not stealing can be a subtle, complicated, and challenging one. For example, is not reporting income for tax purposes a form of stealing? Is copying a commercial computer disk, audio cassette, or video tape a form of stealing? While not stealing is the restraining aspect of this precept, its active expression is reflected in generosity and selflessness. (See Part 6, section titled "Generosity and Selflessness" page 207.)

THE THIRD PRECEPT
REFRAIN FROM FALSE SPEECH

IN A SUCCINCT teaching on when to speak and when not to speak, the Buddha offered the following advice:

"If you know anything that's hurtful and untrue, don't say it. If you know anything that's helpful and untrue, don't say it. If you know anything that's hurtful and true, don't say it. And if you know anything that's helpful and true, be sure to find the right time to speak."

When I look back over my life, I remember occasions when I wish I had not said what I did, occasions when I wish I had spoken up instead of remaining silent. There are times, too, when I wish I'd said something a little differently. It is clear that the effects of an ill-chosen word can last for years, or even a lifetime.

Words can create well-being or destroy it. Our words, language, and communication are conditioned by powerful forces within us, energies that may be damaging or healing, confused or clear. Our communication may leave us with a feeling of harmony, calm, and completion—or we may be left feeling rattled, incomplete, and filled with regret.

Communication has both a strongly determining effect on our inner atmosphere and an enormous impact and influence on other people. Our communication affects those to whom we speak, those who read our writing, and even those who overhear us or observe how we relate to one another. Even without words, our gestures, body language, and overall manner have great impact. Our tone of voice affects animals, and some say even plants respond to the sound of our words. The effects of communication ripple far beyond our immediate vision and context. We form opinions based on what others have said and written. Sometimes we repeat what we hear. We imitate people we admire. What we say and write has enormous effect on the world around us.

In his discourses, the Buddha frequently spoke about "right speech," often translated as "speech that is full, complete, and whole" or "perfect speech." He emphasized that our speech is a central part of awakening to the truth of ourselves and to the ultimate nature of reality.

I have stressed that the training precepts are not absolute commandments. The Buddha strenuously rejected blind obedience to authority. Rather, with the precepts, he indicated areas of our lives in which we might apply the powers of our awareness, sensitivity, and discriminating wisdom. When it comes to speech, our goal is to find true, wholesome, and nonharming forms of expression.

Within our commitment to awareness and compassion, the precept of right speech is a big challenge for many people. It would be easier if we had been given a list of do's and don'ts relating to speech. Awareness of the subtleties and nuances of our speech is a huge responsibility.

Western teachers of insight meditation have recently drafted a set of ethical guidelines for themselves, based on the traditional five precepts, but refined and focused to fit the role of teachers of Dharma at this time, in this culture. Here is the guideline relating to speech:

> *We undertake the precept of refraining from false speech.* We agreed to speak that which is true and useful, to refrain from gossip

in our community, to cultivate conscious and clear communication, and to cultivate the quality of lovingkindness and honesty as the basis of our speech.[6]

Notice that there is emphasis on both avoidance and cultivation, on both silence and the need to speak in ways that manifest caring and cultivate the sense of community.

Traditionally, right speech at first requires avoiding language that is harsh. How does it feel to use swear words and abusive language? How does it feel to hear such talk? Contrast these feelings with those evoked by words that soothe the ear and heart, words that are gentle and loving, and words that are courteous, friendly, and kind.

The second element of right speech is not to gossip. This means not to speak badly of others, to avoid backbiting, talebearing, and any words that cause dissension, conflict, and complication. Emphasized here is the fact that our words have a strong effect on community and friendship. We are asked not to set one person against another with our words.

In the order of monks, speech that causes dissension in the community is one of the most serious offenses, sometimes resulting in suspension from the community. We must be carefully aware of the impact of our speech on our community, associates, and neighbors. Do our words and actions bind us more closely and harmoniously, or do they foster discord and intrigue?

A friend once decided that he would experiment with avoiding gossip by not speaking of other people at all, whether his speech was positive or negative. He reports that, for the duration of the experiment, he stopped talking almost completely! He discovered that the majority of conversations have to do with absent people. He felt much easier and less complicated within himself when he did not participate in gossip of any sort.

Of course, there are times when painful information must be brought forward in order that a situation may be set right and that healing might occur. We may feel that pain could flow from our words. A happy outcome might not be guaranteed. Choosing to speak out in such a situation requires that we trust our careful judgment and be clear about the nature of our intentions. It may be useful to consult with one or more trusted people outside the situation before speaking.

The third aspect of right speech is not to engage in idle or frivolous talk. Often, such talk is a smokescreen that masks both our feelings and perhaps the true nature of a situation. Flippancy can be a mechanism for distraction or avoidance, a way not to deal with the reality of things. If talk has no meaning or real depth, it is said in the texts that it arouses distraction and carelessness in the mind. If there is nothing to say, don't speak. Speaking for the sake of entertainment or passing the time is considered unskillful.

This does not mean that jokes and humor should be avoided. Humor has the power to deflect anger and defuse conflict. Skillfully applied, humor may provide a means of approaching a threatening topic in a way that is more palatable and easier to hear. Laughter can heal both ourselves and the situations we find ourselves in. Obviously the jokes should not be at anyone else's expense, neither abusive, racist, sexist, nor perpetuating oppression and stereotypical perceptions in any way.

The fourth aspect of right speech is not lying. Is our speech honest? We are challenged here to be straightforward, neither lying for our own sake nor for the sake of another. Lying can be subtle tone of voice, a slight shading of the truth, or an exaggeration of the facts. We may defend our exaggerations, but in fact they are a kind of lie. If we carefully examine our motivations, when we do exaggerate, we will probably find something self-serving there, or a feeling of servility toward another person. Perhaps we want something from someone.

If we decide to take up the challenge of right speech, we may find that before we know it, we've said something that leaves us feeling uneasy and uncomfortable. Here, too, humility, patience, and a sense of humor are great allies. It is important to acknowledge the depth and strength of our conditioned speech patterns. Bringing integrity, honesty, and skillfulness to speech is a lifelong endeavor whose very difficulty can develop our capacity for self-love, forbearance, and forgiveness. As we cultivate our willingness to begin again and again, we slowly become more flexible and present. Our sense of purpose deepens as we struggle to be as frank, clear, and loving as we possibly can.

Many of us were brought up in situations where the truth was not directly talked about or valued. For misguided reasons, members of our family or community may have felt a need to protect one another from the difficult truths of life. They considered their silence an expression of love and care. However, to shelter one another from the truth in this way is dangerous. It is painfully self-denying. The silence also violates the right of another to know what is true. If we hide or eclipse the truth, we may deprive someone of the ability to make decisions based on reality.

This kind of lying works on a grand scale, too. Because of our culture's denial of death, when someone dies there is a feeling of injustice and failure, a sense that it is all a dreadful mistake. Imagine how much easier life would be if death under normal circumstances were recognized as natural, inevitable, and right, rather than avoidable, unnatural, and wrong. Similarly, society has drawn a veil over deadly problems like nuclear waste, child abuse, and alcoholism. Fearing the strong disapproval that we might elicit, we find ourselves conditioned to avoid, protect, and deny these realities. We perpetuate the struggle. Bringing these problems into the light is a healing and helpful thing to do. And often the way in which we do this truth-telling deeply challenges our commitment to right and careful speech.

A good way to begin practicing right speech is to start simply. We may commit ourselves to avoiding one or more of the categories of unwholesome speech: harsh speech, gossip, frivolous speech, or lying. On the other hand, we may resolve to be simply more aware as we speak. Once I asked a friend to stop me whenever she suspected that I was exaggerating. This project kept her pretty busy! It was shocking and humbling for me to realize how often, and how subtly, elements of exaggeration found expression in my speech. Of course, the objective is not to hurt ourselves with this information. Rather, we try to open to the truth of what we are saying with both honesty and a sense of forgiveness.

In the natural unfolding of meditation practice, our patterns of speech begin to change by themselves. As our hearts and minds deepen in sensitivity and gentleness, our words echo within us. We feel the jarring resonances of our speech more sensitively than ever before. At a gut level we know that careless words disturb our peace of mind and heart. Conversely, when we communicate in ways that are skillful and wise, we feel the genuine pleasure and happiness this brings. Speech that is useful, timely, and appropriate leaves no flutter in the heart nor any sense of inner disquiet. This lack of residue becomes our direction and compass. We feel joyous and grateful for having said just the right thing at the right time, in the right way.

We learn also that silence can be as true as words. It can be an expression of peace of heart and mind. At times silence is deeply healing. In some situations we may decide to refrain from speaking altogether. This might be the most compassionate and skillful response to a situation, particularly if we suspect that what we have to say would be misunderstood or ignored completely.

One way to refine and deepen our communication is to be aware of intentions (See the section titled "Awareness of Intentions" on pages 39–40.) If we are aware of intentions we are no longer easily victimized or driven into action by whims and desires. We are no longer compelled to shoot off our mouths. Being aware of the intention to speak injects a moment for reflection and choice. We become aware of any hidden agendas that condition our desire to say something. If we find anger, fear, revenge, or self-aggrandizement, we have the opportunity to acknowledge the emotion and perhaps resist speaking, or modify our message toward a more loving and appropriate end.

In the moment before we speak, we can sense our underlying motivation and intention:

- Is our intention manipulative in any way?
- What is the goal of this communication?
- Is this speech divisive or hurtful?
- Are our words a medium for healing and reconciliation?
- What are the emotions behind the words?
- Do we truly need to say this?
- Would silence be a more skillful response?

With time, speech becomes a fully integrated part of a life of awareness. Gandhi says in his autobiography that his speech was always very restrained. Because he spoke little, he could not recollect having said anything he regretted:

> My hesitancy in speech, which was once an annoyance, is now a pleasure. Its greatest benefit has been that it has taught me the economy of words. I have naturally formed that habit of restraining my thoughts, and I can now give myself the cer-

tificate that a thoughtless word hardly ever escapes my tongue or my pen. I do not recollect ever having to regret anything in my speech or writing. I have been spared many a mishap and a waste of time. Experience has taught me that silence is part of the spiritual discipline of the votary of truth. Proneness to exaggerate, to suppress or modify the truth wittingly or unwittingly is a natural weakness of man, and silence is necessary in order to surmount it. A man of few words will rarely be thoughtless in his speech; he will measure every word.[7]

In our practice of communication, it is vital that we have an awareness of the other person also. We ask ourselves whether others seem amendable to listening now. Perhaps their frame of mind is unsuitable for what has to be said, and we then pick a better time for full communication to occur. So, too, as we speak, we notice the effects of our words. If the words are competitive, harsh, or unfairly critical, we observe the nature of their impact. If we gossip or are careless in speaking, we see how others are affected. If our speech is true, kind, and healthy, we see the immediate effect upon the person with whom we are in communication.

The same kind of attentiveness is important when we are listening:

- Do we listen wholeheartedly to what is being said?
- What is our body language communicating to the speaker?
- Are we attentive?
- Do we take full responsibility in our listening?

In speech we have a powerful means for seeing cause and effect at work. We see the effect of the intention behind our words. Bringing awareness to our words, language, and communication deeply fortifies our healing and, at the same time, serves the healing of those with whom we live our lives. We become trustworthy, honorable, and dependable friends, and our relationships become easier and less complicated.

In difficult situations we become willing to put ourselves in the other person's shoes. We may ask, "What would I like to hear if I were the other person? Would I want to hear this, or would I perhaps not?" This does not mean that we become subservient in our wish to protect or placate others or try to make them feel good at the expense of our integrity. Not at all. We simply refine our timing and our message. Perhaps we discover that if we give ourselves the right and the time to speak fully, carefully, and freely, we no longer need to be abusive, manipulative, or controlling in our speech.

Gradually, our speech evolves into a healthy, effective, and powerful vehicle for reconciliation and love. Right speech heals us inwardly, and heals those with whom we share our words.

THE FOURTH PRECEPT
REFRAIN FROM SEXUAL MISCONDUCT

Sexuality is a profound force in the lives of most people. It has the power to damage us or to lift us into selfless love and union. For nuns, monks, and people on retreat the issue of sexuality is simplified by the requirement of celibacy. In silence and with the support of others, they may come to know and understand the workings of sexual energy in the body and the effect it has on the mind. For people living in the world, the challenge is different.

As we observe our sexuality, we see clearly that it is linked with the heart. We may have been profoundly moved and transformed through sexual experience. At times we may have been frightened or even traumatized. We have perhaps been hurt deeply in a sexual relationship. We may have hurt others in turn, in our confusion and pain. There are many lessons that we may learn from the various expressions of our sexual nature, for we have all probably been unskillful in our sexual behavior in some way or other.

Personally, sexual abuse and AIDS have impacted my life in a way that makes this precept a deeply challenging and complicated one for me. How I relate to my homosexuality, how I conduct my sexual relations, and how I relate to others are all affected by what happened in my childhood and by the HIV-positive diagnosis. I would like to share some aspects of my journey with this precept on sexual conduct.

I believe that the abuse in my infancy opened me to the possibility of further abuse as I grew older. The vulnerability and helplessness of my first months became the invitation for additional sexual trauma in my school years. I knew no way other than the one of sexual compliance and submission. I learned a further lesson at school—sex was dirty, forbidden, and something to be ashamed of. At night older boys would force their way into my bed with threats and coercion. By day these same boys were usually the ones who bullied and ridiculed me. There was no sex education at school and no invitation to discuss the question with anyone. At home, my sex education amounted to a blue hardcover book under my pillow when I returned from school one year—"What a Boy Should Know about Sex."

In my teenage years and twenties, I dated women by day and began visiting gay clubs and bars at night. Deeply conflicted I perpetuated the tone of the abuse into adulthood; feelings of shame, guilt, and conflict raged on. I fell in love with a wonderful man, D., in South Africa. When his mother got wind of our relationship, she flew to Johannesburg and told my mother what was happening in an attempt to end the relationship. She did not succeed. I was in my early twenties at the time. My father's response was to write me a letter which I found on my pillow when I came home. He said he was unable to discuss my homosexuality. He couldn't understand it. He would never condone it. Adelaide, my mother, responded very differently—with love, care, and interest.

When I began meditating about ten years later, I was immediately challenged by both the precept on sexual conduct and by the enormous confusion, division, and conflict raging around my sexuality. In my early thirties now, separated from D. after seven years together, I felt desperately alone and filled with regret and confusion for having sabotaged this relationship, which I had valued so much. What I did not realize until several years later was that my love, trust, and respect for D. were fueling the legacy of the years of sexual trauma, and the pain of all that was emerging made it impossible for me to continue with him at that time.

In the beginning years of meditation, when reflecting upon the precept relating to sexual misconduct, it was obviously apparent that I had caused immense harm to both myself and others in the conduct of my sexual relations. I seemed to have little self-reference in making decisions relating to sex, often feeling almost duty-bound to respond to anyone who showed interest in me. Similarly I felt immense sadness and regret for all the people I'd used or taken for granted. It was a time of immense grieving. It was this suffering that culminated in my decision to ordain as a Buddhist monk. In the years of silence and retreat that followed, the practice of celibacy was a huge relief. I considered it a privilege not to have to actively live my sexuality while I was in robes. My life as a celibate monk gave me a breathing space during which I came to understand more deeply the ways I'd been unskillful, uncaring, and harmful, both inwardly and outwardly, in my sexual behavior. I also came to appreciate all the unique and precious aspects of my sexuality. I engaged patterns of resistance to and discomfort about my homosexuality, and when I left the monastery and returned to the world, it was with a new feeling of healthy pride, self-respect, and strength relative to my sexuality. Unknowingly, I had also begun the long journey of healing the legacy of sexual abuse.

Initially my HIV-positive diagnosis in 1989 felt like a return to the closet. Much of the guilt, shame, and confusion of earlier years returned with a vengeance—same emotions, new storyline. I believe I was infected in the early eighties before the virus had been isolated. Safer sex had not even been heard of. Nevertheless the old familiar cycle of self-blame and inner conflict relating to my sexuality returned, fueled by the moral condemnation of AIDS that raged around me.

Slowly, over the years of grappling with both the abuse material and the impact of HIV, I see that for me spiritual practice is not about changing history, fixing myself, or curing myself of what happened; it's about accepting what happened and learning to live with all that is a given in my life now. It may all go away one day, but right now it is here. For a while I felt guilty that I'd contracted AIDS through my sexual behavior. I felt ashamed and shy of my infection, in the same way I once felt ashamed and shy about what happened when the lights went out at school thirty years ago.

Over the years, opening to the truths of my sexual history, identity, and orientation has been the biggest challenge of the spiritual journey—and the one that has brought with it the greatest blessings. The levels of acceptance of my homosexuality, the abuse, and the HIV-positive diagnosis run deep and true these days. This enables me to live this precept with an integrity and authenticity that is altogether new in my life.

In many spiritual traditions homosexuality is considered an impediment of some kind, if not an actual sin or abnormality. The Buddha himself made no specific comment on homosexuality that has been recorded, yet male homosexuality is the only sex act condemned by all schools of Buddhism that arose after his death.[8] A similar negative message was certainly delivered from the Christian pulpits of my youth. My own belief is that every human being has the potential for knowing the deepest truth, because that understanding, that Buddha-nature, is an intrinsic part of our being. Whether one is homosexual, heterosexual, or bisexual, the task of awakening is the same. I don't believe that our sexuality is a problem; rather, conflict with the truth of who we are is the source of suffering. Unquestionably, one of the great blessings of the meditation practice has been the reconciliation, integration, and healing that has happened in the area of my sexuality.

At the monastery where I ordained and lived as a Buddhist monk, my best friend was a lesbian nun. Consequently, our precept on sexuality was firmly in place during all our times together. Yet we were often hounded by some who felt that these times together, sharing Dharma under a tree in the courtyard, were a gross infringement of our vows of purity. Nobody was in the least concerned that a number of my fellow monks would often hold my hand or even stroke my backside, touching gestures of comradeship and friendship.

A consideration at the heart of sexual conduct these days is the issue of safer sex—sexual activity that does not place anyone at risk for sexually transmitted infection. Everyone knows that we should practice safer sex. Yet is the motivation to do so born of a thoughtful, deep consideration of nonharming, lovingkindness, and the interconnection of all life, or is the motivation purely selfish and self-serving without consideration for others involved? Do we who are HIV positive tell others of our infection, even if safer sex is practiced, knowing that this information might jeopardize our sexual opportunities?

Meditation practice enables us to be more aware of the intentions behind our sexual conduct. Understanding more clearly all the motivations behind our sexual activity, we are able to deeply question the spirit in which we engage ourselves in sexual relationships:

- Heterosexual intercourse can lead to the conception of human life. Even if one uses contraception, that potential is still there, implicit in the act. Human life is precious. Would we want to indulge our passions while forgetting this sacred fact of life, and our potential responsibility for it?

- What motivates us to engage in sex? Might it be out of a sense of loneliness or alienation, a wish to relieve tension, pressure from a partner, even hostility? Is there a degree of harmfulness inherent in such motivation?

- Do we engage in sex just to satisfy our own desires? Does this feel selfish? What about the case—perhaps more common among survivors of sexual abuse—where we submit to another's desire out of a confused feeling of compulsion or because we just are not able to say no? Is there a sense of inner compassion, forgiveness, understanding, and patience if this is the case?

- Are we sexually exploitive in any way?

- Do we use other people for our personal gratification?

- Do we think or speak of people as if they were sex objects?

- Is there a place for restraint in the expression of our sexuality? Restraint is not the same as repression, since it is consciously chosen. A period of restraint or celibacy may serve a deeper understanding of how sexual energy works in our life.

On the collective level there are many challenging issues that cannot be ignored. Pornography, adultery, and the exploitation of women's and men's bodies by the advertising world are controversial and difficult issues, clearly related to this precept. The sexual abuse of children is a shattering reality in our society. The precept on sexuality challenges us to bring a true and searching awareness to every aspect of our sexual nature. We open gently to the pain of where we are closed. We engage the fears of intimacy when they arise. We bring the light of awareness to every expression of sexual energy both within ourselves and outside ourselves, in the world, so that here, too, our commitment to lovingkindness and harmlessness is the basis from which our sexuality may be lived in a full and open way.

THE FIFTH PRECEPT
REFRAIN FROM NEEDLESS USE OF INTOXICANTS

A careful, loving, and true awareness is a precious power of mind, and extremely rare in our world. In the bustle of our lives, we are perhaps tempted at times to postpone our periods of meditation. The moments of true awareness are sometimes more fleeting than we would choose. In the light of this, we may consider taking great care with any substance that could potentially disturb or damage our power of awareness.

The Buddha said that intoxication is particularly dangerous because it opens the door to breaking all the other precepts. If we get drunk or high, our judgment is impaired, and often we are not able to skillfully place limits on our behavior. We may be thoughtless or harsh in our speech. We might hurt someone in our drunken carelessness. We may forget to take the necessary precautions we ordinarily would use during sexual relations. We may spend money that we have been saving for our children. We may become unclear and unavailable for respectful and loving interaction with the people in our life.

Apart from the question of whether our use of intoxicants is harmful to both the quality of our consciousness and our state of health, there remains the issue of why we use these substances. Often the reason is to escape suffering. For people who have been abused, the everyday experience of living can be very difficult, and substance abuse is frequently one way of responding to the pain. In meditation, as we open to the magnitude of this pain, we see that it is possible to be aware of the suffering without avoidance or denial. This engagement of the present reality may open us to the source of the pain, which perhaps originated long ago. As the ramifications of early trauma emerge into the light of our awareness, we engage the legacy of our history in a way that frees us from the need to hide from the truth of what happened and the effect it has had on our lives. This understanding helps loosen the grip of any addictive patterns of substance abuse with which we may be grappling. Thus, in a clear way, this precept and the meditation practice serve our recovery and healing from the unskillful use of intoxicants.

If one does choose to use intoxicants, important questions may arise:

- Do I lie to myself about substance abuse, either mine or that of another?
- Am I willing to give attention to the effects of whatever intoxicants and stimulants I use?
- Am I willing to reduce or eliminate my intake of intoxicants?
- Is a commitment to a life of awareness compatible with the use of intoxicants?
- Apart from intoxicants, do I choose activities that create unnecessary confusion and chaos in my life?

Once again, in relationship to this precept, compassion and lovingkindness are the bottom line. Each of us must frankly and honestly ask ourselves whether our use of intoxicants is harmful either to ourselves or to others.

For me, this precept has broad implications. Over and above drugs and intoxicants, there are so many facets and aspects of life that dull the mind and distract attention. What we read and watch can be as numbing and dulling, in its own way, as the strongest drug. Television viewing requires great discernment. The diet of violence, deceit, and greed that so often pours forth from the TV screen is potentially very disturbing to the heart and mind. On the other hand, judicious discernment in the use of television can serve a peace of heart and mind. For our children, television can be a blessing or a powerful force of negativity and delusion. For me this precept is a strong call to discrimination and wisdom. Do our choices in life serve calmness, clarity, and understanding? Or do we choose to disturb and destroy our peace of mind?

With mindfulness, we address every aspect of our life. We become increasingly sensitive to the potential toxicity that surrounds us, and with the protection of awareness we have a choice whether or not to engage something that might be harmful.

Many of us have been deeply affected by the use of alcohol in our families and in society at large. Often, abuse of all kinds arises in situations where alcohol is wantonly consumed. Under the influence of intoxicants, traffic accidents can so easily occur. Is any consumption sufficiently moderate to protect us and others from the fruits of a dulled mind? We live in a world where alcohol, tobacco, and drugs are widely accepted and used. Most people are totally unaware of the immense dangers involved. If we choose to smoke, the toxins we blithely exhale into the atmosphere can potentially kill those around us. A single beer we choose to drink may tragically dull our ability to avoid a child who suddenly steps in front of our car. The fifth precept is deeply challenging if we choose to live carefully and wakefully in our crazy world.

FAMILY AND COMMUNITY

WHILE TOURING THE monastery one day, the Buddha, accompanied by the Venerable Ananda, came upon the dwelling place of a monk who was very ill with dysentery. So sick was the monk that he had fallen and was lying in his own excrement.

The Buddha approached the monk and asked, "Have you anyone who tends you?"

"I have not," replied the sick man. "I am of no use to the monks; therefore they do not tend me."

The Buddha asked Ananda to fetch water, and together they bathed the sick monk from head to toe. They laid him down on a couch and made him as comfortable as possible before leaving.

A meeting of the community was convened, and the Buddha spoke of the sick monk:

"Monks, you have not a mother nor a father who might tend you. If you do not tend one another, then who will tend you when you are sick also? If the community does not tend the sick and infirm, an offense of wrongdoing has occurred."

Over the years the Buddha gave much consideration and great care to the healthy functioning of the community of nuns, monks, and laypeople.

The goal of meditation is not isolation or escape. Neither is it to embellish the idea of "I," "me," and "mine." We do not meditate to impress others with our dedication, our exoticism, or our spiritual attainments. Perhaps the central mission is to recognize and live our interconnection and interdependence with all that exists, and to feel and express this bond as love. The Buddha taught that we can experience peace and connection here and now, within this moment.

Nonetheless, for some reason, when we close our eyes to meditate, we often forget this. Perhaps it is because we feel that when we meditate, we are withdrawing from the heart of activity to do our daily sitting practice. When we go on meditation retreats which take place in silence and seclusion, we may similarly hold the idea of disconnection from life. Perhaps the issue is complicated by friends, family, and work associates who are unable to understand why we meditate. It is not surprising that there are sometimes feelings of isolation and aloneness.

Once upon a time an elderly woman visited her travel agent and asked for a ticket to Tibet. Her travel agent looked at her askance and said, "Madam, why don't you try Florida or a Caribbean cruise? Tibet has very few conveniences."

The old woman knew her mind, however. "No," she replied firmly. "Tibet is my destination. There's a guru there I wish to see, so please arrange my ticket."

Soon she flew off to Nepal. She traveled on a series of trucks to the Tibetan border, waded across rocky rivers, walked through passes, traveled across the plateau, and finally reached the capital of Lhasa. There she announced, "I'm here to see the guru."

The local people responded, "You are not even halfway there yet! It's a long and difficult journey to the guru's cave. Furthermore, after you arrive, you will only be allowed to share three words with him."

"Fine," she replied. "Three words will be sufficient."

So they put her on a yak and she rode off across the plateau toward the mountains. Reaching the monastery, high up in the Himalayas, she immediately joined the long line of devotees who were waiting for an audience.

Slowly, the line crept forward toward the mouth of the guru's cave. Near the front, a monk said to her, "Do you know how to do a prostration? And are you aware that you are only allowed to speak three words to the guru?"

The old lady responded, "Yes, I'm aware of all that." When her turn came, she walked through the curtains and, without prostrating, she stood before the guru and spoke her three words, clearly and firmly:

"Sheldon. Come. Home!"

This joke has all the elements of a parable. Though our spiritual journeys may lead us out of our comfortable and habitual residences, in the end we must come home.

A sense of spiritual community undoubtedly supports our efforts to be free. When we have the company of like-minded friends, we understand the priceless value of sharing our spiritual life with others. It is a gift to have people in our lives whom we trust, people who encourage us when we are down. It is a blessing to be able to share our insights with others and to have people to whom we can give and receive in ways that are healthy and loving. Meditation fundamentally questions the powerful tendency toward separation that governs so much of our world. So many of us feel disconnected both from those around us and from a deeper understanding of who we are. It truly helps to have understanding companions when we feel as though we are swimming against the current.

Ananda, the chief disciple of the Buddha, once said:

Friendship with what is beneficial,
association with what is beneficial,
intimacy with what is beneficial
—this is half the holy life, master.

The Buddha replied:

Don't say that, Ananda, don't say that!
Friendship with what is beneficial,
association with what is beneficial,
intimacy with what is beneficial
—this is the whole of the holy life.[9]

For thousands of years, women and men have gathered together in silence and community, in support of one another to question the deeper currents of life. This still happens, in monasteries, retreat centers, and living rooms all over the world. Together, we strive to discover a deeper purpose in life. In community we question who we are.

The Buddha lived in various communities during his lifetime, both before and after his enlightenment. Over the years of his teaching, a huge community of nuns, monks, and lay practitioners gathered around him. Although he exhorted all to become responsible for their own individual enlightenment, he also established rules of behavior so that the community could define and perpetuate itself. His order has lasted for some twenty-five hundred years, up to the present day.

As a monk I lived in a forest with many other nuns and monks. Early each morning we would come down from our tents in the woods into the meditation hall, where we stayed for several hours, meditating and chanting. The aesthetics of the hall were rather vivid. A great big statue of the Buddha sat in front of us, surrounded by blinking festive lights. Each morning we chanted a list of the qualities of the Buddha. My best friend, an American nun with a strong irreverent streak, used to joke with me about the sound-and-light show. At first I felt a little cynical and resistant to getting up that early, sitting and chanting with the psychedelic lights. Gradually this time of day began to seem precious and even exquisite to me. In fact, it was the thing I missed most when I left the monastery, the feeling of being together. We monks and nuns shared a commitment to knowing the deepest truths possible. We held one another in this wish. Holding our collective hearts together made such a difference.

As laypeople, we can still support one another. In community we come together and practice meditation in silence. We search and look within our hearts and minds together. Those who read and use this book, though not visible to one another, probably have common interests, yearnings, and goals. In a way, we share community too.

These days, much of the world operates on the basis of a fiercely individualistic philosophy. This individualism has brought a measure of freedom to the world, giving us the option to define ourselves independently of what others think or wish. We have the right to seek our true path to happiness. However, individualism can fall out of balance. Many people yearn to belong and feel connected. So many feel lonely and isolated.

In the West we often envy people who are born into societies that provide a deep sense of community and family. We feel an instinctual wish to build, create, or consciously adopt the communities that we perhaps never had. Can we now create communities that support our spiritual commitment and at the same time provide that sense of connection and respect for which we all thirst?

Sadly, many people have grown up in homes that were dysfunctional. Possibly alcoholism was a part of the fabric of family life. Perhaps there was abuse too. Such woundedness often arouses a powerful yearning for healthy community, one we have not known before. This movement toward togetherness and communion can be difficult and challenging. Can we, in community, hold one another as we take our faltering steps toward healing the forces within us that have separated us from one another for so long?

One of the most powerful levels of purification that we experience in meditation is the shedding of the idea that we are separate. When we look inward, many of us experience a pain and suffering born of the separation that we find. We discover that we are deeply conflicted within. We are often filled with self-hatred, nonacceptance, and inner violence that is crippling and relentless. The depth to which we can open to this pain is the degree to which healing is possible. We sense that conflict with others can be healed. We cease to accept the inevitability of living at odds with the people who share our lives.

Yet there may be rifts within our family, separation from neighbors and members of our community, rivalry and dislike among the people we work with. There may be real hatred and deep wounds. As we become more sensitive and awake, we feel more and more acutely the pain of all separation that exists in our world, and we feel the suffering born of that separation.

In South Africa I lived a privileged white life. I believed in the dreams I had for myself and my country. I believed that I was going to live long there, and that I was going to be happy. I believed that the abundance that surrounded me was going to serve me for as long as I lived. Slowly, excruciatingly, I awakened to the fact that so much of what I valued was founded on oppression, greed, and injustice. The crumbling of the world I grew up in was one of the most painful processes of my life. I eventually left South Africa and vowed never to live there again. The turmoil and confusion that persist in my country today, despite the huge changes, are powerful expressions of the depth of separation and division that have existed there for so long.

It is a courageous step when one confronts and begins to grapple with all the ways in which separation occurs in life—separation and conflict within oneself and also in any feelings of alienation from others that may exist. At the heart of Buddhist practice there is a ritual which, over the years, has directly helped me as I have opened to the divisions in my life and slowly begun to heal them. This ritual of taking refuge has its own meaning for each person, but in general, as the word *refuge* implies, it means trusting in some kind of protection.

The first refuge is in the Buddha. For me, this means taking refuge in the possibility that I can be free from suffering. The

Buddha was a human being like any other woman or man in the world today. Since he came to know the deepest truth, it is also possible for each of us to do the same. The potential for freedom from suffering is the birthright of us all.

The second refuge is in the Dharma. This means taking refuge in truth. For me it means taking refuge in the experience of each moment and endeavoring to live by the truth of that experience. This refuge protects me from being in conflict with myself and with life.

The third refuge is in community. Traditionally, this refuge referred to the community of nuns and monks. One could either ordain or take refuge in the inspiration and guidance of those in robes. When reflecting on the meaning of community in our lives, we may wish to expand the idea to include all people who are seekers of the truth. Perhaps we can open our hearts even wider and take refuge in all of humankind. Everybody wants to love and be loved. Everybody yearns for happiness. We can expand our sense of community even more, by including the creatures of the oceans, rivers, air, and land. For some people community can be even more inclusive. Our refuge embraces all beings both visible and invisible in all of the realms and all of the universes.

I watched the release of Nelson Mandela on television in 1990. I cried when he walked out of Polsmoor Prison near Cape Town, with his wife, Winnie Mandela. I had somehow never believed that his release would ever happen. At the time, it felt like a very personal celebration, a specifically South African event for which many had fought and died. Since Mandela's release, however, it has become clear that his freedom is not exclusively a South African celebration. As he travels around the world and explores the avenues of peace and reconciliation, millions of people are obviously deeply moved by his commitment

and resolve to heal the fragmentation of our country. Many celebrate his liberation from prison. For me this shared happiness
very beautifully expresses the reality of global community and
support. His liberation became the liberation of everybody to
some degree. His twenty-one years spent on Robben Island off
the southern tip of Africa were twenty-one years during which
all of us were to some extent imprisoned.

Can our refuge in one another include all who are imprisoned for their beliefs or for their conscience? Does every bird
drenched in oil, spilled by tankers along our shores, fall within
the embrace of our sense of family? Is the disappearing rain forest a loss that strikes to the heart of our refuge in nature? Meditation is a way of broadening our refuge, until every aspect of life
feels like a part of oneself. Our sensitivity to the well-being of all
creatures becomes deep and true.

As our hearts expand to include all of the world, we may at
times feel a pain that is vast and deep. We may wonder how we
could possibly bear all this suffering, without insulating ourselves or creating some armoring of separation. Yet if we look
back at the places from which we've grown, we probably will
find that separation is, in the end, far more painful than the healing of it. To share in the pain of the world means that we open
to the joy of the world also. All beings suffer, and all beings have
their moments of happiness and relief.

There is a Sufi adage that speaks to the heart of suffering:

> Overcome any bitterness which may come because you are not
> up to the magnitude of the pain that was entrusted to you.
> Like the great mother of the world who carries the pain of the
> world in her heart, each one is a part of her heart and each of
> us endowed with a certain measure of cosmic pain. You are
> sharing in the totality of that pain and are called upon to meet
> it in joy instead of self-pity.

In 1989, when I resolved to be tested for HIV, I told a number of friends of my decision. With the positive test result, these friends gathered around me, and since then they have supported and loved me in ways that have made a huge difference. Any feelings of isolation and disconnection are contradicted by the love and care I receive. Over the years the composition of this group has changed and grown. Together we have weathered harsh storms and enjoyed times of joy and ease. In community we have looked at uncomfortable issues seldom confronted by people in this busy and distracted world. And in doing so we have all grown, personally and as a family. With these beloved friends I have been able to share many difficult issues that could otherwise have left me feeling very separate and lonely. I speak more easily of my despair and grief now. I share my distress at sleeplessness and nightmares. I have been able to express feelings of loss and rage for the difficulties of my childhood. We discuss health-care options, physical symptoms, and whatever everyday support I may need, like lifts to the doctor, shopping, and a buddy to accompany me to the hospital.

At every gathering we ensure that each person in the support group has opportunity to speak personally of his or her own life with all its ups and downs. The attention is not exclusively directed to me. What this has meant, over the years, is that I do not feel alone on my journey with HIV. Many treasured friends, both within my support group and beyond, all over the world, have joined me as I grapple and dance with this virus.

The ever-present love, care, and support heals the dream that I am isolated, alone, abandoned. Within the fire, a spirit of community has arisen that feels like a blessing beyond measure. In community we hold one another as together we move closer to the healing for which we all took birth. In true community, when one person suffers we all hurt. And when one person is free we all breathe easier. When one person awakens, we are all awakened a little more. When we awaken, we open to the truth of our place within the vast web of interconnection that holds us all and out of which none of us can ever fall.

Albert Einstein wrote:

> A human being is part of the whole called by us universe, a part limited in time and space. He experiences himself and these thoughts and feelings as something separated from the rest, a kind of optical delusion that is consciousness. This delusion is a kind of prison for us, restricting us to our personal desires and to affection for a few people nearest to us. Our task must be to free ourselves from this prison by widening our circle of compassion to embrace all living creatures and the whole of nature in its view.

DANCING WITH LIFE
AND DEATH

In his eightieth year, the Buddha informed Ananda that he would soon die. Ananda was grief-stricken. He wept profusely as he told the other monks, "Alas, the enlightened one will soon die. I am still a student with much yet to learn. He who has been so kind to me will shortly pass utterly away!"

The Buddha, learning of Ananda's anguish, called him to his bedside. "Enough, Ananda," admonished the Buddha. "Cease this weeping. Have I not again and again reminded you that all conditioned things, including our most beloved friends, are subject to dissolution and death? That which is born must someday die. It is the nature of things. Not even a buddha is exempt from these laws."

"Ananda, be diligent, make appropriate effort, and you shall attain enlightenment after my death." And he added:

> Be an island unto yourself.
> Be your own refuge.
> Make the Dharma your island.
> Make the Dharma your refuge.
> Take no other refuge!

Shortly afterward, an assembly of monks gathered at the bedside of the Buddha. His last words before dying alerted them to the fragility of life:

"Again I remind you: Subject to decay are all composite things. Strive diligently for liberation."

At the moment of his death a massive earthquake shook the ground. Terrible and awful were the tremors. A huge sound poured forth from the depths of the earth, moving through all of nature and rising in crescendo to the skies. Ear-shattering thunder covered the universes in a paroxysm of grief that gripped all who heard it.

Sometime later the body of the Buddha was cremated. After everyone had left the charnel ground, Ananda sat down within sight of a heap of ashes that had once been the funeral pyre of his teacher. Grieving and tearful, he reflected on all that had happened.

In this deep contemplation, suddenly the veils of delusion lifted, and as promised, Ananda attained full enlightenment.

With unutterable gratitude and humility he stood up and left the ashes of the Buddha behind him.

A few years ago I felt strongly stirred to prepare for death in every way possible. All that was unresolved, unplanned, and unsettled in my life seemed very weighty and sticky. On the one hand I sensed the ripening of a surrender to the realities in my life; on the other hand, I felt undermined by all that impeded my letting go. Again and again, in many different ways, I felt called to prepare fully for death and then live from that preparedness. This endeavor has been both the challenge and celebration of the last years.

On a practical level there was much to do. I settled into accommodations that are simple, private, and adequate. I am surrounded by beloved friends. Members of my support group are close by. My health-care providers are a short distance away. I am linked with the local AIDS agency and other organizations that provide support.

I redrafted my wills, powers of attorney, and other legal documents and carefully arranged my personal affairs in a way that will serve those who will deal with my estate someday. I have continuing discussions with friends and family about my wishes and priorities related to dying, life support, and the prolongation of life. My ashes will be sprinkled upon the grounds of the two spiritual communities in Africa and America where I have lived and loved.

The immediate effect of beginning this project was surprising. Rather than engendering gloom, it has brought an ever-increasing sense of lightness and relief. As each piece falls into place, I slip a little more easily into an ease of well-being. I some-times wish I had not waited so long to begin this process. This movement toward readiness for death has clearly impacted my personal relationships. One of the realities that my mother, Ade-laide, and I share is the constant reminder of our mortality. We are more and more able to share our thoughts, fears, and hopes about dying. This has further deepened our love and connection. What a blessing!

In friendships the question of unfinished business arises fre-quently. When I say goodbye to friends, there is no assumption that I will see them again, especially those who live a distance away. The gift of time together feels more precious than ever. Increasingly, I am stirred to regard these times as our final mo-ments together, and I am drawn to use the opportunity to ap-preciate the friendship and express all that has not yet been said.

These days I feel better able to clearly discern what is au-thentic and honest for me in relationship to people in my life. I value and nurture friendships with a wholeheartedness, largely free of the fears that kept me separate and divided for so long. More than ever before, friendships are one of the great happi-nesses of my life.

Yet letting go of relationships feels easier too. Allowing peo-ple to move on, for whatever reason, is no longer a scary and threatening occurrence. Some friends are just not able to walk this HIV path with me. For me this is more and more OK. Understandably, this disease is a terrifying mirror for some peo-ple. At one time the fear of friendlessness required that I desper-ately hold on to the friendships I had. Nowadays it feels alto-gether different. I am grateful for the feeling of space, joy, and acceptance that surrounds the coming and going of people in my life.

I have come to see that there can be an inner tyranny related to the question of unfinished business. Sometimes there is an idea that the resolution of an interpersonal situation must always culminate in a hand-in-hand walk into a glorious sunset. I have grappled seriously with this notion and now realize that for me the completion of interpersonal business sometimes necessitates that I abandon my wish that all be set right and healed between those involved. There is an important distinction between resolution and reconciliation. Business is sometimes resolved when a situation is clearly comprehended with discrimination and care, when all personal work relating to the situation is done and one realizes that, for whatever reason, full reconciliation is just not possible right now. For the abused person, the motivation for reconciliation may emerge from a deep need to associate with an energy that is abusive. This association may provide a sense of being in control of the abusive situation. For me, letting go of the idea of full reconciliation has been the final step to a peaceful resolution of a difficult part of my history.

Over time it becomes increasingly clear that very little is known about what causes AIDS, what aggravates it, and what hinders the disease process. Drugs that have been championed for years are now abandoned, used more cautiously, or not prescribed at all. People develop AIDS who do not even test positive for HIV! The politicking, competition, and self-interest that pervades the medical, pharmaceutical, and scientific communities is heartbreaking, maddening, and unconscionable.

I see that the most workable response to this tragedy is for me to hold true to what I believe are the important facts about AIDS. I don't believe that being HIV positive automatically leads to death. There is overwhelming evidence to support this view. Conventional medical opinion veers in this direction from time to time. The cover of the *Maryland Medical Journal* of February 1990 states: "AIDS does not inevitably lead to death. . . . It is simply not true that the virus is 100 percent fatal."

For me there are two challenges. On the one hand, I must face the fact of my unquestionable mortality. One day death will surely come. AIDS does kill vast numbers of people. I could become a further statistic. On the other hand, I live with hope. Maybe I can dance with Sipho, the virus, until a cure is found. Maybe a remission will happen. Perhaps a miracle is possible. I try to live with a sense of the miraculous. I certainly do not wish to be closed to a possibility that may someday ripen in my life. For me, balancing hope and reality is the only sane response in the world that has largely turned its back on the immense tragedy of AIDS.

In recent years, five friends have committed suicide. Two were living with AIDS. My feelings about suicide have changed over the years. At first I felt angry and betrayed. How could they do that? How selfish! Now I feel differently. With the passing of time, I believe I understand, at least to some degree, the hellish ground from which the decision to take one's life can come. There are considerations and reflections on suicide that engage me from time to time. AIDS-related dementia involves severe or complete deterioration of the mind. Might it not be better to die before that happens, when one's mind can still be clear and awake? Karmic results flow from intention, not from the action itself. If the intention to take one's life is a decision born of compassion, kindness, and clarity, will the consequences necessarily be negative? Is any person ever in a position to judge the decision of someone who decides to take her or his life?

The traditional Buddhist attitude to suicide is clearly stated. Suicide is born of the three qualities of mind that create suffering: desire, aversion, and ignorance. One desires death, one has aversion to life, and one is ignorant of the full consequences of the suicide.

Up until today the deeper voices of my heart whisper that for me suicide will not be an option. I have taken no practical steps to be prepared should I decide to take my life. I do know that I would like to die with full clarity of mind. This feels very important. Yet in the end I just don't know what lies ahead for me.

Recently I spent a weekend with twenty-five friends. We gathered, as a community, to explore the Tibetan Buddhist teachings on life and death. The objective was to explore the possibility of extending the commitment of community support through and beyond the dying process.

The time together was an extraordinary combination of seriousness, investigation, interest, and a lot of fun. We engaged the one certainty that we all share. It was one of the most loving and moving times of my life.

I felt very empowered by the exploration. Fundamental to the dying process is the practice of awareness, as outlined in this book. Whatever happens after death is obviously affected by the degree and quality of balance and wakefulness that there is through the dying process. Every time we meditate, each time we return to the truth of the moment, we prepare to die.

At the moment of death I would like to be with friends who both accept and are at peace with my death. I'd like someone to remind me to let go as I go through the process of dying.

"Let go."

"Let go."

"Don't hold on to anything!"

Many inspiring and moving books about death and dying have been published. I have read stirring accounts of women and men who enter sublime states of love, receptivity, compassion, and acceptance while they are ill, or just before they die. Steel-hearted people are transformed into sweet, all-caring saints who shower love and blessing upon those whom they terrorized all their lives. As I feel my way across the landscape of AIDS and as the healing from abuse broadens and deepens, what emerges is not always sweetness and light. When I first began meditation, I imagined that after a decade and a half, I'd surely be dwelling in celestial harmony of mind. Well, in reality I live some distance from those mansions, and it is humbling.

It is exciting, though, too. True acceptance is a state that is broader and vaster than my wildest dreams. I have accepted more aspects of my life and of myself than I ever could have imagined. I probably shan't get a mention as a model patient in an inspiring book on death and dying one day. Instead, I'm faced again and again with the challenge to trust the only thing I have found trustworthy. And that is the process of opening now, in each moment, to what is given, letting go of all images and ideas that prevent full acceptance of what is true.

I suspect there is no correct or honorable way of dealing with illness and death. One's death is fiercely personal. As best I can, I choose to step into the mystery of acceptance, faith, and trust, and let go as much as possible of all that obscures what is true, no matter how difficult the truth may be. I suspect that at the moment of death, we can be hoodwinked by a noble wish to do things properly and right. I would certainly like to be all-loving and all-light, but far more tantalizing is the possibility of living a life that is authentic, true, and real—and of dying in the same way.

When visiting South Africa recently, I entered into a world of AIDS that is largely hidden from Westerners. In my country, an estimated three hundred people are infected with the virus each day. Hospitals overflow with patients, and these hospitals are primarily rural and ill-equipped. Their staffs are inexperienced and often very frightened. Specific AIDS medication is nonexistent. Drugs and therapies that are commonplace in the West are unheard of there. AIDS-specific drugs are prohibitively expensive for most people. All that can be done is to medicate the pain.

Perhaps worst of all, ignorance and fear of AIDS pervades Africa. It is immensely more difficult being HIV positive there than in countries where the reality of AIDS is being somewhat more directly addressed.

After this visit, I feel my privileges with keen gratitude. I will never again take medication without conscious appreciation. Neither can I mindlessly swallow all the vitamins, remedies, herbs, and tinctures without taking the time for a moment of conscious appreciation and gratitude.

Before taking any medication, I now pause to fully acknowledge the tablet: to observe it, feel it in my hand, and give thanks and perhaps express a wish or say a prayer. I reflect on the incredible chain of interconnected commitment, resolve, and love that lie behind each tablet, tincture, and salve. While it is clear that many people prey financially on the AIDS crisis, I focus on those who make drugs and treatment possible out of their genuine concern, commitment, and loving care. As I swallow the medication, I have a clear intention to let the healing in, along with the medication. Taking medicine has become a sacred ritual in my life.

Although there are limitations in my life now, I feel deeply grateful for the blessings of relatively stable health and all the new possibilities that are present. In Africa the place and people of my childhood mirrored me in ways that were vivid and revealing. My time there was filled with an enduring sense of gratitude for what is possible in spite of the challenges. I know more deeply than ever that a true love resides within the heart of suffering. I feel deep appreciation for the meditation practice and all that it has meant in my life over the years. On evening walks in the hills around my mother's home, I drank the fragrances of flowers with a joy and ecstasy born of this gratefulness. Many of my close friends in South Africa are dead now from AIDS. Sometimes each step, each vista, each birdcall is received with a thankfulness for the borrowed time on which I feel I am living.

While in Africa I participated in AIDS-related projects, training and educating support groups. One afternoon, in a group of about twenty people, one man told me of his revulsion, disgust, and aversion toward me. He was certainly honest! However, nothing that was said touched me personally or negatively. I was amazed. It was utterly clear and palpable that the suffering was entirely his lot. His words expressed the pain that was there. The homophobia and discrimination passed me by without trace. It was an exhilarating and freeing moment. I found myself able to respond forcefully, helpfully, and clearly. I gave silent thanks that I was able to discern the truth of the situation so vividly. I gave thanks for the ability to open to the pain expressed in that room, a pain born of all the attachments, opinions, and prejudices involved. I gave thanks for the ability to respond with discriminating wisdom and care, in a way that was helpful. This incident reminded me that I am now able to live the truth of my sexuality and disease without shame, guilt, or inner conflict. My gratitude is immeasurable.

A while ago I began attending church. After a discussion with the priest, I again started taking the sacrament. Each time I participate in this ritual it stirs places of mystery, depth, and possibility within me. The crucifix, the suffering and death of Christ, and the ensuing ressurection and promise of eternal life strike to the heart of my life again and again, in ways I certainly don't fully understand. The following excerpts from the Bible touch a deep chord within me:

> Do you not know that all of us who have been baptized into Christ were baptized into his death? Therefore we have been buried with him by baptism into death, so that, just as Christ was raised from the dead, so we too might walk in newness of life. For if we have been united with him in a death like his, we will certainly be united with him in a resurrection like his. If we have died with Christ, we believe that we will also live with him. We know that Christ, being raised from the dead, will never die again; death no longer has dominion over him . . . the life he lives, he lives to God. So you also must consider yourselves . . . alive to God in Christ. [Romans 6:3–11][10]

Being able to open, with love and celebration, to the heart of Christianity, without being waylaid by all that seems questionable and uncomfortable to me, is a healing that helps close one of the most difficult chapters in my life. Reconnecting with the spirit of Christ after having shrugged off all the enforced and hypocritical religiosity of my school years has been a great happiness. I don't feel any more or less Buddhist or Christian. In fact these labels feel rather suffocating and limited. However, I do feel more authentic to the emerging truth of what fires this heart and mind. I pray that I may pursue that truth, wherever it leads me.

In the last year, amid the various difficulties that come and go, a sense of childlike effervescence, wonder, and joy has slowly emerged into my life. This playfulness is intoxicating. It feels like the best medication available. What is most remarkable is that these feelings are clearly not conditional upon the absence of physical pain and difficulty. They are increasingly the playmates of all that is happening.

Until fairly recently, I believed that the experience of abuse had fundamentally damaged me in a way that was irrevocable and absolute. While I still believe that the impact of what happened will always be part of the patterning of my life, what I now realize, to my great surprise and delight, is that when the abuse took place, the development of the essential spirit of the violated child was interrupted but not destroyed, and that it is possible to move on again, in adulthood, from that point where I was forced to shut down and armor myself from a pain that was intolerable then. As I take these faltering and wondrous steps into a world largely free of the guilt and terror of those years, I feel those parts of me, frozen and squashed by the abuse, now coming forward into life with great spirit, joy, and celebration. I sense that it was precisely for this integration and reconnection that I began meditating when I stepped into the darkness of my history with the hope of knowing again the light that went out so long ago.

With this birthing have come interludes of the deepest sense of contentment and surrender that I have ever known. This sweetness unquestionably helps make the difficult times more bearable and workable. It also feels easier to die, knowing that parts of me that were dead, are alive again today. In spite of the facts, as I write this in my forty-fourth year, I am happier and more at peace with both myself and the circumstances of my life than I have ever been before.

Rainer Maria Rilke died after a long and very painful illness. In a letter to a friend, he wrote of the importance of opening to suffering. He emphasized the possibilities that are awakened when one faces the difficulties and mysteries of life:

> It is true that these mysteries are dreadful, and people have always drawn away from them. But where can we find anything sweet and glorious that would never wear this mask of the dreadful? Whoever does not, sometime or other, give his

full and joyous consent to the dreadfulness of life, can never take possession of the unutterable abundance and power of our existence; can only walk on its edge, and one day, when the judgement is given, will have been neither alive nor dead.[11]

In the last year, renewed passion, zeal, and interest have flowered in the meditation practice, where this whole journey began. True awareness and meditation have become the deepest and purest expression of love that I know. This love and awareness seem to highlight the blessedness and preciousness of life as I slip through the ups and downs of my days. I feel deep and abiding gratitude for the teachings of the Buddha and a boundless gratitude to my teachers and all who have inspired and helped me along the way. The flower bud that felt so tight when I began this journey long ago now feels wide open, filled with color, and showered with blessing for all that has been possible in my life.

Notes

1. APPROACHING SUFFERING

1. E. M. Coetzee, *Waiting for the Barbarians* (New York: Penguin Books, 1980), p. 8.
2. Chögyam Trungpa, *Shambhala: The Sacred Path of the Warrior* (Boston: Shambhala Publications, 1988), pp. 45–46.

2. OPENING TO SUFFERING

1. World Food Council, 17th Session, Helsinki, June 5–8, 1991.
2. Mark Sommer, "Opinion: Who Will Pay for Peace?" *Christian Science Monitor*, February 19, 1992, p. 18.
3. John Stevens, trans., *One Robe, One Bowl: The Zen Poetry of Ryokan* (New York & Tokyo: John Weatherhill, 1977), p. 75.
4. Shunryu Suzuki, *Zen Mind, Beginner's Mind* (New York and Tokyo: John Weatherhill, 1970), p. 21.

3. ASPECTS OF MEDITATION

1. Robert Bly, trans., *The Kabir Book* (Boston: Beacon Press, 1977), p. 24.
2. Trungpa, *Shambhala*, pp. 48–49.
3. Rainer Maria Rilke, *Letters to a Young Poet*, trans. Stephen Mitchell (New York: Random House, 1984), pp. 34, 35.
4. Trungpa, *Shambhala*, p. 49.
5. Ibid., p. 50.
6. Ibid., p. 46.
7. Meher Baba, *Discourses* (Myrtle Beach, S.C.: Sheriar Press, 1987), p. 362.
8. Jae Jah Noh, *Do You See What I See?* (Wheaton, Ill.: Quest Books, 1977), p. 113.
9. "The Love of God and Affliction," in George A. Panichas, ed., *The Simone Weil Reader* (Mt. Kisco, N.Y.: Moyer Bell, 1977), p. 440.
10. Carlos Castaneda, *Journey to Ixtlan: The Lessons of Don Juan* (New York: Washington Square Press, 1972), pp. 33, 34,
11. *Visuddhimagga* 16.90, trans. by Andrew Olendzki.

12. Excerpted from "The Questions," in John Moyne and Coleman Barks, *Open Secret: Versions of Rumi* (Putney, Vt.: Threshold Books, 1984) p. 76.
13. Thich Nhat Hanh, *Peace Is Every Step* (New York: Bantam Books, 1991), pp. 59–60.
14. Shunryu Suzuki, *Zen Mind, Beginner's Mind*, p. 36.
15. Nisargadatta Maharaj, *I Am That* (Durham, N.C.: Acorn Press, 1992).
16. *Samutta Nikaya* 35.95.12–13, trans. by Andrew Olendzki.
17. David Finkelhor, "Answers to Important Questions about the Scope and Nature of Child Sexual Abuse," article prepared for *The Future of Children* special issue on child abuse, University of New Hampshire, Durham, N.H., October 1993.
18. Wayne Muller, "Beginning the Journey," in *Inquiring Mind* 8, no. 2 (Spring 1992), p. 5.
19. Quoted in Joseph Goldstein, *Insight Meditation: The Practice of Freedom* (Boston: Shambhala Publications, 1993), p. 13.
20. Ina Hughes, "A Prayer for Children," from an undated Children's Defense Fund brochure.

4. MEDITATIONS OF THE HEART

1. Nisargadatta Maharaj, *I Am That*.
2. Lance Morrow, " 'I Spoke as a Brother': A Pardon from the Pontiff, A Lesson in Forgiveness for a Troubled World," *Time* 123 (January 9, 1984), p. 26.
3. Excerpted from *Call Me by My True Names: The Collected Poems of Thich Nhat Hanh* (Berkeley: Parallax Press, 1993), p. 20.
4. Mohandas K. Gandhi, *An Autobiography: The Story of My Experiments with Truth* (New York: Dover, 1948).

5. QUESTIONING

1. Jae Jah Noh, *Do You See What I See?*, p. 95.
2. Trungpa, *Shambhala*, pp. 84–85.
3. Rilke, *Letters to a Young Poet*, trans. Stephen Mitchell (New York: Vintage Books, 1986), pp. 91–93.
4. Peter Matthiessen, *Nine-Headed Dragon River: Zen Journals, 1969–1982* (Boston: Shambhala Publications, 1987), pp. 129–130.
5. In Christopher Titmus, *Spirit of Change* (Alameda, Calif.: Hunter House, 1993), pp. 112, 124.
6. Ken Wilber, *Grace and Grit: Spirituality and Healing in the Life and Death of Treya Killam Wilber* (Boston: Shambhala Publications, 1991), p. 265.
7. Yael Bethian, "The Unhealed Life," in *The Sun*, no. 158 (January, 1989), pp. 37, 39.

6. LIVING WITH LOVE

1. Kahlil Gibran, *The Prophet* (New York: Alfred A. Knopf, 1923) pp. 19–20.
2. Robert Aitken, *The Mind of Clover* (Berkeley: North Point Press, 1984), p. 136.
3. Gandhi, *An Autobiography.*
4. Castaneda, *Journey to Ixtlan*, p. 69.
5. Gandhi, *An Autobiography.*
6. *Inquiring Mind* 8, no. 1 (Fall 1991), p. 19.
7. Gandhi, *An Autobiography.*
8. John Stevens, *Lust for Enlightenment: Buddhism and Sex* (Boston & London: Shambhala Publications, 1990), pp. 139–40.
9. *Samyutta Nikaya* 45.2.2–3, trans. Andrew Olendzki.
10. New Revised Standard Version.
11. Rainer Maria Rilke, *The Sonnets to Orpheus*, translated by Stephen Mitchell (New York: Simon and Schuster, 1985), p. 162.

Suggested Reading

BUDDHISM

Batchelor, Stephen (trans.). *Meaningful to Behold*. Dharamsala: Library of Tibetan Works and Archives, 1979.

——. *The Faith to Doubt: Glimpses of Buddhist Uncertainty*. Berkeley: Parallax Press, 1990.

Feldman, Christina. *Woman Awake: A Celebration of Women's Wisdom*. London: Arkana, Penguin, 1990.

Goldstein, Joseph. *The Experience of Insight: A Simple and Direct Guide to Buddhist Meditation*. Boston & London: Shambhala Publications, 1976, 1987.

——. *Insight Meditation: The Practice of Freedom*. Boston & London: Shambhala Publications, 1993.

Goldstein, Joseph, and Jack Kornfield. *Seeking the Heart of Wisdom: The Path of Insight Meditation*. Boston & London: Shambhala Publications, 1987.

Kabat-Zinn, Jon. *Wherever You Go, There You Are*. New York: Hyperion, 1994.

Kornfield, Jack. *A Path with Heart*. New York: Bantam, 1993.

Kornfield, Jack, and Paul Breiter. *A Still Forest Pool*. Wheaton, Ill.: Theosophical Publishing House, 1985.

Levine, Stephen. *A Gradual Awakening*. New York: Doubleday, 1979.

Surya Das. *The Snow Lion's Turquoise Mane: Wisdom Tales from Tibet*. San Francisco: HarperCollins, 1992.

Suzuki, Shunryu. *Zen Mind, Beginner's Mind*. New York & Tokyo: John Weatherhill, 1970.

Thich Nhat Hanh. *The Miracle of Mindfulness: A Manual on Meditation*. Boston: Beacon Press, 1975.

——. *Being Peace*. Berkeley: Parallax Press, 1987.

——. *Old Path, White Clouds: Walking in the Footsteps of the Buddha*. Berkeley: Parallax Press, 1991.

——. *Touching Peace*. Berkeley: Parallax Press, 1992.

Trungpa, Chögyam. *Shambhala: The Sacred Path of the Warrior.* Boston: Shambhala Publications, 1985.

AIDS

AIDS Project Los Angeles. *AIDS: A Self-Care Manual.* Santa Monica: IBS Press, 1987.

Callen, Michael. *Surviving AIDS.* New York: HarperCollins, 1990.

Kaiser, J. *Immune Power: Comprehensive Treatment Plan for HIV.* New York: St. Martins Press, 1993.

Markoff, Niro, and Paul Duffy. *Why I Survive AIDS.* New York: Simon & Schuster, 1991.

Melton, George R., with W. Garcia. *Beyond AIDS: A Journey into Healing.* Beverly Hills, Calif.: Brotherhood Press, 1988.

Peavey, Fran. *A Shallow Pool of Time.* San Francisco: Crabgrass Publications, 1989.

Root-Bernstein, Robert. *Rethinking AIDS.* New York: Free Press/Macmillan, 1993.

Schneider, David. *Street Zen: The Life and Work of Issan Dorsey.* Boston & London: Shambhala Publications, 1993.

Shilts, Randy. *And the Band Played On.* New York: Penguin, 1987.

Sontag, Susan. *AIDS and Its Metaphors.* New York: Farrar, Straus & Giroux, 1988.

ABUSE

Bass, Ellen, and Laura Davis. *The Courage to Heal.* New York: HarperCollins, 1988.

Lew, Mike. *Victims No Longer.* New York: Nevraumont Publishing Co., 1988.

Miller, Alice. *The Drama of the Gifted Child.* New York: Basic Books, 1981.

———. *For Your Own Good.* New York: Farrar, Straus & Giroux, 1983.

DEATH AND DYING

Chokyi Nyima Rinpoche. *The Bardo Guidebook.* Kathmandu: Rangjung Yeshe Publications, 1991.

Fremantle, Francesca, and Chögyam Trungpa, trans. *The Tibetan Book of the Dead.* Boston & London: Shambhala Publications, 1975.

Kapleau, Philip. *Wheel of Life and Death.* New York: Doubleday, 1989.

Kübler-Ross, Elisabeth. *On Death and Dying.* New York: Macmillan, 1970.

Levine, Stephen. *Healing into Life and Death.* New York: Doubleday, 1987.

———. *Meetings at the Edge.* New York: Doubleday, 1984.

————. *Who Dies?* New York: Doubleday, 1982.

Sogyal Rinpoche. *The Tibetan Book of Living and Dying.* San Francisco: HarperCollins, 1992.

White, John. *A Practical Guide to Death and Dying.* Wheaton, Ill.: Quest Books, 1980.

Wilber, Ken. *Grace and Grit: Spirituality and Healing in the Life and Death of Treya Killam Wilber.* Boston & London: Shambhala Publications, 1991.

OTHER

Casarjian, Robin. *Forgiveness.* New York: Bantam Books, 1992.

Chopra, Deepak. *Quantum Healing.* New York: Bantam Books, 1989.

Daumal, René. *Mount Analogue.* Boston & London: Shambhala Publications, 1980.

Jae Jah Noh. *Do You See What I See?* Wheaton, Ill.: Quest Books, 1977.

Kabat-Zinn, Jon. *Full Catastrophe Living.* New York: Delacorte Press, 1990.

Kornfield, Jack, and Christina Feldman (eds.). *Stories of the Spirit, Stories of the Heart.* New York: HarperCollins, 1991.

Lerner, Harriet Goldhor. *The Dance of Anger.* New York: Harper and Row, 1985.

Gandhi, Mohandas K. *An Autobiography: The Story of My Experiments with Truth.* New York: Dover, 1983.

Merton, Thomas. *The Seven Storey Mountain.* New York: Harvest/Harcourt Brace Jovanovich, 1946, 1978.

Moyne, J., and Coleman Barks. *Open Secret: Versions of Rumi.* Brattleboro, Vt.: Threshold Books, 1984.

Ram Dass and Paul Gorman. *How Can I Help?: Stories and Reflections on Service.* New York: Alfred A. Knopf, 1985.

Rilke, Rainer Maria. *Letters to a Young Poet.* Trans. Stephen Mitchell. New York: Vintage Books, 1986.

Rodegast, Pat, and Judith Stanton (eds.). *Emmanuel's Book: A Manual for Living Comfortably in the Cosmos.* New York: Bantam Books, 1985.

————. *Emmanuel's Book II: The Choice for Love.* New York: Bantam Books, 1989.

Titmuss, Christopher. *Freedom of the Spirit.* London: Green Press.

————. *The Profound and the Profane: An Inquiry into Spiritual Awakening.* Totnes: Insight Books, 1993.

————. *Spirit of Change.* Alameda, Calif.: Hunter House, 1993.

Walsh, Roger N., and Frances Vaughn (eds.). *Beyond Ego: Transpersonal Dimensions in Psychology.* Los Angeles: Jeremy P. Tarcher, 1980.

———. *A Gift of Peace: Selections from a Course in Miracles*. Los Angeles: Jeremy Tarcher, 1986.

Tapes of Gavin Harrison's talks and those of other meditation teachers associated with the Insight Meditation Society in Barre, Massachusetts, as well as books on insight meditation, are available from:

Dharma Seed Tape Library
Box 66
Wendell, MA 01380

Insight Meditation Center Information

United States

Cambridge Insight Meditation Center
331 Broadway
Cambridge, MA 02139
(617) 491-5070

Cloud Mountain Retreat Center
c/o Northwest Dharma Association
311 W. McGraw
Seattle, WA 98119
(206) 286-9060

Dhamma Dena Desert Vipassana
HC-1, Box 250
Joshua Tree, CA 92252
(619) 362-4815

Insight Meditation Society
Pleasant St.
Barre, MA 01005
(508) 355-4378

Southern Dharma Retreat Center
Route 1, Box 34H
Hot Springs, NC 28743
(704) 622-7112

Spirit Rock Meditation Center
P.O. Box 909
Woodacre, CA 94973
(415) 488-0170

Canada

Karuna Meditation Society
19-555 West 12th Ave.
Vancouver, B.C. V5Z-4L6
(604) 222-4941

England

Amaravati Buddhist Centre
Great Gaddesden, Hemel Hempstead
Hertfordshire HP1 3BZ
044-284-3239

Gaia House Trust
Woodland Rd.
Denbury Nr Newton Abbot
Devon TQ12 6DY
Tel. Ipplepen 080-381-3188

South Africa

Buddhist Retreat Centre
Box 131
Ixopo, Natal 4630
033-612-2203

Heldervue Homestead
16 Prunus Street
Heldervue
Somerset West 7130
024-651-297

Australia

Buddha Sasana Association
c/o Graham White
P.O. Box 64
Thirroul, NSW 2515
Australia
(04) 267-3240

Buddhist Practitioner's Network
P.O. Box 993
Byron Bay, NSW 2481
Australia
(06) 685-6608

Eric Harrison
P.O. Box 1019
Subiaco, WA 6008
Australia
(09) 381-9689

New Zealand

Te Moata
c/o Tim Wyn-Harris, Enid Roberts
Box 100
Tairua, Thames Cty.
New Zealand
(7) 868-8798

Acknowledgments and Credits

I wish to thank the publishers who granted permission to reprint the following excerpts:

From *The Kabir Book* by Robert Bly, copyright © 1971, 1977 by Robert Bly. Reprinted by permission of Beacon Press.

Excerpt from "The Questions," reprinted from *Open Secret: Versions of Rumi*, translated by John Moyne and Coleman Barks. Reprinted by permission of Threshold Books, RD 4, Box 600, Putney, VT 05346.

Excerpt from "Recommendation" by Thich Nhat Hanh, from *Call Me By My True Names: The Collected Poems of Thich Nhat Hanh*. Reprinted by permission of Parallax Press, Berkeley, California (1993).

Excerpts from *Shambhala: The Sacred Path of the Warrior* by Chögyam Trungpa. © 1984 by Chögyam Trungpa. Reprinted by arrangement with Shambhala Publications, Inc., 300 Massachusetts Avenue, Boston, MA 02115.

Each step in the birthing of this book has involved many people. A community of generous, tireless, and kind people have loved and encouraged both me and the book all along the way. To all I humbly and gratefully extend my deepest thanks and appreciation.

Rand Engel initially suggested that a book might be lurking somewhere within my crazy life. Without his indefatiguable support, love, and encouragement this book probably would not have happened.

During all the stages of the book, Eva Gumprecht has been a steady, patient, and sure ally and friend. Amidst the hell realms of wiped discs, wayward manuscripts, and frayed nerves, her quiet wisdom and care have made a huge difference.

JoAnna Schoen has magically, lovingly, and efficiently choreographed disks, transcripts, and the chaos of an emerging manuscript.

George Fowler, Eva Gumprecht, Anne Lewis, Michelle Palmer, Steve Proskauer, JoAnna Schoen, Anne Spanel, and Andi Werner transcribed the Dharma talks and processed the manuscript. May you never have to commit a South African accent to paper again!

Kate Lila Wheeler reviewed and edited the initial transcripts. Her wholehearted commitment to and belief in the book made a huge difference at the beginning of the project.

Joseph Goldstein, Adelaide Harrison, and Eric Kolvig read the manuscript and provided invaluable feedback that has strengthened and served this book.

George Bowman, Joseph Goldstein, Trudy Goodman, my brother Craig Harrison, Narayan Liebenson-Grady, Chris Macek, Liza Murrow, Andy Olendzki, Sarah Doering, Louis and Chrissie van Loon, Heila and Rodney Downey, Michael Shandler, and Lucy Tinkcombe have given abundant energy, support, encouragement, and love to the project.

John White, my agent, provided valuable guidance and advice each step along the way.

This book has been deeply enriched by the vision, expertise, patience, and wisdom of my editor, Kendra Crossen. To her and all at Shambhala Publications I extend my sincere thanks and great respect.

Many other people have directly and indirectly served the evolution of this book. With deep gratitude I thank my teachers, Michele McDonald-Smith and Joseph Goldstein, for their love, support, and guidance over the years.

The teachings of Ajahn Anando, Christina Feldman, Aya Kema, Jack Kornfield, Larry Rosenberg, Sharon Salzberg, Steven Smith, Ajahn Sumedo, Godwin Samaratna, and Christopher Titmuss have profoundly touched my life. To each I extend my thanks.

My beloved support group have held, loved, and cheered me on over the last years. My gratitude is beyond words. Stephen Berman, Marilyn Bradley, Rebecca Bradshaw, Beth Craddock, Emily Fox, Vicki Gabriner, Paula Green, Joe Goren, Linda Harris, Karen Levine, Rhonda Marianni, Kevin McVeigh, Ellen Mooney, Susan O'Brien, Jim Perkins, Sarah Pirtle, Marcia Rose, Trudy Godman, George Bowman, Liza Murrow, Stewart McDermet, and Carolyn Sadeh.

Louis van Loon and Molly van Loon built the Buddhist Retreat Centre in South Africa where I began my journey and to where I often return home. My gratitude for all they made possible is immeasurable.

Carol Drexler, Barry Elson, Paul Epstein, Tom Hoskins, Nanette Keith, Jonathan Klate, Charles Liggins, Judy McKeon, Jonathan Miller, Steven Miller, Rob Rechtschaffen, Ray Rethman, Molly Scott, Nancy Sunflower, Edith Sullwold, Bob Weitzman, Martin Wohl, Jan de Vries, Eva Mondon, Rupa Cousins, Bonnie Hill, Joan Miller, Mary Kraisen, Thomas Herman, Jill Elkington, and Mimi Bergstrom are all friends, healers, and health-care allies who have loved, guided, and joined me on the journey.

Over the last twelve years the staff, board, and teachers at the Insight Meditation Society in Barre, Massachusetts, have in many ways extended great kindness, support, and care to me. I thank them all from the bottom of my heart.

I would like to pay tribute to the enthusiasm and dedication of the meditation community in southern Vermont where I began teaching.

To all my beloved friends, far too numerous to mention,

May we and all beings be happy

May we and all beings be peaceful

May we and all beings be filled with love, kindness, and compassion

May we and all beings be free from suffering and the causes of suffering

May all share the fruits, blessings, and merit of this book.

Index